# NBA Basketball

## AN OFFICIAL FAN'S GUIDE

**To my grandfather, Sam Mabel.**
**The blessing is in knowing him.**

THIS IS A CARLTON BOOK

This edition published by Carlton Books Limited 1994

10 9 8 7 6 5 4 3 2 1

ISBN 1-85868-031-X

A CIP catalogue record for this book is available from the British Library


Project editor: Martin Corteel
Project art editor: Zoë Maggs
Designer: Jon Lucas
Production: Sarah Schuman

Printed and bound in Italy

**PREVIOUS PAGE** Houston superstar Hakeem Olajuwon registers
another rejection

**Author's acknowledgments**

Special thanks to Jim O'Donnell and Jeanne Frederick for their tireless research and attention to detail. And to the NBA's Frank
Fochetta, Diane Naughton, Lee Newell, Brian McIntyre, Terry
Lyons, Jan Hubbard, Pete Steber and Alex Sachare for their remarkable ability to bring compassion and support to their commitment
to quality. To Martin Corteel at Carlton Books for making the
process so smooth and professional. And finally, to my wife, Laura,
for all the coffee and care. This project couldn't have been done
without all these people in place. My thanks.

# CONTENTS

# INTRODUCTION

On and off the court and all around the globe, the evolution of the NBA now seems more like a revolution.

A game once confined to a small group of major American cities and carried most often via radio, now reaches into 27 major United States markets with television providing action to more than 140 countries around the world.

New franchises have been added in Toronto and Vancouver, Canada and NBA players, once banned from international competition, captured the imagination of fans from Spain to Australia, Japan to South Africa as members of the Dream Team at the 1992 Barcelona Olympics.

When NBA Commissioner David Stern visited China, officials asked him to bring the "Red Oxen," or the Chicago Bulls as they are known in the U.S. When he spoke with government leaders in Russia they asked about playing an NBA game in Red Square. When the league decided to take the game international, season-opening games were played in Japan.

Indeed, the game and its players has caused a stir well beyond the traditional boundaries of North America. And with good reason.

After veteran stars such as Wilt Chamberlain, Bill Russell, George Mikan, Jerry West, Oscar Robertson and Elgin Baylor carried the league through the 1950s and 1960s, a whole new wave of talent took over and set the stage for an unprecedented explosion in worldwide interest.

Julius Erving became one of the first players to stretch the imagination with his performances. His high-flying style and acrobatic dunks helped "Dr. J" establish a whole new standard for the next generation of players.

And they must have been paying attention because the 1980s proved to be the dawn of a new age. Larry Bird and Magic Johnson came into the league together and landed with tradition-rich franchises in Boston and Los Angeles, respectively.

Next came Michael Jordan, who turned Chicago, yet another major media market, into an NBA power. Then Patrick Ewing, the 7–0 center with a soft jump shot, went to the New York Knicks, whose history matches that of the league itself.

Other stars such as Charles Barkley, Dominique Wilkins, Chris Mullin, Scottie Pippen, Hakeem Olajuwon and David Robinson joined in and helped turn the NBA game into a non-stop show.

**Known as the "Human Highlight Film" for his acrobatic and dramatic dunking ability, former Atlanta Hawk, Dominique Wilkins has become one of the greatest offensive players in NBA history**

He stands just 6–6 and has more than 250 pounds backed onto his compact frame, but Charles Barkley remains among the most dynamic rebounders and scorers the game has ever known

Major television contracts brought the NBA to more homes than ever and widened the audience to viewers in virtually every country of the world. NBA arenas turned into miniature theme parks, each with its own attractions, and attendance for regular season games exploded.

Most importantly, the players didn't disappoint. Bird's Boston Celtics and Johnson's Los Angeles Lakers spent much of the 1980s fighting off challengers for NBA championships. Then came the Detroit Pistons of Isiah Thomas and finally, after a glorious rise, Jordan's Chicago Bulls who reeled off three consecutive titles.

The players became some of the most recognizable athletes in the history of professional sports, their exploits and personalities making the NBA experience as great off the court as on.

And as the 1980s gave way to the 1990s, the league's popularity appeared to only gain more steam. The Dream Team became the talk of the 1992 Olympic Games and Dream Team II, which includes yet another group of NBA stars, was expected to do the same in Toronto in 1994. The revolution rolls on.

With the speed and quickness of a guard and the scoring ability of a small forward, David Robinson has redefined the center position. At 7–1, Robinson is a force at either end of the floor

# THE HISTORY OF THE NBA

It all started with a peach basket and a round ball more than 100 years ago. But in the decades since Dr. James Naismith created the first rough version of basketball, the National Basketball Association has become home to the greatest players in the history of the game. From the NBA's first great big man, George Mikan, to the Boston Celtics dynasty and the great 1980s run of Larry Bird, Magic Johnson, Isiah Thomas and Michael Jordan, the league has become an international show and one of the most popular spectator sports of all time.

## The Birth of a League

Dr. James Naismith couldn't have known that his simple idea would lead to the creation of a game played around the globe by some of the most gifted athletes sports had ever seen.

In 1891, Dr. Naismith had two peach baskets nailed to a gymnasium balcony at the Springfield Young Men's Christian Association Training School. Dr. Naismith was hoping to create an indoor activity during the cold winter months, and by hanging the baskets high off the ground he sought to promote finesse and agility over mere size and strength.

In less than 50 years, however, the game came to revolve around players with a variety of all-around skills. And by the spring of 1946, the beginnings of the NBA were firmly in place.

Although college basketball dominated the interest of fans in America, the professional game started coming together. Though teams had been organized and playing for nearly 40 years, the level of interest rarely extended beyond the team's immediate geographical area.

**Dr. Naismith holds an early model basketball**

# THE BAA

The Basketball Association of America was no different, at least in its first season in 1946–47. There were 11 teams divided into two divisions, the Western and Eastern, and they were situated in some of the country's biggest cities, including New York, Chicago, Boston, Philadelphia, Detroit and Cleveland. The league even had a franchise in Toronto.

The BAA also had a legitimate star in "Jumpin'" Joe Fulks, a 6–5 forward from Kentucky. At a time when no team was averaging as many as 80 points a game, Fulks was a sensation.

Fulks was the only player to average more than 17 points a game as he led the BAA with a 23.2 points per game average during the league's inaugural season.

But neither Fulks nor the all-star lineup of cities garnered the kind of fan support necessary for a fledgling league. Although more and more people became aware of the professional game, television barely existed and radio supplied only spotty coverage. Even big city newspapers treated the league with passing interest.

Not surprisingly, the BAA ran into immediate problems. By the start of the league's second season only seven teams remained. Baltimore eventually was added to even the divisions. But problems persisted and no one was sure whether a professional basketball league, particularly in a climate dominated by the college style and game, could flourish.

The concept needed help at virtually every turn. Six of the eight BAA teams were in the East, which shut out most of the rest of the country. And while Fulks and Max Zaslofsky were legitimate early stars, the league needed a high profile draw.

The BAA got significant boosts on both fronts starting with the 1948–49 season when four teams from the National Basketball League, which operated primarily in the Midwest, joined forces with the BAA. Suddenly, the BAA had some of the highest profile players in some of the best basketball markets in the country.

**Joe Fulks was one of the game's first great high-scoring forwards**

# THE NBA LEAPS FORWARD

And, perhaps as important as anything that had happened to date in professional basketball, the BAA had George Mikan.

The BAA changed its name to the the National Basketball Association for the 1949–50 season when the surviving teams from the National Basketball League merged with the BAA. Though the league had plenty of problems to iron out, not the least of which was an awkward 17-team roster divided into three divisions, the professional game was gathering momentum.

Syracuse had a budding superstar in Dolph Schayes, whose son Danny would have a solid NBA career in the 1980s; Minneapolis had Mikan; New York had legendary coach Joe Lapchick; and Chicago had Zaslofsky.

But the growing pains were long from over. After one year, six teams were gone. Though more managable and logical given the two-division format, the NBA continued to struggle.

The league, rugged and prone to fouls because of some of its early rules, continued to fight through its problems as more and more stars emerged. Players such as Neil Johnston, Ed Macauley, Bill Sharman, Bob Cousy, Bob Pettit and Paul Arizin were highly skilled for any era.

The game itself, however, needed refinement. And the first move in that direction came prior to the 1954–55 season when owners from the nine remaining NBA teams adopted two radical, and equally important, rules changes.

Syracuse owner Danny Biasone had dabbled with the concept of putting a time limit on ball possession. The idea was to keep teams from stalling, particularly at

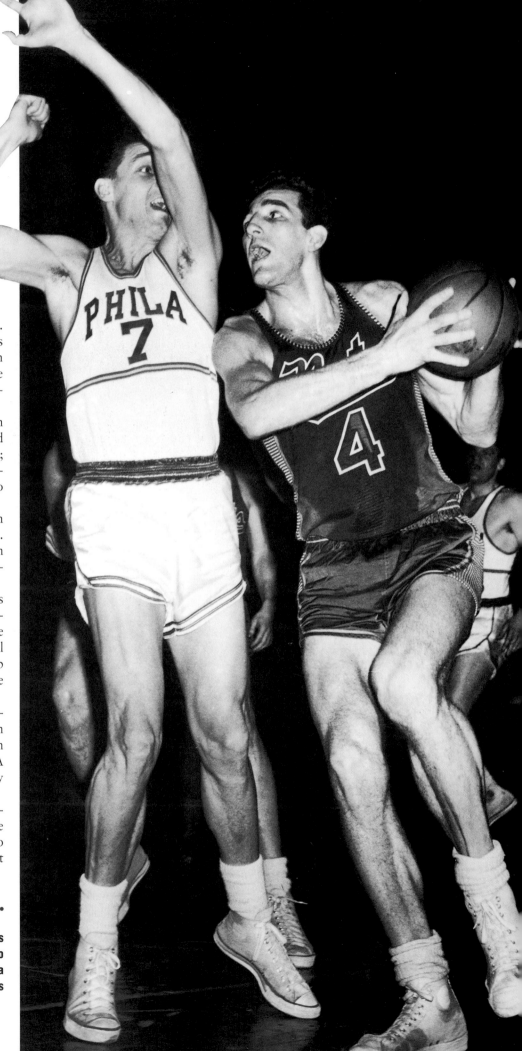

Syracuse superstar Dolph Schayes (4) blows past a Philadelphia defender on his way to another basket. His son, Danny, played for a number of NBA teams in the 1980s and 1990s

the end of games. Not only was the tactic boring, but it disrupted a game that revolved around scoring. Biasone arrived at 24 seconds by figuring teams normally average 60 shots a game. Thus, 120 shots divided into 2,880, the number of seconds in a 48-minute game, came out to 24. The idea caught on quickly. If the offensive team didn't get off a shot that hit the rim within 24 seconds of taking possession, the defensive team would be awarded possession of the ball.

The other rule involved the number of fouls teams could commit in any one quarter. Now teams that committed more than six fouls in a quarter were penalized. Instead of shooting two free throws, opposing players would shoot three for every foul after the sixth one in a given period. Not only did it succeed in making fouling an expensive tactic to keep the opposition from scoring, but it helped keep the game moving.

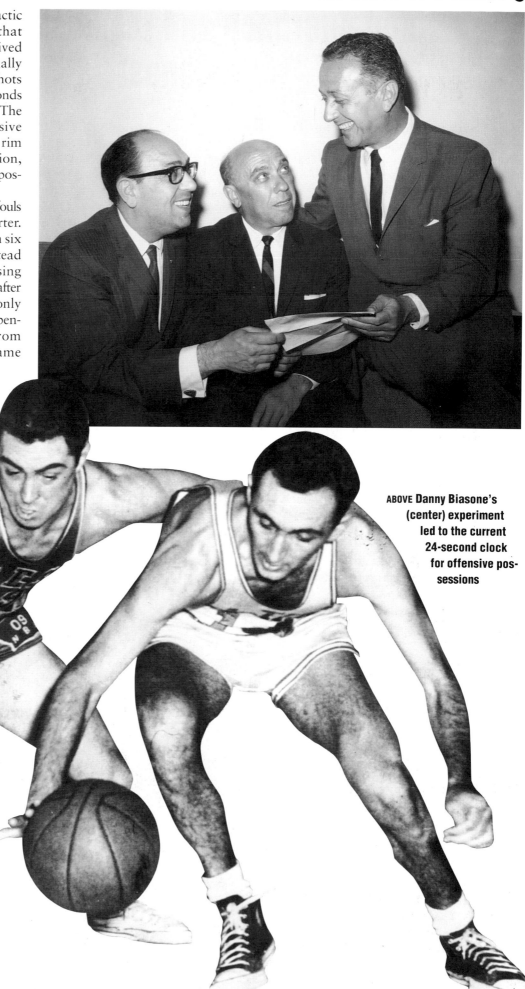

**Boston's Bob Cousy (right) was one of the greatest point guards in NBA history**

ABOVE **Danny Biasone's (center) experiment led to the current 24-second clock for offensive possessions**

# Red Auerbach and the Boston Celtics Dynasty

Unlike modern teams, those of the late 1950s had virtually no scouting system in place to evaluate talent. When a team chose a college player in the draft, the coach or general manager making the choice many times had never seen the player play.

All of which underscores the brilliance of Arnold "Red" Auerbach. By the start of the 1956–57 season, the league had been reduced to eight franchises—Boston, Philadelphia, Syracuse and New York in the Eastern Division and Fort Wayne, Minneapolis, St. Louis and Rochester in the Western Division. Over the next four seasons, however, three of greatest players in history would join the league. The first of these was Bill Russell, a slender, 6–9 center who had turned the University of San Francisco into a national college power. In fact, San Francisco went two straight seasons without losing a single game. Back in Boston, Auerbach took

notice. The Celtics had led the NBA in scoring during the 1955–56 season, averaging 106 points a game. They had three solid scorers in guards Sharman and Cousy and forward Macauley. The team also had the rights to 6-4 Cliff Hagan, whom Boston had drafted in 1953, and whose military commitment was coming to a close.

But Auerbach needed a rebounder and he needed the kind of defense Russell could provide. While the Celtics scored a lot of points, they also gave up plenty, 105.3 a game during the 1955–56 season.

That Russell would be tied up with the Olympics in Melbourne, Australia, until December didn't matter to Auerbach. He knew what he wanted even though not even Auerbach knew what he was getting.

So in a move that would impact the entire league for 13 seasons, Auerbach gambled. He agreed to send Macauley and the rights to Hagan, both future Hall of

Famers, to St. Louis for the right to draft Russell.

Almost as important to the Celtics' future was the addition of high scoring rookie Tom Heinsohn. Auerbach used Boston's regular pick to choose Heinsohn, who immediately stepped into the scoring void left by Macauley's departure. With All-Stars Cousy and Sharman out front, Heinsohn at forward and Russell in the middle, the Celtics were suddenly covered at all spots.

Though the first installment on Auerbach's winnings came immediately, no one knew what was ahead. The Celtics, with Russell at center, beat St. Louis 4–3 in the 1957 Finals with a dramatic 125–123 double overtime victory in Game 7 to claim their first NBA Championship.

A year later, however, St. Louis got even. Hagan and Macauley teamed with superstar Bob Pettit and the Hawks eliminated Boston 4–2 in the 1958 Finals.

Nothing of the sort would happen again for eight years. Not only was Russell more brilliant and driven to succeed than anyone imagined, but Auerbach continued to load the roster with stars.

Players such as Frank Ramsey, K.C. Jones, Sam Jones, Tom "Satch" Sanders, John Havlicek and Don Nelson carried Boston through a league maturing quickly.

Though Elgin Baylor, perhaps the most acrobatic scorer the league had seen to that point, arrived in Minneapolis in 1958, Wilt Chamberlain in Philadelphia in 1959 and Oscar Robertson in Cincinnati in 1960, the Celtics marched on.

**The Men In Charge: Bill Russell and Red Auerbach led the Boston Celtics to eight straight championships**

## EIGHT CONSECUTIVE CHAMPIONSHIPS

Auerbach, perhaps the greatest coach the league has ever known, proved equally brilliant behind the scenes. His ability to spot talent and blend diverse personalities

# THE FIRST GREAT SEASON

The 1966–67 season marked the first real peak for the NBA. Not only was fan interest at an all-time high, but the league was filled with some of the greatest players in history.

Rick Barry, a sharp-shooting 6–7 forward, was in San Francisco. Oscar Robertson had averaged 31.3 points the previous season for Cincinnati, Jerry West had matched Robertson's scoring with the Los Angeles Lakers and Wilt Chamberlain remained the most dominant offensive force in the game.

And Boston, with Bill Russell now coaching and playing, took on a whole new intrigue.

More importantly, the league was looking at expanding from 10 to 12 teams. And players, particularly the big names, were earning big money. Chamberlain earned $100,000, the first player to hit that level, during the 1965–66 season. Boston pulled a public relations coup by agreeing to pay Russell $100,001 for the 1966–67 campaign.

The rivalry between the players and their teams caught the imagination of an entire country. So too had Philadelphia's record-setting performance during the 1966–67 regular season. The 76ers, with Chamberlain in the middle, won a staggering 68 games to end Boston's string of eight straight titles.

For the first time in Chamberlain's career, his team went on to win a championship with a victory over Barry's San Francisco squad in the Finals.

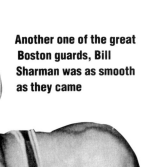

Another one of the great Boston guards, Bill Sharman was as smooth as they came

into the Celtics system turned the Boston franchise into one of the greatest in all professional sports.

The Celtics averaged a remarkable 57.6 regular season victories during the eight-year championship run. Not once did Boston lose more than 26 games in any one season. And when it mattered most, the Celtics never lost.

When the 1960 Finals went to Game 7 against St. Louis, Boston responded with a 122–103 victory. When the 1962 Finals went to Game 7 against Los Angeles, which is where the Minneapolis franchise moved, Boston pulled out a 110–107 victory in overtime.

In fact, once the Celtics reached the playoffs they seemed to lift their game even higher. During the 1963–64 season, Robertson, who had developed into a remarkable all-around player, led Cincinnati to a 55–25 record, just four games behind Boston in the Eastern Division.

Once the playoffs started, however, Cincinnati didn't have a chance. In a 4–1 semifinal round blitzing, Boston beat the Royals by an average of almost 13 points a game.

The beat went on through the 1965–66 season. But the last Boston championship proved to be one of the most difficult and required every ounce of Auerbach's genius.

Philadelphia, with Chamberlain winning his seventh straight scoring title, had added rookie Billy Cunningham through the draft. Cunningham could run the floor, jump as well as anybody in the league and he knew how to score. The 76ers finally appeared to have enough guns to shoot down Russell's Celtics.

Indeed, Philadelphia finished the regular season with 11 straight victories to win the Eastern Division by a game, with Boston finishing second for the first time no one seemed very interested in Auerbach's successor.

But after the Celtics were upset at home in the first game of the Finals, Auerbach decided to let the world in on a secret of historic magnitude. Auerbach announced that Russell would become the first black head coach in NBA history when he took over coaching duties at the start of the 1966–67 season.

The stunning announcement had an uplifting affect on the Celtics. They beat Los Angeles three straight games and eventually held off the Lakers in a tough Game 7 for the franchise's eighth straight championship.

## DYNASTY ENDS

Though the Boston dynasty would carry on after a one-year lapse, the end was clearly in sight. Auerbach moved to the Celtics' front office and the roster he had created was beginning to show its years.

Boston finished eight games behind Philadelphia in the Eastern Division in 1967–68 only to rally past the 76ers in the playoffs and win another championship.

But in 1969, the last breaths of dynasty were there for all to see. And with the American Basketball Association heading into its second full season, changes were on

the horizon. Nowhere was that more apparent than in Boston. The Celtics' regulars averaged 31 years of age, with Sam Jones nearly 36 and Russell 35 when the playoffs started.

The Celtics had finished back in fourth in the Eastern Division behind the Baltimore Bullets, Philadelphia 76ers and New York Knicks. These three teams had the fire of youth while Boston continued the fight with reputation and sheer intensity.

In Baltimore, rookie cen-

in 10 years. The immediate result was that the Celtics had to play a first-round playoff series against Cincinnati while the 76ers rested.

Boston fought through a tough five-game series and was battle-tested, if not rested, when it met Philadelphia in the Eastern Division Finals. Whatever the reason, the 76ers fell apart. Boston dusted off Philadelphia 4–1 and coasted into the Finals against a Los Angeles Lakers team it had beaten before.

Still, the Celtics struggled. Auerbach had announced early in the season that his coaching career would end following the 1966 playoffs. He had not announced a replacement and early in the NBA Finals

**The Shooter: Sam Jones redefined the shooting guard position with a soft jump shot and remarkable all-around scoring ability**

ter Wes Unseld made one of the league's most dramatic debuts. He averaged 13.8 points and 18.2 rebounds and led the Bullets to the Eastern Division title. Although standing just 6–7, Unseld's body was packed with 245 pounds of solid muscle.

Combined with unusual mental toughness, Unseld immediately established himself as a presence under the basket, and Baltimore as a force to be reckoned with, which is why Unseld received both the Most Valuable Player and Rookie of the Year awards in 1969.

In New York, the Knicks were coming together quickly thanks to another undersized center, Willis Reed. With flashy Walt Frazier at guard, steady Bill Bradley at forward and Dick Barnett occupying the point, the Knicks were one of the league's best all-around teams. And they became significantly better after trading for forward Dave DeBusschere midway through the 1968–69 season. The Knicks, as it turned out, were only a season away from taking over where the Celtics left off.

Philadelphia, led by Cunningham, Hal Greer and Chet Walker remained solid as well. So, as the aging Celtics walked softly into the 1969 playoffs, the NBA's past, as well as its future, was there for all the world to see.

But the last gasp of champions proved to be just enough. Boston knocked off Philadelphia 4–1 in the semifinals, New York 4–2 in the Eastern Conference Finals and, matched once more against the Los Angeles Lakers, rolled into the NBA Finals.

Though the Lakers had Chamberlain this time, nothing changed. The Celtics came back from an early 2–0 deficit and won the deciding Game 7 by a single basket. The 11th championship in 13 years was the last for Russell, who retired as player and gave up the coaching reins at the same time.

"He was the greatest defensive player I have ever seen," states current Chicago General Manager Jerry Krause. "A lot of people say Russell couldn't play in today's game. A lot of people don't know Russell. He would have found a way. He knew how to win. And he would have found a way to adapt."

● ● ● ● ● ● ● ● ● ● ● ● ● ● ● ● ● ● ●

**One of the greatest shooters of his era, Rick Barry had virtually unlimited range. Here he is playing for the Oaks in the old ABA**

# The 1970s—The Changing of the Guard

After years of dominance by Boston in particular and the Eastern Division in general, the balance of power shifted almost annually during the 1970s. Eight different teams won championships including Seattle and Portland. The Los Angeles Lakers ended a run of futility in the Finals by winning one title while New York and Boston captured two apiece. Off the court, the American Basketball Association ceased operations in the middle of the decade with four teams joining the NBA.

Although the New York Knicks, coached by Red Holzman, took the decade's first championship, the biggest story of the season unfolded in Milwaukee.

Prior to the 1969–70 season, the Bucks and Phoenix Suns flipped a coin to determine the first pick in the 1969 NBA Draft. The coin flip had become an annual event between the two worst teams in the league, one each from the Western and Eastern Divisions.

But this one became one of the most important in basketball history. Lew Alcindor, or Kareem Abdul-Jabbar as he would be known later, had been one of the greatest players in college history at UCLA. With an unstoppable "sky-hook" and unusual agility given his slender 7-2 frame, Abdul-Jabbar was considered likely to become professional basketball's next dominant player.

Milwaukee won the flip and the NBA rights to Abdul-Jabbar. After the ABA failed to come up with a suitable financial package, Abdul-Jabbar agreed to sign with the Bucks. His impact, as expected, was immediate. He finished second in scoring (28.8) and third in rebounding (14.5) while lifting Milwaukee from 27 to 56 victories in his first season.

"He was an incredible player from the minute he joined the league," says former NBA player and current coach Kevin Loughery. "There wasn't anything he couldn't do. And he had that shot that no one could stop."

The Knicks meanwhile had put together a team as fundamentally sound as any in history. Smart, disciplined, versatile and focused, New York had the league's best record and went on to record the franchise's first championship with a rousing seven-game Finals victory over the Lakers.

A year later Oscar Robertson, who had failed to win a single title during his brilliant career in Cincinnati, joined Milwaukee and provided all the help Abdul-Jabbar needed. The Bucks won a stunning 66 games during the regular season and breezed through the playoffs.

Boston, after a down period following Russell's retirement, came back strong starting with the 1971–72 season. The Celtics had players such as John Havlicek, Jo Jo White, Dave Cowens and Don Chaney leading yet another Eastern Division charge.

## THE GREATEST SEASON

But no team could stop the last, and one of the greatest, runs put together by Chamberlain's 1971–72 Los Angeles Lakers. At 35, Chamberlain was now more of a defender and rebounder. The Lakers' offense revolved around sharpshooting guards Gail Goodrich and veteran Jerry West; Happy Hairston and Jim McMillian, solid players, manned the forward spots, and the bench included future coach Pat Riley.

For all the dominance displayed by Boston during the 1960s and Milwaukee during the previous season, nothing could compare to Los Angeles' record-shattering assault.

They won an NBA-record 33 straight games during one stretch and finished 69–13 during the regular season, marks that still stand. The Lakers were so dominant that they won by an average of more than 12 points a game while leading the league in scoring (121.0).

The playoffs weren't much different. Los Angeles had lost seven times in the championship round in nine years before 1972. Matched against the New York Knicks, that string stopped quickly. The Lakers knocked off New York 4–1 for the franchise's first title since the team moved from Minneapolis in 1960.

Over in the ABA, the league had discovered the one player who would eventually become its savior. After his junior season at the University of Massachusetts, Julius Erving was signed by the Virginia Squires. Erving became an instant sensation, averaging 27.3 points and 15.7 rebounds a game.

But it was not what Erving did as much as the flash and flair of the process. His dunks were thundering and came from everywhere. He slammed on the run, under the basket and over everyone, including 7–2 Kentucky center Artis Gilmore.

Though the ABA and NBA continued to talk about a merger, Erving would be the one player to eventually push the process forward.

Back in the NBA, the Boston Celtics were once again riding high in the East. Led by Havlicek's scoring and Dave Cowens' aggressive play in the middle, Boston averaged a league-high 59 victories from the start of the 1971–72 season through the 1976 Finals.

But unlike their predecessors, these Celtics didn't always get it done in the playoffs. During the five-season sprint Boston reached the Finals only twice, winning in 1974 and 1976.

● ● ● ● ● ● ● ● ● ● ● ● ● ● ● ● ● ● ● ● ● ● ● ●

**LEFT Kareem Abdul-Jabbar; (RIGHT) Wilt Chamberlain rises above the crowd**

# EXPANSION

The league, loaded with talent, expanded to 18 teams for the 1974–75 season, adding New Orleans, which would later become the Utah Jazz. More importantly, the power was distributed evenly among a handful of teams.

The Chicago Bulls, coached by Dick Motta, remained one of the league's toughest defensive teams. The Buffalo Braves, with high-scoring Bob McAdoo, improved to 49 victories while the Washington Bullets, with Elvin Hayes on board, were the East's best team.

But out West, three teams had emerged. Golden State, with Rick Barry back in the fold, won the Pacific Division and put together a brilliant postseason run that took the Warriors all the way to the Finals.

Right behind them, however, were Seattle and Portland. The SuperSonics were slowly building toward a title run of their own later in the decade while the Trail Blazers had won the 1974 coin flip for center Bill Walton.

**Julius Irving in his ABA days with the Squires**

Golden State's title romp past Washington only delayed the Bullets' own championship. After Boston took the 1976 title, Portland, Washington and Seattle followed with championships.

Off the court, the last major piece of business was finally resolved when four ABA teams—Denver, Indiana, New York and San Antonio—were admitted into the NBA prior to the 1976–77 season. It seemed only fitting that as the NBA celebrated its 30th season the ABA would be suffering through the last of its problems. The NBA started the 1976–77 season with 22 teams and a whole new group of potential stars.

A controversial trade landed Erving in Philadelphia, while Denver had David Thompson, the first No. 1 draft pick to ever sign with the ABA, and Dan Issel. San Antonio had high-scoring guard George "Ice" Gervin and high-flying Larry Kenon and Indiana had high-scoring Billy Knight.

The Trail Blazers appeared to be on the verge of a dynasty thanks to Walton's presence. But the oft-injured center, who had been compared to everyone from Abdul-Jabbar to Russell, stayed healthy long enough for only a single championship.

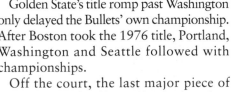

## SHINING STARS

Though four teams ultimately moved from the ABA to the NBA, the biggest winners proved to be basketball fans.

Now, for the first time, fans all over the country were able to see players like Julius Erving, 7–2 center Artis Gilmore, 6–4 scoring machine David Thompson, Dan Issel, Larry Kenon and George Gervin, a smooth-scoring 6–7 guard.

All of those former ABA players had an immediate impact on the NBA. Erving helped Philadelphia to the Atlantic Division title in 1977 while Thompson and Issel keyed Denver's Midwest Division title.

Individually, Indiana's Billy Knight finished second in scoring, Thompson fourth, Gervin ninth and Issel 10th in their first NBA season. Gilmore ranked fourth in rebounds while Indiana's Don Buse led the NBA in assists.

A year later, Gervin and Thompson finished first and second in scoring in one of the most dramatic head-to-head competitions in history. As if in memory of the old ABA and its high-flying, wide-open game, Thompson and Gervin decided the scoring title on the final day.

Thompson made his bid with a brilliant, 73-point performance in an afternoon game. Later that night, Gervin—needing 59 points—scored 63 to win the title, 27.21 ppg to 27.15.

With Walton controlling the middle offensively and defensively, Portland rallied to knock off Julius Erving's Philadelphia 76ers for the 1977 crown.

Seattle and Washington, both led by veteran talent, closed out the decade by meeting back-to-back in the 1978 and 1979 Finals with the Bullets winning the first round and the SuperSonics the second.

With those championships, however, came the end of an era. The next decade would be defined by spectacular worldwide growth off the court and the brilliant play of a whole new generation of players on the court.

The Iceman Cometh: Smooth and graceful, George Gervin often appeared to be gliding through games. Gervin won NBA scoring titles with a unique combination of jump shots, finger rolls and dunks. But it was his cool, almost serene manner, that earned him the nickname "Ice"

# The greatest show on—
# and off—Earth

It all started where it had all started before. Red Auerbach, using a rule that would later be eliminated, selected 6–9 forward Larry Bird as a "junior eligible" in 1978. A year later, the Los Angeles Lakers won the 1979 coin flip and selected 6–9 guard Earvin "Magic" Johnson with the No. 1 pick in the draft. Once again, the league's premier franchises were headed into a decade-long battle with two of the greatest players in history leading the charge. By 1985, the NBA found itself positioned for the most lucrative period of its history. Michael Jordan landed in Chicago and Patrick Ewing in New York, giving the league superstars in its four major markets. The game would never be the same.

The twist and turn of an entire league's future fortunes hung on the flip of a coin in 1979.

By the end of the 1970s, the NBA found itself dominated by secondary markets. The Seattle SuperSonics won the 1979 championship, with Washington, San Antonio and Kansas City winning the other three divisions. The major media centers had dropped back in the pack with Chicago finishing last in the Midwest Division, New York and Boston fourth and fifth, respectively, in the Atlantic and Los Angeles third in the Pacific.

Over the next five seasons, however, luck and Red Auerbach's genius would go a long way toward changing all that.

Boston's Auerbach, as he had done time and again over the previous 30 years, made two moves that transformed the Celtics from a troubled franchise with a dark future into an instant contender.

Coming off a 32–50 season in 1978, Auerbach decided to use the Celtics' first-round draft pick, No. 6 overall, on a 6–9 forward at Indiana State University. Auerbach, invoking a rarely used rule, selected Larry Bird as a junior eligible. Bird had transferred to Indiana State early in his college career, so while his original college class graduated 1978, Bird still had a year of collegiate playing eligibility remaining.

Auerbach didn't care. As with Russell back in the 1950s, Auerbach saw something special in Bird. So while Bird stayed in school for another season, the Celtics limped to a 29–53 record during the 1978–79 season.

But the gamble paid off. Bird arrived for the 1979–80 season after one of the most widely watched college championship games in history. Bird led Indiana State into the NCAA championship game opposite Earvin "Magic" Johnson's Michigan State team.

With two future NBA players surrounding him, Johnson's Spartans cruised past Bird to the 1979 national championship. It proved to be only the beginning of an often brilliant, decade-long battle played out across the entire country.

## THE CELTICS AND LAKERS RISE AGAIN

The Los Angeles Lakers, thanks to a previous trade that gave them Utah's first-round selection, won the annual coin flip for the NBA Draft's first pick and took Johnson. Boston then signed Bird and the league's two most storied franchises were

## "SHOWTIME" IN LOS ANGELES

Hollywood couldn't have made a better casting call. When the Los Angeles Lakers decided to change coaches 11 games into the 1981–82 season they called on Pat Riley, a former player and one of the most intense competitors the game had ever known.

Riley had been a teammate of Lakers General Manager Jerry West and was a reserve on the 1971–72 Lakers team that won 33 straight games. So Riley, like his star Magic Johnson, knew how to win.

With slicked-back hair, a wardrobe full of Italian suits and a style all his own, Riley became the perfect compliment to Johnson's wide-eyed enthusiasm. Riley turned the Lakers into an end-to-end attack, the offense quickly becoming known as "Showtime" for all the points it scored.

When the roster changed later, Riley went back to a low-post attack utalizing Johnson and Kareem Abdul-Jabbar. The Lakers also played solid defense when it mattered most and executed with precision.

Riley left Los Angeles following the 1989-90 season, having guided the Lakers to four championships and seven trips to the Finals in eight years.

back in business.

Very big business.

The coast-to-coast rivalry gave the league a boost no one could have expected. Bird and Johnson had captured the imagination of a nation during college and now they would carry on as professionals in environments perfectly suited to their respective styles. Bird, almost fundamentally perfect, was the ideal match for Boston's proud tradition built on fundamental concepts. As for Johnson, he had a nickname and a personality made for the high glitz Hollywood atmosphere that surrounded Lakers games.

Magic became "the man" in Los Angeles and the Lakers, with legendary Kareem Abdul-Jabbar in the middle, were now a team for the ages.

With the addition of two marquee names in the same season, particularly in Boston and Los Angeles, interest in the league exploded. And the players didn't disappoint.

The Lakers won the first championship of the Magic era with a dramatic Game 6 victory over Philadelphia in 1980. Johnson, forced to play center after Abdul-

**OPPOSITE Magic Johnson; (RIGHT) Larry Bird**

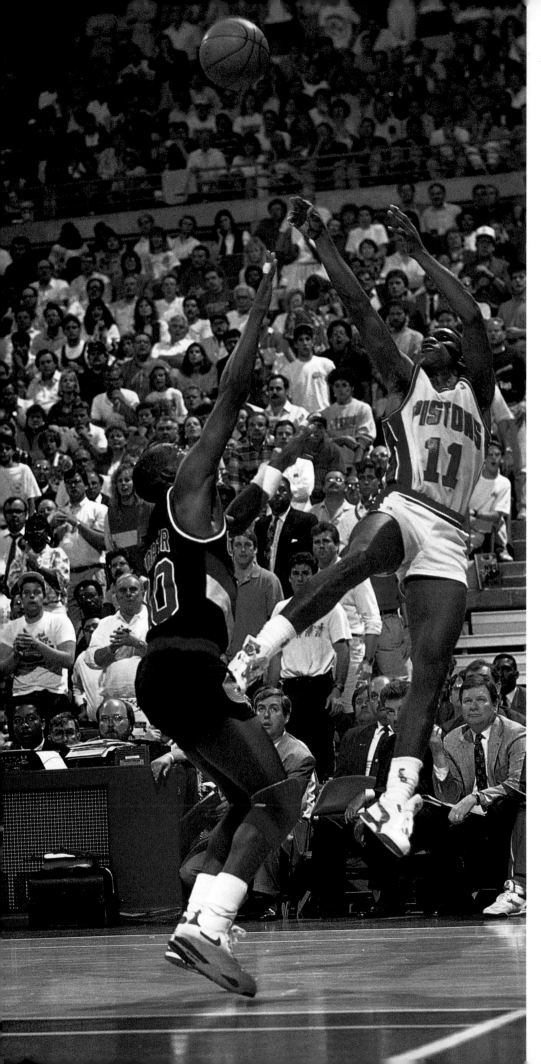

Jabbar was injured in Game 5, scored 42 points, grabbed 15 rebounds and handed out seven assists in a stunning 123–107 victory over the 76ers and Julius Erving at Philadelphia.

While Johnson had been solid during the regular season, nothing marked his legend like that championship performance. Bird, however, edged Johnson for Rookie of the Year by leading the Celtics to a 61–21 record and the Atlantic Division title.

"Magic was the only player who could take three shots and still dominate a game," Erving said later.

Indeed, Magic and Bird went on to dominate the first half of the decade, with the Celtics winning their first title in 1981. And once more, Auerbach was in the middle of it all.

Prior to the season, Auerbach sent the No. 1 pick in the draft, which the Celtics had acquired in a trade, plus the No. 15 choice to Golden State for center Robert Parish and rights to the No. 3 pick, which turned out to be Kevin McHale. With Cedric Maxwell occupying the forward spot opposite Bird, Boston rolled.

The Celtics rallied past Philadelphia in the Eastern Conference Finals before dismissing Houston for the 1981 title.

## TWO GREAT TEAMS

For Bird and Johnson, the real showdown didn't come until 1984. Erving's 76ers, including center Moses Malone, made back-to-back Finals appearances in 1982 and 1983 against the Lakers, with each team gaining a championship.

But it was the 1983–84 season that really kick-started professional basketball into a whole new gear. The high-scoring Denver Nuggets, coached by Doug Moe, led the league in scoring by averaging an amazing 123.7 points per game. Included in the Nuggets' season-long sprint was one of the more remarkable games in NBA history.

Matched against the Detroit Pistons, Denver scored 184 points and still managed to lose. The Pistons, led by Isiah Thomas,

**Little Big Man: Size was never an issue for 6–1 superstar Isiah Thomas**

scored 186 and won in triple overtime in the highest scoring game of all time.

Elsewhere, the heavyweight bout everyone wanted to see slowly started to form. Boston breezed through the Eastern Conference and the Lakers did the same in the West.

For the first time since college, Bird and Johnson faced one another with a championship on the line as the 1984 Finals unfolded. This time, however, Bird found a measure of revenge.

And he had plenty of help.

One more move by Auerbach solidified the roster and set the process in motion. The Celtics acquired guard Dennis Johnson, a defensive specialist and former All-Star, in a steal of a deal with Phoenix before the season.

The Lakers, having gained James Worthy in the 1982 NBA Draft, were just as loaded with talent. So when the two teams opened the Finals in Boston, the eyes of an international audience were fixed on them.

The series embodied all the elements that had turned the NBA into the hottest professional sports league in the world. The three-point shot, an ABA feature instituted prior to the 1979–80 season, proved to be an exciting weapon in crunch time.

There were blowout victories by both teams, two dramatic overtime games and an even more compelling Game 7 showdown inside fabled Boston Garden. When it ended, Bird was named the Finals' Most Valuable Player and the NBA, already expanding rapidly beyond the United States, hit another new high in fan interest.

# THE JORDAN PHENOMENON

As it turned out, the 1984 Finals were only the beginning. Chicago, using the No. 3 pick in the 1984 Draft, selected Michael

**Dream Maker: Hakeem Olajuwon lifts another jump hook**

Jordan in a move that rocked the record books and changed history.

For the second straight season Houston gained the No. 1 pick in the draft and selected a center. This time, the Rockets landed Hakeem Olajuwon. With 7–4 Ralph Sampson arriving the previous season, Olajuwon completed the "Twin Towers" in Houston.

Meanwhile, Portland decided to gamble with the No. 2 choice. The Trail Blazers had Clyde Drexler on their roster and desperately needed a center. So intead of taking Jordan, Portland chose 7–1 center Sam Bowie, who had missed two entire college seasons with leg injuries.

Unfortunately for the Trail Blazers, Bowie's problems weren't behind him. Bowie missed an average of nearly 55 games a season during his five years in Portland.

With Jordan, the Bulls couldn't have been happier. He pumped life into a franchise that was near collapse and turned the cold and empty Chicago Stadium into one of the loudest arenas in all of sports. He also helped turn the league into a marketing phenomenon.

Jordan's shoe and apparel deal with Nike established a whole new commercial presence for professional athletes. Jordan, unlike Bird, Johnson or Erving before him, had a personalized shoe that sold millions of pairs before the 1984–85 season ended.

Jordan finished third in the league in scoring behind New York's Bernard King and Bird, averaging 28.2 points.

More importantly for the league, Jordan turned the Bulls into a wondrous road show despite an otherwise ragged roster.

The Bulls finished third in the Central Division and reached the playoffs for only the second time in eight years. Off the court, Jordan turned into a household name with major marketing and advertising deals covering everything from soft drinks to fast food and automobiles.

"He's the real thing, no question," said Kevin Loughery, Jordan's first NBA coach. "He understands the entire game, on and off the court. No one knows how good this kid is

going to be. He's a killer. This guy will be one of the greatest players to ever play the game if he stays healthy."

Meanwhile another Lakers-Celtics championship showdown ended with the title going back to Los Angeles. But not for long.

The Celtics added the often-injured veteran center Bill Walton for the 1985–86 season and came within two games of the regular-season victory record. Boston finished 67–15 and roared into the Finals against Houston's towering frontline of 7-foot Olajuwon, 7–4 Sampson and 6–8 Rodney McCray.

First, however, Boston had to dismiss Jordan's pesky Bulls. Jordan had missed all but 18 games of the regular season due to a broken foot. He returned for the first round of the playoffs and put on one of the greatest one-man shows in history.

Playing against the eventual champs with a thin supporting cast, Jordan bombed Dennis Johnson and the Celtics for 49 points in a Game 1 loss. Then, before a national television audience on a warm Sunday afternoon, Jordan exploded for 63 points and carried the Bulls into double overtime before the Celtics prevailed.

Although Boston went on to sail through the Eastern Conference playoffs, Bird had seen more than enough of Jordan.

"Maybe it was God disguised as Michael Jordan," quipped Bird after the Game 2 scare, the highest scoring playoff performance in history.

## THE LOTTERY

Houston's ability to land consecutive No. 1 picks led to the creation of the lottery for the 1985 Draft. And that's when the final piece of the puzzle fell in place for the NBA.

New York, the league's primary media market, had finished 23-59 and needed help. More specifically, the New York market needed a star. And they got one when

the Knicks ended up with the No. 1 pick and landed 7–0 center Patrick Ewing.

For the league, the circle was virtually complete. With Johnson in Los Angeles, Bird in Boston, Jordan in Chicago and Ewing in New York, the NBA became an even more lucrative television draw. On the marketing side, the league was moving outside the United States and into countries all over the world with sales of league merchandise spiraling.

"This is the best game in sports," said former Bulls Coach Stan Albeck at the time. "You have everything. The game is fast, the players are incredibly skilled and going to an NBA arena is fun. The whole thing is entertainment."

It wasn't until the 1987–88 season that a slow changing of the guard started to take place. Detroit, with a tough and disciplined lineup keyed by Thomas, finally knocked Boston out of the playoffs and reached the Finals. In terms of championships, the Bird era ended when the Pistons closed out the Eastern Conference Finals with a 4–2 decision over the Celtics in 1988.

Although Johnson helped the Lakers rally to a 4–3 victory over Detroit in the 1988 NBA Finals, his championship dreams ended as well. The Lakers had become the first team since the Celtics in 1968 and 1969 to win consecutive championships.

## A NEW ERA DAWNS

But the pages were turning. Kareem Abdul-Jabbar retired the following season after 20 brilliant seasons and 44,149 points.

"It couldn't have been any better," said Abdul-Jabbar. "Not when I can remember growing up on the streets of Manhattan and hoping I got to play one pro season. I outlasted everybody. I got to play with the greats of the game. I realized all my professional goals."

The times, as evidenced by the Pistons' 4–0 pasting of the Lakers in the 1989 Finals, were indeed changing.

Nowhere was that more evident than in Detroit. Known for their rough and tumble defense, the Pistons made a third straight trip to the championship round in 1990 after yet another bruising Eastern Conference playoff match with Jordan's Bulls.

LEFT Michael Jordan sails in for another slam; (OPPOSITE) John Paxson launches a three-pointer

With Thomas leading the Pistons' charge, Detroit knocked off Portland for a second straight championship. Like the Lakers before them, the Pistons felt they had left their mark by winning two in a row. But unlike the Lakers, the run came to a close quickly.

With solid support in Scottie Pippen, Horace Grant and Bill Cartwright and the steady leadership of Coach Phil Jackson behind him, Jordan guided the Bulls to the promised land in 1991. Chicago won 61 regular season games, a franchise record, and then marched through the playoffs.

The Bulls pounded Charles Barkley's Philadelphia 76ers 4–1, then crushed the arch-rival Pistons 4–0 before knocking off Johnson's Lakers 4–1 in the 1991 Finals.

As it turned out, the league would never be the same. In a stunning development prior to the 1991–92 season, Johnson announced he had the HIV and would retire from basketball.

Though he immediately went to work raising money and awareness of HIV, the basketball world shook. Johnson, one of the classiest players sport had ever known, left with five championships rings and nine trips to the Finals. His smile and enthusiasm had turned a game into entertainment and his ability had turned the Lakers into a remarkable end-to-end show.

"Describing Earvin Johnson is more complicated than one might guess because the man is more complicated than he at first seems," says Abdul-Jabbar. "The whole world knows about his sense of showmanship and his flair for the spectacular, but the inner man, the fierce competitor with the iron will to win, is often concealed by the smile and the easy demeanor."

As Johnson left the game, Bird limped on behind him. Though Boston remained among the East's strongest teams, Bird missed 45 games during the 1991–92 season due to injury.

## THE BULLS DOMINATE

The future suddenly moved to Chicago.

With Jordan winning his sixth straight scoring title and the roster staying healthy, the Bulls sprinted to a 67–15 regular season record. But they didn't stop there. After rolling through the East on its way to the Finals, the Bulls upended Portland with a dramatic fourth-quarter comeback in Game 6 inside Chicago Stadium.

"Can they win three in a row?" Magic Johnson considered the thought as USA Basketball's Dream Team prepared for the Barcelona Olympics following Chicago's dumping of the Trail Blazers.

"They could, but I don't know," said Johnson. "If they thought winning two in a row was tough, winning three is even harder. I know. I tried."

Though Johnson flirted briefly with a comeback, he remained a key member of the gold medal winning Dream Team and nothing more. Bird too announced his retirement after a long summer of soul-searching, his sore back too far gone to be of any use to the Celtics. Meanwhile, Jordan and the rest of the NBA prepared for yet another battle.

Phoenix pulled off one of the biggest trades in NBA history prior to the 1992–93 season by dealing three players to Philadelphia in return for Charles Barkley. The New York Knicks, which had narrowly missed knocking the Bulls out in 1992, added Charles Smith and Doc Rivers. And Coach Pat Riley, who had presided over four titles with the Lakers, sensed his first in New York.

But Jordan had other ideas. Although tired and fighting nagging injuries, Jordan won his seventh straight scoring title to match Wilt Chamberlain's league record. Then in the playoffs, with the Bulls fighting fatigue and long odds, Jordan grabbed hold of the team and never let go.

Chicago fought off the Knicks by rallying from a 2-0 deficit to win four straight games in the Eastern Conference Finals. In the 1993 Finals, Jordan came through one last time against Barkley, perhaps his best friend in the league.

A John Paxson three-pointer with 3.9 seconds left in Game 6 at Phoenix provided the margin of victory as Chicago became the first team in 27 years to win three consecutive titles.

Less than two months later, Jordan retired and turned the league over to a whole new group of rising stars.

"It's their turn now," says Jordan. "I've had my fun. I loved it while I was there, but it's time to move on."

# THE NBA FINALS

| YEAR | WINNER | SERIES | LOSER |
|------|--------|--------|-------|
| 1947 | Philadelphia | 4–1 | Chicago |
| 1948 | Baltimore | 4–2 | Philadelphia |
| 1949 | Minneapolis | 4–2 | Washington |
| 1950 | Minneapolis | 4–2 | Syracuse |
| 1951 | Rochester | 4–3 | New York |
| 1952 | Minneapolis | 4–3 | New York |
| 1953 | Minneapolis | 4–1 | New York |
| 1954 | Minneapolis | 4–3 | Syracuse |
| 1955 | Syracuse | 4–3 | Fort Worth |
| 1956 | Philadelphia | 4–1 | Fort Worth |
| 1957 | Boston | 4–3 | St. Louis |
| 1958 | St. Louis | 4–2 | Boston |
| 1959 | Boston | 4–0 | Minneapolis |
| 1960 | Boston | 4–3 | St. Louis |
| 1961 | Boston | 4–1 | St. Louis |
| 1962 | Boston | 4–3 | Los Angeles |
| 1963 | Boston | 4–2 | Los Angeles |
| 1964 | Boston | 4–1 | San Francisco |
| 1965 | Boston | 4–1 | Los Angeles |
| 1966 | Boston | 4–3 | Los Angeles |
| 1967 | Philadelphia | 4–2 | San Francisco |
| 1968 | Boston | 4–2 | Los Angeles |
| 1969 | Boston | 4–3 | Los Angeles |
| 1970 | New York | 4–3 | Los Angeles |
| 1971 | Milwaukee | 4–0 | Baltimore |
| 1972 | Los Angeles | 4–1 | New York |
| 1973 | New York | 4–1 | Los Angeles |
| 1974 | Boston | 4–3 | Milwaukee |
| 1975 | Golden State | 4–0 | Washington |
| 1976 | Boston | 4–2 | Phoenix |
| 1977 | Portland | 4–2 | Philadelphia |
| 1978 | Washington | 4–3 | Seattle |
| 1979 | Seattle | 4–1 | Washington |
| 1980 | Los Angeles | 4–2 | Philadelphia |
| 1981 | Boston | 4–2 | Houston |
| 1982 | Los Angeles | 4–2 | Philadelphia |
| 1983 | Philadelphia | 4–0 | Los Angeles |
| 1984 | Boston | 4–2 | Los Angeles Lakers |
| 1985 | Los Angeles Lakers | 4–2 | Boston |
| 1986 | Boston | 4–2 | Houston |
| 1987 | Los Angeles Lakers | 4–2 | Boston |
| 1988 | Los Angeles Lakers | 4–3 | Detroit |
| 1989 | Detroit | 4–0 | Los Angeles Lakers |
| 1990 | Detroit | 4–1 | Portland |
| 1991 | Chicago | 4–1 | Los Angeles Lakers |
| 1992 | Chicago | 4–2 | Portland |
| 1993 | Chicago | 4–2 | Phoenix |
| 1994 | Houston | 4–3 | New York |

# THE TEAMS

For all the individual demands, basketball has always revolved around the rhythm of a team. From the beginning the NBA has been identified by its teams, those great and those in pursuit of greatness.

The record books are full of names and numbers, superstars and stats. Individuals win scoring titles, rebounding titles and block all the shots. They pass out assists and lead the league in steals. But all of them operate within the context of a team. And the greatest of those teams – the Boston Celtics, Los Angeles Lakers and Chicago Bulls – managed to combine diverse individual talents into a singular battle plan.

In the 1950s, every NBA team chased the Minneapolis Lakers. But for all George Mikan's brilliance, not even he could have carried the Lakers to championship after championship by himself. When the Celtics came together under the guidance of Arnold "Red" Auerbach, they came together as a cohesive unit with stars at virtually every position. The Los Angeles Lakers, with Magic Johnson leading the charge in the 1980s, relied on a selfless approach that mirrored that of Auerbach's Celtics. Even with Michael Jordan, perhaps the greatest player to ever play the game, the Chicago Bulls didn't win a single title until Scottie Pippen, Horace Grant and others filled in around him. From East to West, NBA teams have fought to create their own history, each of them traveling the same road in search of championships.

**Alonzo Mourning tries to score on New York's Patrick Ewing**

# Forward March!

**Atlanta Hawks**

For many of their early NBA years, Atlanta was a franchise on the move. The Hawks played in Moline, Milwaukee and St. Louis before landing in Atlanta. The common thread in all those stops has been the presence of a high-scoring forward. In the early years it was Bob Pettit. Most recently, the team has been led by Dominique Wilkins, one of the greatest showmen the league has ever seen.

Few NBA teams have had as many lives as the Atlanta Hawks. And few have had a more colorful past. Though blessed with a rich history that includes some of the league's most noted players and coaches—Arnold "Red" Auerbach coached the team briefly before it moved from the old National Basketball League to the NBA—Atlanta spent its early years moving through the Midwest in search of a home.

The Hawks made their NBA debut in 1949, coming from the old NBL as the Tri-City Blackhawks. They moved to Milwaukee two years later and legendary coach Red Holzman, who would become one of the most successful leaders in history while running the New York Knicks, eventually came on and guided the Hawks

**Spud Webb: 1986 Slam-Dunk Champion**

through the first of many difficult transitions. Holzman actually started out as a player/coach for the Hawks, but neither his playing nor his coaching could pull the team above the .500 mark.

Then the Hawks got a break. Though the struggle would continue, the 1954 NBA Draft produced one of the game's greatest players. Bob Pettit, a brilliant scorer and perhaps the greatest forward of his era, arrived from Louisiana State University. Not even Pettit's star power, however, could keep fan interest in Milwaukee.

So owner Ben Kerner moved the Hawks, complete with Pettit and Holzman, to St. Louis where the franchise flourished. But not before the Hawks participated in one of the most famous trades in NBA history. In April, 1956, the Hawks sent their first-round draft choice to Boston for Ed Macauley and Cliff Hagan. Though Macauley and Hagan became Hall of Famers, Boston ended up getting the better of the deal. That first-round pick produced Bill Russell, who would lead the Celtics to a remarkable 11 NBA titles.

The first of those came at the expense of the Hawks. Boston beat St. Louis for the 1957 NBA title. But a year later, with Pettit leading the way, the Hawks won their first and only championship by downing Russell's Celtics. Boston won the next eight titles while the Hawks remained strong, but never quite good enough.

The team eventually moved again, this time to Atlanta in 1968. The next great wave came during the mid 1980s when Dominique Wilkins, one of the most exciting players ever, became the team's leading scorer. Wilkins, combined with players

| ROLL OF HONOR | | | | |
|---|---|---|---|---|
| **Conference/Division** | Eastern/Central | | | |
| **First NBA year** | 1949-50 | | | |
| **Home Arena details** | The Omni (built 1972, capacity 16,510) | | | |
| **Former cities/nicknames** | Tri-Cities Blackhawks (1949-51), Milwaukee Hawks (1951-55), St. Louis Hawks (1955-68) | | | |
| **NBA Championships** | 1958 | | | |
| **Playing Record** | **G** | **W** | **L** | **Pct** |
| **Regular Season** | 3550 | 1796 | 1754 | .506 |
| **Playoffs (Series 17-30)** | 233 | 105 | 128 | .451 |

# LENNY WILKENS
## A Coach's Coach

Lenny Wilkens always played the game as if he were a coach on the court.

He displayed an unusual ability to break down defenses as evidenced by a 15-year career that included nine All-Star Game appearances. Fundamentally strong and given to a quiet leadership, Wilkens actually started coaching before he ever finished playing.

Wilkens' first coaching assignment came at Seattle in 1969. Twice during three seasons as player/coach he led the league in assists while never averaging less than 17.8 points per game.

Wilkens eventually continued his playing career at Cleveland and then Portland, where he once again became a player/coach. In 1975, a brilliant playing career behind him, Wilkens turned his attention to coaching full time.

Wilkens returned to Seattle and led the SuperSonics into the NBA Finals two consecutive seasons, the second of which produced the first championship in franchise history in 1979.

such as Kevin Willis, Tree Rollins and Glen "Doc" Rivers, led a spirited run during the 1986–87 season. But once again, the Boston Celtics were there to answer.

The Hawks, like their days in St. Louis, ran into a Boston franchise in high gear. Though Atlanta won 50 or more games four straight seasons in the 1980s, the Celtics were in the midst of a rebirth behind Larry Bird and dominated the Eastern Conference for much of the decade.

Atlanta could be headed toward higher ground, however. Danny Manning, acquired from the L.A. Clippers for Wilkins in 1994, is an All-Star forward who can score and pass effectively. And Lenny Wilkens has proven to be among the greatest coaches in history. He entered the 1993-94 season just 69 victories short of Red Auerbach's NBA record of 938.

**Ballhawking: Dominique Wilkins (front), Andrew Lang and Kevin Willis secure two points**

# Basketball's Greatest Franchise

No team in the history of professional sports in America dominated more completely than the Boston Celtics of the late 1950s and 1960s. With a legendary coach in Arnold "Red" Auerbach on the sidelines and Bill Russell, perhaps the greatest big man ever to play the game, playing center, the Celtics won 11 championships in 13 years including an NBA record eight straight. Boston has won more regular season games and postseason titles than any team in NBA history.

By the time Arnold "Red" Auerbach turned over the day-to-day operations of the Boston Celtics, no one doubted the genius of the NBA's most successful coach.

As a coach, Auerbach presided over the greatest dynasty in the history of professional sports in America. His Celtics won nine championships including a stunning eight straight during the late 1950s and early 1960s. But that was only part of Auerbach's contribution to Boston's storied history.

His greatest attribute might have been making deals and evaluating talent. The first of three franchise-shaking moves came prior to the 1956–57 season when Auerbach traded veteran stars Ed Macauley

**Dynamic Duo: Bill and "Red" celebrate!**

and Cliff Hagan to St. Louis for the Hawks' first-round pick in the 1956 Draft.

The player Auerbach wanted was 6–10 center Bill Russell. He also selected K.C. Jones and made Tommy Heinsohn a territorial pick. A year later, with his first pick,

Auerbach added shooting guard Sam Jones. These eventual Hall of Famers helped turn Boston into a dynasty.

During the 1960s, Auerbach continued to build the team through the draft. In 1962, following the Celtics fourth straight title, Boston selected John Havlicek in the first round.

Following the 1965–66 season, Auerbach turned the coaching duties over to Russell, who became the NBA's first black head coach. Russell's teams won two more titles in his three seasons in the dual role of player/coach.

Boston won two more titles in the 1970s with Heinsohn coaching a team dominated by Havlicek and Dave Cowens. But just as the Celtics appeared headed for an extended lull following a sub-.500 season in 1977–78, Auerbach made another round of off-court moves that would define yet another era.

Auerbach used the team's first-round draft pick to select Larry Bird. It was a gutsy move, since Bird wasn't eligible to join the Celtics for a year. It was also the second great move of Auerbach's career. Although the Celtics suffered another losing season waiting for Bird's arrival, he would prove to be well worth the wait.

With another high draft pick, Auerbach made his third franchise-changing move. He traded two first-round picks to Golden State for center Robert Parish and the No. 3

## ROLL OF HONOR

| | | | | |
|---|---|---|---|---|
| **Conference/Division** | Eastern/Atlantic | | | |
| **First NBA year** | 1946-47 | | | |
| **Home Arena details** | Boston Garden (built 1928, capacity 14,890) | | | |
| **Former cities/nicknames** | None | | | |
| **NBA Championships** | 1957, 1959, 1960, 1961, 1962, 1963, 1964, 1965, | | | |
| | 1966, 1968, 1969, 1974, 1976, 1981, 1984, 1986 | | | |

| **Playing Record** | G | W | L | Pct |
|---|---|---|---|---|
| **Regular Season** | 3723 | 2354 | 1369 | .632 |
| **Playoffs (Series 63-24)** | 457 | 271 | 186 | .593 |

★ ★ ★ ★ ★ ★ ★ ★ ★

# RED AUERBACH
## A Basketball Genius

If Arnold "Red" Auerbach had only coached, he would be remembered as one of the NBA's true legends.

But Auerbach did much more than that during a career that started in the 1940s and continues into the 1990s. As Coach, then General Manager, Auerbach knew exactly the kind of player that could make it in the NBA.

Auerbach shipped two future Hall of Fame players to St. Louis for the rights to the Hawks' first pick in the 1956 Draft. Auerbach then used that pick to select Bill Russell, who would turn Auerbach's gamble into a monumental payoff.

With Auerbach coaching and managing the team's roster, Boston won nine NBA championships in 10 years, including a remarkable string of eight straight.

Auerbach moved to the front office following the 1965–66 season. But his moves help produce seven additional championships.

And at the end of all of them, Auerbach could be found lighting a gigantic "victory cigar", which became as much a symbol of the Celtics success as the man himself.

pick overall, which Auerbach then used to select Kevin McHale. Auerbach eventually landed guards Dennis Johnson and Danny Ainge in separate deals, all of which made Boston the Eastern Conference's dominant team yet again during the 1980s.

The Bird era produced three championships and five more trips to the NBA Finals.

And the dominance might have continued had tragedy not dealt the franchise two major blows. Young Len Bias, considered the link to yet another golden era, died in 1986 before playing a single game for the Celtics. Then in the summer of 1993, Reggie Lewis, Boston's leading scorer, died unexpectedly while preparing to play in a pick-up game.

Whether the Celtics return to their championship form anytime soon remains to be seen. One thing seems sure: If it can be done, Auerbach probably knows the way.

● ● ● ● ● ● ● ● ● ● ● ● ● ● ● ● ● ● ● ● ● ● ●

Celtics Trio: Pinckney (54), Fox (55), Gamble (31)

# The NBA's Buzz

Considered a long shot when the most recent expansion process started, Charlotte put together a solid plan and found itself with one of four new franchises. With smart marketing moves and even brighter player decisions, the Hornets have become one of the most successful young teams in the league. With young superstars in Larry Johnson and Alonzo Mourning, no one doubts Charlotte now.

They came out of nowhere in 1988, and the Charlotte Hornets haven't stopped rolling since.

One of two franchises added to the league prior to the 1988–89 season, Charlotte started making all the right moves immediately. On the court, the Hornets drafted wisely and moved patiently while building one of the league's best young teams. Off the court, Charlotte became one of the NBA's most popular franchises by combining basketball success with brilliant marketing.

As a result, Charlotte led the league in attendance in four of its first five seasons. The 23,698-seat Charlotte Coliseum is one of the NBA's largest and loudest arenas, its fans packing the "Hive" for virtually every home game since the team arrived.

**Gattison's Got It: Kenny grabs a rebound**

But there are at least a couple reasons for all the noise and notice. One of those is All-Star forward Larry Johnson. A rugged rebounder and powerful scorer, Johnson became the team's first real pillar. Charlotte used the first pick in the 1991 Draft to select Johnson from the University of Nevada-Las Vegas (UNLV). And he didn't disappoint.

Johnson quickly became recognized as one of the best power forwards in the league. He averaged more than 20 points and 10 rebounds in each of his first two seasons. Johnson was named NBA Rookie of the Year and a year later was chosen to the All-NBA Second Team.

"He's a great player," says former Chicago Bulls Coach Doug Collins. "Larry Johnson isn't afraid to mix it up inside or move outside and take the big shot. He's going to be a star in this league, no question."

But Johnson couldn't get it done alone. Although high draft picks like J.R. Reid and Kendall Gill had preceded Johnson, the Hornets struggled through their first four seasons.

Then came Alonzo Mourning. Although Orlando's Shaquille O'Neal gained more notoriety during the 1992–93 season, Mourning established himself as one of the best young centers to enter the NBA in years.

"Alonzo is a force," says Johnson. "He's the kind of player that can take the pres-

## ROLL OF HONOR

| | | | | |
|---|---|---|---|---|
| Conference/Division | Eastern/Central | | | |
| First NBA year | 1988-89 | | | |
| Home Arena details | Charlotte Coliseum (built 1988, capacity 23,698) | | | |
| Former cities/nicknames | None | | | |
| NBA Championships | None | | | |
| Playing Record | G | W | L | Pct |
| Regular Season | 492 | 181 | 311 | .368 |
| Playoffs (Series 1-1) | 9 | 4 | 5 | .444 |

sure off me and help us win a championship."

The year before Mourning arrived, Charlotte had stumbled to a 31–51 record. Kenny Gattison, though a solid competitor, had been forced to play the middle despite standing just 6–8. Opposing teams had taken advantage, which forced Johnson to carry much of the offensive and defensive load.

But all that changed with Mourning. The Hornets, under new Coach Allan Bristow, won 44 regular-season games to make the playoffs for the first time.

Charlotte more than passed its first playoff test. The Hornets blew by Boston in the First Round of the 1993 postseason and fought the powerful New York Knicks hard before getting eliminated in the Eastern Conference Semifinals.

Still, vestiges of Charlotte's embryonic era remain. Tyrone "Muggsy" Bogues, the league's smallest player at 5–3, and Dell Curry, a long-range shooter, have been with the team since the opening season.

For the Hornets, a five-year plan was all they needed. Now skeptics can only wonder how long will it be before Charlotte can be found buzzing around the NBA Finals?

The Long And Short Of It: 5–3 Muggsy Bogues and 6–10 Alonzo Mourning

## ALONZO MOURNING
### A Man In The Middle

Alonzo Mourning arrived overshadowed by Orlando's Shaquille O'Neal. At 7–1 and 301 pounds, O'Neal figured to dominate the 6–10, 240-pound Mourning.

Mourning, however, had something no one could measure. Defiant and driven by a deep competitive streak developed at Georgetown University, Mourning attacked the league with a vengeance.

He averaged 21.0 points, 10.3 rebounds and 3.47 blocked shots a game, impressive numbers for a veteran, much less a rookie. Mourning immediately established himself as one of the NBA's next great players, dueling head-to-head with O'Neal and leading Charlotte to three straight victories over O'Neal's Orlando Magic.

Still, that wasn't enough for Mourning. He spent much of the 1993 summer working out with former Georgetown star Patrick Ewing. If the Charlotte Hornets are going anywhere, it's a good bet Alonzo Mourning will be the one directing them.

# CHICAGO BULLS

# Defending The Throne

With one of the game's greatest players in Michael Jordan, the Chicago Bulls became the first team in more than 25 years to win three straight NBA Championships. Jordan turned a struggling franchise into the dominant team of the early 1990s with a spectacular combination of style and substance that made the Bulls one of the best teams in league history.

The Chicago Bulls story is a tale of two eras, with defense the single thread connecting them.

When Coach Dick Motta took over the Bulls in 1968, the franchise was entering its third season. Johnny "Red" Kerr had guided the expansion Bulls into the playoffs in their first two seasons, but management wanted a fresh young coach and hired Motta.

Within a year, Motta had built the offense around a pair of high-scoring forwards in Bob Love and Chet Walker. The defense revolved around Jerry Sloan, whose competitive intensity intimidated many opponents.

From 1970 to 1975, Chicago led the league in defense twice and never finished lower than third. Still, the Bulls were never quite good enough. They reached the

**Sky High: Bearded Bill Wennington makes space**

Western Conference Finals in 1974 and then again in 1975.

After Motta left for Washington in 1976, management acquired aging stars like Artis Gilmore and Larry Kenon. When that didn't work, ownership compounded the

problem with poor draft choices.

By 1984 the Bulls were in desperate need of a savior.

They got three of them.

First, Michael Jordan arrived in the 1984 Draft. Then Jerry Reinsdorf bought the team midway through the 1984–85 season and inserted Jerry Krause as general manager. Krause, who had been a Bulls scout in the late 1960s and early 1970s, knew exactly the kind of team he wanted. He had watched Motta win games with defense and like Reinsdorf, who had long admired Red Holzman's New York Knicks, wanted a team that could play both ends of the court.

Though it took two coaching changes and nearly six seasons, Krause eventually built a team to complement Jordan's extraordinary talents. The key moves came on a single day in 1987. The Bulls made a deal with Seattle to acquire the draft rights to Scottie Pippen and then selected Horace Grant with their own first-round pick.

A year later the final piece to a championship puzzle arrived in the form of aging 7–1 center Bill Cartwright. Coach Phil Jackson, a player on those Knicks teams that Reinsdorf remembered, built the defense around Jordan, who had become the league's best defensive guard as well as its premier scorer.

So it wasn't surprising that the Bulls turned in one of the most dominating play-

## ROLL OF HONOR

| | | | | |
|---|---|---|---|---|
| Conference/Division | Eastern/Central | | | |
| First NBA year | 1966-67 | | | |
| Home Arena details | Chicago Stadium (built 1929, capacity 17,339) | | | |
| Former cities/nicknames | None | | | |
| NBA Championships | 1991, 1992, 1993 | | | |

| Playing Record | G | W | L | Pct |
|---|---|---|---|---|
| Regular Season | 2295 | 1197 | 1098 | .522 |
| Playoffs (Series 21-17) | 185 | 97 | 88 | .524 |

# BOB LOVE
## A Love Story

That Bob Love, who came from a small Louisiana town with a severe stutter, ever made it in the NBA, much less a record book, is one of the league's great stories of pride and perseverance.

In 1965, Love, a brilliant player at Southern University, wasn't drafted until the fourth round by Cincinnati.

Cut by the Royals, Love ended up in the old Eastern League playing for $50 a game while working part time in a hospital. In 1969, Love joined Chicago.

A year later, Love played all 82 games for the Bulls and led the team in scoring with 21.0 points per game. He went on to lead Chicago in scoring seven straight seasons, never averaging less than 19.1 points a game. Love also made the NBA All-Defensive Second Team three times.

Chicago retired his uniform No. 10 early in the 1993–94 season.

off performances in history in 1991. Chicago won 15-of-17 playoff games and defeated Magic Johnson's Los Angeles Lakers in the NBA Finals for its first title.

A year later, with the starting lineup intact, the Bulls won their second straight championship by blitzing Portland. And then, in what turned out to be Jordan's final season, Chicago made history. The Bulls marched back into the NBA Finals for the third consecutive year. Once there, Jordan refused to let his team lose. He averaged 41 points in six games against Phoenix, including 55 in Game 4 alone.

Then, thanks to a game-winning three-pointer from John Paxson in Game 6, the Bulls joined the Boston Celtics (1959–66) and Minneapolis Lakers (1952–54) as the only teams in NBA history to win as many as three consecutive championships.

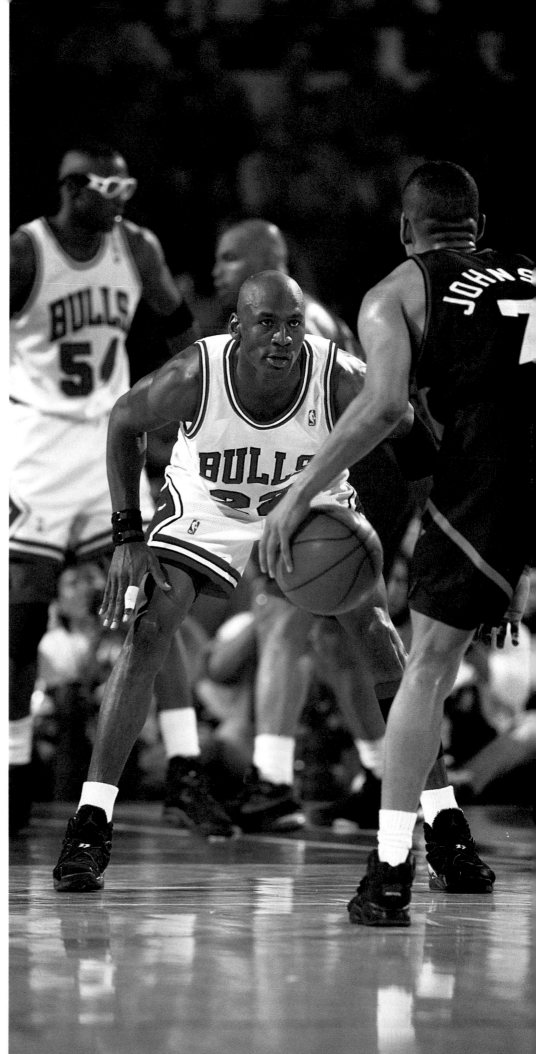

**Eye Of The Tiger:** Michael Jordan focuses on another victim — this time the intended prey is Phoenix guard Kevin Johnson

# Back From The Brink

A little more than a decade after nearly collapsing beneath the weight of bad decisions on and off the court, Cleveland has become one of the NBA's most solid franchises. With a revamped front office, committed ownership and stars like Mark Price and Brad Daugherty, the Cavaliers have become an Eastern Conference power.

For a while, the Cleveland Cavaliers looked like basketball's version of a roller-coaster. The only problem was no one knew for sure whether the Cavaliers would ever pick up enough steam to climb back up after crashing on the way down.

Like most expansion teams, Cleveland started slowly when it got the green light to take off in 1970. Under Coach Bill Fitch, the Cavaliers stumbled early and often. They lost the first 15 games in franchise history before slowly gaining ground during their first four seasons.

Players such as Bobby "Bingo" Smith, Walt Wesley and Butch Beard, along with top draft picks Austin Carr, Jim Brewer and Campy Russell, helped fuel a steady climb. After winning 15 games in their first season, the Cavaliers improved to 40 by 1974–75.

And a year later, thanks to a timely trade, the team really started rolling. After a 6–11 start to the 1975–76 season, the Cavaliers traded for aging center Nate Thurmond, a future Hall of Famer. Thurmond's influence helped steady the team, particularly young Jim Chones, and Cleveland began to come together.

The Cavaliers won 43 of their last 65 games to finish 49–33 and charged into the playoffs. Once there, Cleveland dispatched the Washington Bullets in a dramatic seven-game series. The Cavaliers lost to eventual champion Boston in the Eastern Conference Finals after Chones was sidelined with a broken foot.

It would be the first in a series of bad breaks for Cleveland. Injuries pushed the team on a downhill course that only gathered steam in 1979 when the franchise was sold to Ted Stepien.

Under Stepien's erratic hand, Cleveland went through seven head coaches (including Bill Musselman twice) and never won more than 28 games from 1980 through 1983. Stepien so mismanaged the team that the NBA executive office actually stepped in and awarded the Cavaliers a "bonus" first-round pick in 1983 in an attempt to salvage the franchise.

By then, however, the Cavaliers had bottomed out. When new owners took over in 1983, the only way to go was up and that's exactly where Cleveland headed once Wayne Embry joined the front office and Lenny Wilkens took over as head coach.

Cleveland traded for center Brad Daugherty on Draft Day in 1986 and never looked back. The Cavaliers added All-Stars Mark Price and Larry Nance via trades and bolstered the bench with draft choices such as John "Hot Rod" Williams and Terrell Brandon.

The combination of off-court leadership and on-court talent made Cleveland one of the most successful teams of the late 1980s. Led by Wilkens' even-handed approach, the Cavaliers became one of the Eastern Conference's most dynamic teams.

The offense, keyed by Price and Daugherty, was smooth and efficient. Wilkens, a former All-Star point guard, developed an unselfish approach that made Cleveland among the most difficult teams in the league to defend. Concentrate too

## R O L L   O F   H O N O R

| | | | | |
|---|---|---|---|---|
| **Conference/Division** | Eastern/Central | | | |
| **First NBA year** | 1970-71 | | | |
| **Home Arena details** | The Coliseum (built 1974, capacity 20,273) | | | |
| **Former cities/nicknames** | None | | | |
| **NBA Championships** | None | | | |
| | **G** | **W** | **L** | **Pct** |
| **Playing Record** | | | | |
| **Regular Season** | 1968 | 863 | 1105 | .439 |
| **Playoffs (Series 4-10)** | 66 | 26 | 40 | .394 |

Cleveland Cleaning: Larry Nance, one of the NBA's greatest leapers, clears the boards for the Cavaliers

★★★★★★★★★★★

# MARK PRICE
## Quietly Courageous

Mark Price had established himself as Cleveland's point guard when his left knee popped 16 games into the 1990–91 season.

Standing just 6 feet tall and weighing less than 180 pounds, Price had been the Cavaliers' silent warrior. He took over the point full-time his second season and quickly developed into a near perfect leader. Price had developed one of the league's best jump shots and could connect from virtually anywhere on the court.

After taking nearly a year to recover from the knee injury, Price returned early in the 1991–92 season as if he'd never left. He was named to the Eastern Conference All-Star team for the second time in his career and led the NBA in free-throw shooting (.947).

He also proved to be one of the league's most valuable players. During those two seasons, Cleveland was 29–47 with Price out of the lineup. When Price played, the Cavaliers were 61–27.

much on Daugherty and Price, one of the NBA's finest outside shooters, would bomb away from the outside.

The Cavaliers appeared on the verge of a championship during the 1988–89 season when they won 57 games and defeated Chicago six times during the regular season.

But the roller-coaster ride headed for another set of dips, virtually all of them created by Chicago's Michael Jordan. Jordan's last-second 16-foot jump shot beat Cleveland in the decisive game of the 1989 First Round Playoff series. Jordan's Bulls struck again in 1992 and once more in 1993, when Jordan's last-second jump shot eliminated Cleveland in the Eastern Conference Semifinals.

In the wake of that defeat, Wilkens resigned as head coach and was replaced by former Atlanta Coach Mike Fratello. But what could give rise to the next Cleveland drive might have happened in Chicago. With Jordan retired, maybe the Cavaliers can find enough steam to climb to the top of the hill.

# DALLAS MAVERICKS

# The Long Road Back

For years the Dallas Mavericks were recognized as one of the most successful expansion franchises in league history. Building with young talent and under the leadership of seasoned Coach Dick Motta, the team charged to the top of the Western Conference before age and disappointing personnel moves led to yet another building program. If history is any indication, Dallas will be back on top before long.

For eight seasons, the Dallas Mavericks pushed all the right buttons and made all the right calls. From their first season in 1980–81, when Coach Dick Motta, for long one of the league's master tacticians, poked and prodded a rag-tag expansion roster to 15 victories, the Mavericks defied the gloomiest of expectations.

They improved quickly, winning 43 games in just their fourth season. Three years later, with Motta still at the controls and the roster loaded with talent, Dallas had arrived. The Mavericks took Magic Johnson's Los Angeles Lakers to the seventh game of the Western Conference Finals in 1988. The rise was so rapid and so perfectly executed that Dallas was considered one of the finest organizations in all of professional sports.

Indeed, representatives from Minnesota, Miami, Charlotte and Orlando queried Mavericks executives prior to joining the league in the NBA's last expansion. How, they all wondered, could a team rise to within a single game of the NBA Finals in just seven seasons?

Thanks to a tight-knit front office, a solid coaching staff and enlightened player selection, Dallas made the process appear effortless. It started with the team's NBA Draft in 1981 which produced Mark Aguirre, Rolando Blackman and Jay Vincent. Aguirre and Blackman eventually became two of the league's finest scor-

**Mash Dash: Mashburn goes into the hole**

ers, Aguirre the versatile small forward capable of scoring from anywhere on the court and Blackman the true shooting guard with deadly accuracy.

The 1984 Draft produced Sam Perkins, a versatile 6–11 forward who added yet another scorer and inside defense. Detlef Schrempf arrived in the 1985 Draft, with towering 7–2 center James Donaldson coming aboard in a trade. The roster appeared virtually complete when the 1986 Draft produced Roy Tarpley, a multi-talented 6–11 forward.

Tarpley, as it turned out, would provide

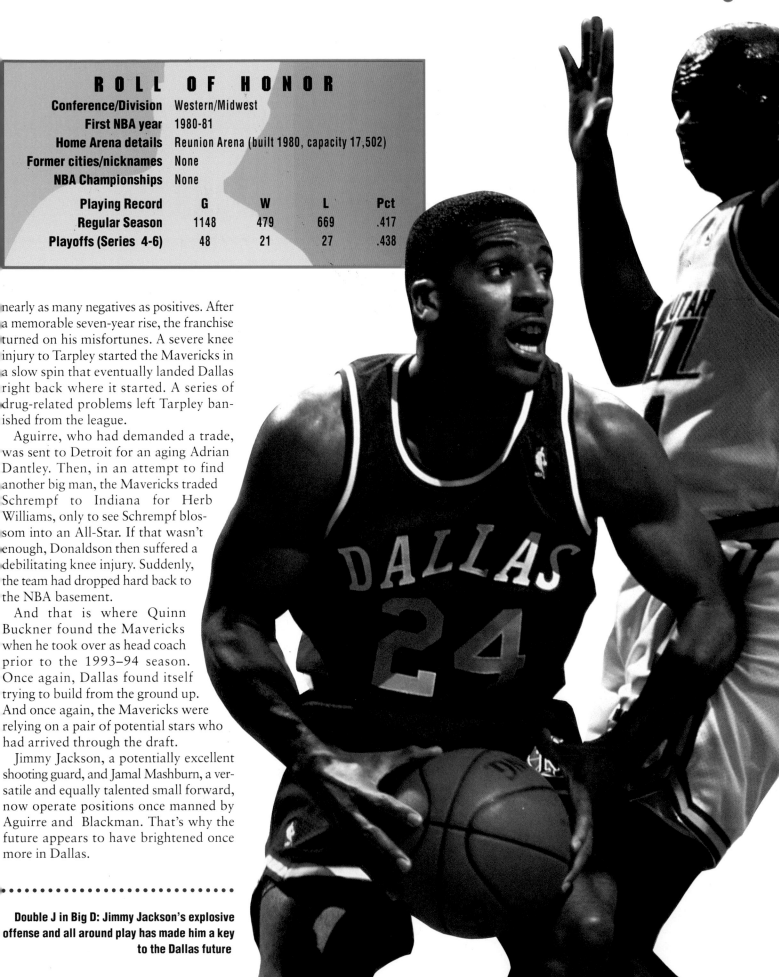

## ROLL OF HONOR

| | | | | |
|---|---|---|---|---|
| Conference/Division | Western/Midwest | | | |
| First NBA year | 1980-81 | | | |
| Home Arena details | Reunion Arena (built 1980, capacity 17,502) | | | |
| Former cities/nicknames | None | | | |
| NBA Championships | None | | | |
| **Playing Record** | **G** | **W** | **L** | **Pct** |
| Regular Season | 1148 | 479 | 669 | .417 |
| Playoffs (Series 4-6) | 48 | 21 | 27 | .438 |

nearly as many negatives as positives. After a memorable seven-year rise, the franchise turned on his misfortunes. A severe knee injury to Tarpley started the Mavericks in a slow spin that eventually landed Dallas right back where it started. A series of drug-related problems left Tarpley banished from the league.

Aguirre, who had demanded a trade, was sent to Detroit for an aging Adrian Dantley. Then, in an attempt to find another big man, the Mavericks traded Schrempf to Indiana for Herb Williams, only to see Schrempf blossom into an All-Star. If that wasn't enough, Donaldson then suffered a debilitating knee injury. Suddenly, the team had dropped hard back to the NBA basement.

And that is where Quinn Buckner found the Mavericks when he took over as head coach prior to the 1993–94 season. Once again, Dallas found itself trying to build from the ground up. And once again, the Mavericks were relying on a pair of potential stars who had arrived through the draft.

Jimmy Jackson, a potentially excellent shooting guard, and Jamal Mashburn, a versatile and equally talented small forward, now operate positions once manned by Aguirre and Blackman. That's why the future appears to have brightened once more in Dallas.

**Double J in Big D: Jimmy Jackson's explosive offense and all around play has made him a key to the Dallas future**

# Rocky Mountain Highs

The Denver Nuggets' success in the old ABA had started to fizzle by the time they joined the NBA in 1976. Even the franchise's high-scoring teams under Coach Doug Moe came during a decade dominated by Magic Johnson's Los Angeles Lakers. That could change soon, however, as Denver has once more started building a contender with young stars like Dikembe Mutombo, LaPhonso Ellis and Mahmoud Abdul-Rauf.

For all the flash and dash the golden years have often come at the wrong time for the Denver Nuggets.

When Coach Larry Brown and high-flying superstar David Thompson were crafting 60-win seasons in the mid-1970s, the Nuggets were one of the most exciting shows in the American Basketball Association. Though the team remained strong after merging with the NBA prior to the 1976–77 season, the next surge didn't come until Doug Moe brought his version of run-and-gun basketball to the Mile High City.

The Nuggets reached the playoffs for nine straight seasons under Moe, but ran

**Mahmoud Abdul-Rauf looking for an opening**

into dominant Western Conference teams like Dallas, Houston and the Los Angeles Lakers.

Still, the Nuggets have rarely not shined. As one of the 11 charter members of the ABA in 1967, Denver was recognized as one of that league's best run organizations. Originally called the Rockets, Denver stunned the basketball world in 1969 by signing college undergraduate Spencer Haywood. Haywood, star of the U.S. men's gold medal team at the 1968 Mexico City Olympics, played only one season for Denver. But his signing put the franchise on the professional basketball map while also leading to changes in college eligibility rules, many of which are in place today in the NBA.

The franchise got a face-lift in 1974, when Carl Scheer, an innovative general manager, took over the team and hired Brown as coach. The Nuggets had a new name and a front office full of new faces, plus they became instant contenders on the court.

After winning 65 games during the 1974–75 season, Denver loaded up for an ABA title run. North Carolina State sensation Thompson became the first No. 1 NBA draft pick to sign with the rival ABA. The same season, Denver landed another rookie, Marvin Webster, and veteran Dan Issel. With Thompson and Issel leading the way, Denver went to the ABA championship series before losing to the New

# DIKEMBE MUTOMBO
## An African Nugget

The full name—Dikembe Mutombo Mpolondo Mukambra Jean Jacque Wamutombo—has 49 letters. For Dikembe Mutombo, as he's known around the NBA, remembering his name is as easy as blocking a shot.

Mutombo, who attended Georgetown University, grew up in Kinshasa, Zaire and speaks five different African dialects in addition to English, French, Portuguese and Spanish.

The Nuggets made Mutombo the No. 4 pick in the 1991 Draft and they haven't been disappointed. Mutombo became the only rookie selected to the 1992 All-Star Game. He led the team in shooting, rebounding, blocks and minutes played while averaging 16.6 points a game that first season.

Mutombo also helped turn the entire Denver franchise around. The Nuggets improved 12 games during his second season and, for the first time in four years, appeared to be on the verge of returning to the playoffs.

# ROLL OF HONOR

| | | | | |
|---|---|---|---|---|
| Conference/Division | Western/Midwest | | | |
| First NBA year | 1976-77 | | | |
| Home Arena details | McNichols Sports Arena (built 1975, capacity 17,022) | | | |
| Former cities/nicknames | Denver Rockets (1967-74) | | | |
| NBA Championships | None | | | |

| Playing Record | G | W | L | Pct |
|---|---|---|---|---|
| NBA Regular Season | 1476 | 740 | 736 | .501 |
| Combined NBA/ABA | 2220 | 1153 | 1067 | .519 |
| Playoffs (Series 7-13) | 95 | 39 | 56 | .411 |
| Combined NBA/ABA | 157 | 66 | 91 | .420 |

Jersey Nets and a its young superstar, Julius Erving.

It turned out to be the ABA's finale and Denver's only clear shot at a championship. Ensconced in the NBA's reconfigured Midwest Division, the Nuggets continued a franchise tradition of playoff futility. After winning 50 games in its NBA debut in 1976–77, Denver ran into the championship-bound Portland Trail Blazers in the Conference Semifinals. A year later, Seattle eliminated the Nuggets in the Western Conference Finals.

And despite continued regular-season success under Moe, the Nuggets never reached the NBA Finals. Still, Denver remained one of the greatest scoring shows in league history. During Moe's nine seasons, Denver led the league in scoring five times and never finished out of the top five.

Players like Thompson, Issel, Alex English, Kiki Vandeweghe, George McGinnis and Lafayette "Fat" Lever fueled a relentless offensive attack that didn't run out of steam until Moe left following the 1989–90 season.

Issel, whose No. 44 was retired by the team, took over as head coach prior to the 1992–93 season. With young guns like Mahmoud Abdul-Rauf (formerly known as Chris Jackson), LaPhonso Ellis and Dikembe Mutombo, the Nuggets are back on the playoff trail.

• • • • • • • • • • • • • • • • • • • • • • • • •

**Rising Above: Young Nuggets Brian Williams (8), La Phonso Ellis (20) and Dikembe Mutombo (55) look to get a grip on Denver's future**

# Witnesses For The Defense

They didn't win many friends, but the Detroit Pistons certainly influenced opponents. With limited offensive weapons, the Pistons turned to defense in the late 1980s and put on a clinic. With a tough, no nonsense approach, Detroit became one of the greatest defensive teams in the history of the league. They won a pair of NBA Championships during a rough and tumble five-year run in which they never finished lower than third in overall team defense.

When Detroit won the 1989 NBA title, it ended a 40-year journey that included 21 head coaches, one franchise move and a daunting 15-year stretch without a single winning season. Even after the team moved from Fort Wayne, Indiana, to Detroit for the 1957–58 season, 13 straight losing seasons followed.

The franchise started out as the after-hours avocation of Fort Wayne manufacturer Fred Zollner, who owned a factory that made automobile pistons. Zollner first organized the team in 1937, a decade before the NBA started. Throughout the mid-1940s, Zollner's Pistons were one of the top teams in the National Basketball League, winning consecutive titles in 1944–45.

But all that changed when the NBL survivors, including the Pistons, joined the NBA. The Pistons immediately established what would become a long-running reputation as everyone's favorite opponent despite some solid, early talent. Not even players such as George Yardley, Max Zaslofsky, Larry Foust and Andy Phillip could prevent the Pistons from general mediocrity during their first decade in the league.

Under Coach Charlie Eckman, a former referee, Fort Wayne reached the NBA Finals in 1955 and 1956, but following the move to Detroit in 1957, a .500 playing record was beyond the Pistons.

The first of two major upturns followed with the arrival of 6–11 Bob Lanier, Detroit's No. 1 pick in the 1970 Draft. Three years later, the Pistons finished 52–30, their best record to that point, but fell to the Chicago Bulls in the Western Conference Semifinals.

By 1979 Lanier and long-time backcourt star Dave Bing had been traded and the

Pistons were again one of the league's worst teams. But out of the ashes of a 16–66 1979–80 season rose a Detroit team that

**Full Stretch: Olden Polynice (0) tries to grab one**

# ROLL OF HONOR

| | | | | |
|---|---|---|---|---|
| Conference/Division | Eastern/Central | | | |
| First NBA year | 1948-49 | | | |
| Home Arena details | The Palace of Auburn Hills (built 1988, capacity 21,454) | | | |
| Former cities/nicknames | Fort Wayne Pistons (1948-57), | | | |
| NBA Championships | 1989, 1990 | | | |
| **Playing Record** | **G** | **W** | **L** | **Pct** |
| Regular Season | 3612 | 1709 | 1903 | .473 |
| Playoffs (Series 23-25) | 216 | 111 | 105 | .514 |

would come to dominate the 1980s. The Pistons used their No. 1 pick in the 1981 Draft to select Isiah Thomas, who would become one of the most accomplished point guards in NBA history. Joe Dumars arrived in the 1985 Draft followed by Dennis Rodman and John Salley in 1986. Trades produced Bill Laimbeer, Vinnie Johnson, Mark Aguirre and James Edwards.

**Joe Cool: Dumars has one of the sweetest jump shots in all of basketball**

Coach Chuck Daly then molded the team into a bruising defensive squad built on strength and toughness. They pushed, shoved, scratched and clawed their way to consecutive championships, winning their first in 1989 by sweeping the Los Angeles Lakers and Magic Johnson 4–0 in the best-of-7 NBA Finals.

But Detroit's ascent coincided with the arrival of Michael Jordan in Chicago, which in turn created one of the most heated rivalries in all of American sports. The end of the Pistons' reign finally came in 1991 when Jordan, whose Bulls had been eliminated the two previous seasons by Detroit, led a 4–0 thrashing of the Pistons in the Eastern Conference Finals.

Since then, the Pistons have had three coaches, and veterans such as Vinnie Johnson and Bill Laimbeer have retired. The team, as it has done before, is trying hard to rebuild. This time it's with a mixture of young and old, Joe Dumars from the old regime with Sean Elliott, Lindsay Hunter and Allan Houston representing the future.

# Shooting Stars

Before Coach Don Nelson took over at Golden State, the Warriors were suffering through the worst period of their existence. But Nelson brought new life to the once proud franchise with a wide-open offense that more than made up for the lack of a big-time center. He used shooters like Chris Mullin and Tim Hardaway to make the Warriors one of the most dangerous teams in the league.

I f Coach and General Manager Don Nelson has his way, Golden State is headed toward another championship season.

The Philadelphia Warriors began play in 1946 as charter members of the 11-team Basketball Association of America. Under the leadership of local basketball legend Eddie Gottlieb and with players such as Joe Fulks, Howie Dallmar and George Senesky, those Warriors won the first BAA title.

It took nine years for the Warriors to capture another championship, this one in the reconfigured NBA. With Senesky as Coach, legendary players such as Paul Arizin and Neil Johnston led Philadelphia

to a 45–27 regular-season record and an easy rout of the Fort Wayne Pistons in the 1956 Finals.

In 1959, Gottlieb convinced his fellow owners to allow Philadelphia a non-traditional "territorial" draft pick. In that era, each NBA team was allowed to choose one college player from the geographic area of the team's dominant fan base. Gottlieb's coup was predicated on the fact that Wilt Chamberlain had played high school ball in Philadelphia, although he was attending college at the University of Kansas.

Wilt "the Stilt" would become the greatest scoring machine in NBA history. Chamberlain, who stood 7–1 and weighed

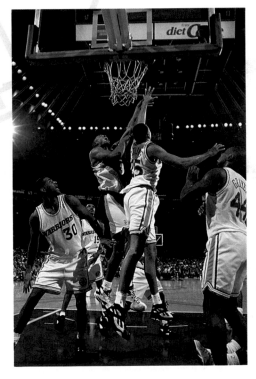

**Chris Gatling defends against the Pacers**

275 pounds, immediately became the most dominant individual player the league had ever known. He averaged a phenomenal 50.4 points a game during the 1961–62 season for Philadelphia.

But not even Chamberlain could carry an entire franchise by himself. With attendance lagging, Gottlieb sold the team to a San Francisco group that moved the Warriors west for the 1962–63 season.

## ROLL OF HONOR

| | | | | |
|---|---|---|---|---|
| Conference/Division | Western/Pacific | | | |
| First NBA year | 1946-47 | | | |
| Home Arena details | Oakland Coliseum Arena (built 1966, capacity 15,025) | | | |
| Former cities/nicknames | Philadelphia Warriors (1946-62), San Francisco Warriors (1962-71) | | | |
| NBA Championships | 1947, 1956, 1975 | | | |

| Playing Record | G | W | L | Pct |
|---|---|---|---|---|
| Regular Season | 3718 | 1816 | 1902 | .488 |
| Playoffs (Series 22-24) | 214 | 99 | 115 | .463 |

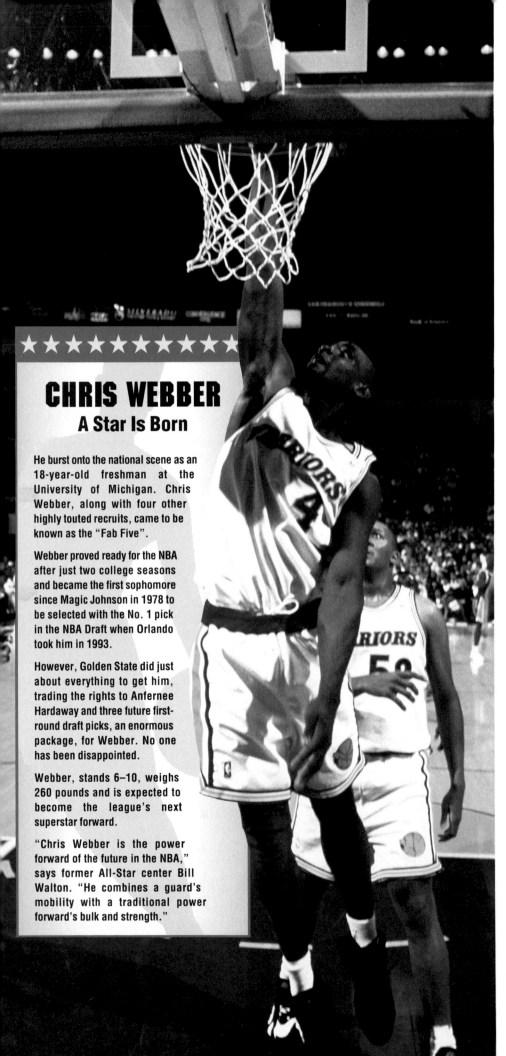

# CHRIS WEBBER
## A Star Is Born

He burst onto the national scene as an 18-year-old freshman at the University of Michigan. Chris Webber, along with four other highly touted recruits, came to be known as the "Fab Five".

Webber proved ready for the NBA after just two college seasons and became the first sophomore since Magic Johnson in 1978 to be selected with the No. 1 pick in the NBA Draft when Orlando took him in 1993.

However, Golden State did just about everything to get him, trading the rights to Anfernee Hardaway and three future first-round draft picks, an enormous package, for Webber. No one has been disappointed.

Webber, stands 6–10, weighs 260 pounds and is expected to become the league's next superstar forward.

"Chris Webber is the power forward of the future in the NBA," says former All-Star center Bill Walton. "He combines a guard's mobility with a traditional power forward's bulk and strength."

Two years later, the Warriors were once again building for a championship run. Nate Thurmond, who would become another of the great NBA centers, arrived. San Francisco then dealt Chamberlain to the new Philadelphia franchise. Thurmond was soon surrounded by players such as Rick Barry, Jeff Mullins, Al Attles and Clyde Lee. And in 1967, the Warriors found themselves back in the NBA Finals, this time against Chamberlain's Philadelphia 76ers, who took the championship 4–2.

It took another 10-year cycle before Golden State reached the Finals again. With Attles now coaching and Barry leading the team in scoring, Golden State, which moved to Oakland from San Francisco prior to the 1971–72 season, swept the Washington Bullets 4–0 for the 1975 NBA Championship.

As before, however, another downturn started gradually over the next decade. It wasn't until another new ownership group hired Nelson that the franchise took off again.

Nelson, who entered the 1993–94 season ranked eighth on the all-time career victories list, brought the Warriors back to life. Young, talented players such as Chris Mullin, Tim Hardaway, Sarunas Marciulionis and Billy Owens combined to win 55 games during the 1991–92 regular season.

Though injuries have slowed the Warriors since, Nelson has managed to make the team even stronger with the addition of potential superstars Chris Webber and Latrell Sprewell.

Once more all signs point to another Warriors uprising as they approach the mid-point of another decade. After all, the franchise has a tradition to follow.

**No Miss For Chris: Webber finishes off another fastbreak with a one-hand slam against the Los Angeles Lakers**

# The Dream is Real

Houston used one of the biggest front lines in NBA history to reach the 1986 NBA Finals. But after Larry Bird's Boston Celtics ended those title dreams, the Rockets are still trying to find a way back. Now, with former star player Rudy Tomjanovich coaching and superstar Hakeem "the Dream" Olajuwon doing just about everything else, Houston could be headed for another championship run.

How could any team have had players such as Elvin Hayes, Moses Malone, Ralph Sampson and Hakeem Olajuwon, all as rookies, and reach the early 1990s without a single NBA championship?

The San Diego Rockets joined the league in 1967 along with the Seattle SuperSonics as the 11th and 12th NBA teams. As with most expansion teams, the first season was a long one. The immediate result, however, was that San Diego had the No. 1 pick in the 1968 Draft which produced the multi-talented Hayes. Though Hayes led the league in scoring his first season, teams started double and triple-teaming the 6–9 forward. Opposing teams decided to let the other Rockets beat them, which rarely happened. By 1971, the Rockets were still

**Scott Brooks leads Rockets celebration**

a sub-.500 team and attendance had fallen off in San Diego.

A move to Houston followed, but so too did the losses. A feud between Coach Tex Winter and Hayes eventually led to Hayes being traded in 1972. Despite the pres-

ence of budding stars like Calvin Murphy and Rudy Tomjanovich, the Rockets would need four years and some luck to recover from the Hayes trade.

It wasn't until rookie John Lucas and a 21-year-old Moses Malone arrived in 1976 that the franchise moved over the .500 mark for the first time in its history. Malone helped lead Houston to 49 victories and the Central Division title.

But once again, the future wasn't nearly as bright as expected. And this time a near tragedy played a part. On Dec. 9, 1977 in a game at Los Angeles, a fight broke out between the Rockets and Lakers. Tomjanovich, trying to be a peacemaker, ran into a punch thrown by Kermit Washington. Tomjanovich ended up in critical condition with shattered bones throughout his face. Though Tomjanovich eventually recovered, the team limped to 54 losses.

In 1981, with Malone and Murphy leading the way, the Rockets upset Magic Johnson's Los Angeles Lakers in the First Round of the Playoffs. Then they dispatched Midwest Division champion San Antonio and rival Kansas City before losing to Boston in the Finals.

Once more success was fleeting. Within two years, the Rockets were the worst team in basketball. Malone signed with Philadelphia and Houston found itself looking for another great, young center.

Thanks to the NBA Draft the Rockets

## ROLL OF HONOR

| | |
|---|---|
| Conference/Division | Western/Midwest |
| First NBA year | 1967-68 |
| Home Arena details | The Summit (built 1975, capacity 16,279) |
| Former cities/nicknames | San Diego Rockets (1967-71) |
| NBA Championships | None |

| Playing Record | G | W | L | Pct |
|---|---|---|---|---|
| Regular Season | 2214 | 1073 | 1141 | .485 |
| Playoffs (Series 12-15) | 144 | 70 | 74 | .652 |

found two of them. They drafted 7-4 Ralph Sampson with the No. 1 pick in 1983 and then Hakeem Olajuwon with the first pick in 1984, that duo combining with young Rodney McCray to create one of the most imposing front lines of that era.

Houston, however, remained a team of potential. The Rockets did reach the 1986 NBA Finals and fought the Boston Celtics valiantly before losing in six games. But within three years, the "Twin Towers" were disbanded with the trade of Sampson. The Rockets remained dangerous thanks to Olajuwon, but the team didn't come together completely until Tomjanovich took over as head coach prior to the 1992–93 season. With Olajuwon, Otis Thorpe, Vernon Maxwell and Kenny Smith leading the way, Houston won 55 games and reached the Western Conference Semifinals.

## RUDY TOMJANOVICH
### Blast From The Past

Midway through the 1991–92 season the Houston Rockets were out of experiments. They had tried virtually everything in search of an elusive NBA championship.

With the team stuck with a 26–26 record, the franchise finally decided to try one of its own. Rudy Tomjanovich had been a member of the organization since 1970 when he joined the Rockets as a rookie sharpshooter out of the University of Michigan.

By the time Houston named Tomjanovich interim head coach Feb. 18, 1992, he had been involved in the franchise's only two division championships and ranked third on the team's all-time scoring list. The team finished an encouraging 16–14 under Tomjanovich.

As it turned out, the Rockets had found the man they needed. Houston finished 55–27 in 1992–93 to easily win the Midwest Division. Meanwhile, Tomjanovich was named IBM NBA Coach of the Year.

For Houston, the experiments were over.

**California Dreamin':** Hakeem Olajuwon slaps away a Los Angeles Clippers shot

# Picking Up The Pace

**Pacers**®

The Indiana Pacers have one of the more storied histories in all of basketball, but virtually all of it occurred before the team joined the NBA in 1976. As a charter member of the American Basketball Association, Indiana had some of the most dominant teams in that league's brief history. Since joining the NBA, however, the Pacers have worked hard to reclaim their past success.

Despite being situated in a state known for its wildly devoted basketball fans, the Indiana Pacers have spent much of their NBA existence trying to develop a following.

High school basketball has its roots in the small towns of Indiana, while Indiana University has one of the most visible programs in the country. So when the Pacers entered the old ABA as a charter member in 1967, they had much to prove.

They never blinked.

With stars like Mel Daniels, Roger Brown and Freddie Lewis, Indiana won 59 games and the ABA championship in 1970. One year later, the Pacers tapped neighboring Indiana University by sign-

7–4 Rik Smits controls the middle

ing undergraduate George McGinnis, a brilliant young forward.

And McGinnis paid off immediately. He led the Pacers to consecutive ABA titles. Under the leadership of Coach Bobby "Slick" Leonard, the Pacers were a hit on and off the court. That's why Indiana was one of the four surviving ABA franchises to join the NBA in 1976.

But that signaled the end of an era for the Pacers. Leonard was faced with a massive rebuilding job after McGinnis signed with the Philadelphia 76ers in 1975 and age

## ROLL OF HONOR

| Conference/Division | Eastern/Central | | | |
|---|---|---|---|---|
| First NBA year | 1976-77 (ABA 1967-76) | | | |
| Home Arena details | Market Square Arena (built 1974, capacity 16,530) | | | |
| Former cities/nicknames | None | | | |
| NBA Championships | None (ABA – 1970, 1972, 1973) | | | |
| **Playing Record** | **G** | **W** | **L** | **Pct** |
| NBA Regular Season | 1476 | 633 | 843 | .429 |
| Combined NBA/ABA | 2220 | 1060 | 1160 | .477 |
| Playoffs (Series 2-7) | 37 | 14 | 23 | .378 |
| Combined NBA/ABA | 156 | 83 | 63 | .532 |

caught up with the rest of the ABA cast.

Selfless Don Buse and high-scoring Billy Knight were the Pacers' early NBA stars, but the franchise never quite got rolling. Entering 1993–94, Indiana finished above .500 only twice and never won more than 44 games.

The team's first NBA Playoff game didn't come until 1981 and the Pacers didn't win a playoff game until 1987. Along the way there were seven coaches and a four-year period in the early 1980s when Indiana averaged 58 losses per season.

It only seems fitting that the Pacers were slapped out of that first playoff experience by one of their own. McGinnis led Philadelphia to a quick blitz of the Pacers in the First Round of the 1981 Eastern Conference Playoffs.

The Pacers, however, were not without some individual gems even during the most difficult times. Players such as Clark Kellogg, Herb Williams, Steve Stipanovich, Detlef Schrempf, Wayman Tisdale, Chuck Person and others, have passed through the franchise.

But when Indiana needed a couple breaks, there were none. The team, coached by the legendary Jack Ramsay, finished 41–41 and reached the Playoffs in 1987. Indiana not only earned its first playoff victory, but it appeared to have finally turned itself around.

But Kellogg, who had suffered a severe knee injury four games into the 1986–87 season, never returned. A year later, Stipanovich, a 7-foot center who had developed into a solid player, suffered a career-ending injury. Suddenly, the Pacers were losing games in bunches once more. Another injection of young talent has helped bring Indiana back into the playoff picture. Reggie Miller, one of the league's finest shooters, and 7–4 center Rik Smits helped the Pacers into the playoffs four

straight seasons through the 1992–93 campaign.

With Coach Larry Brown assuming control of the team prior to the 1993–94 season and Derrick McKey arriving in a trade for Schrempf, the Pacers are hopeful of advancing in postseason play.

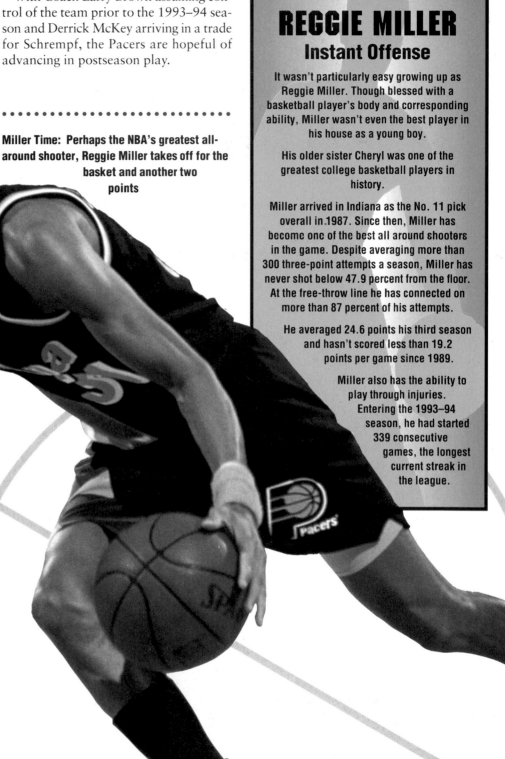

**Miller Time:** Perhaps the NBA's greatest all-around shooter, Reggie Miller takes off for the basket and another two points

★ ★ ★ ★ ★ ★ ★ ★ ★ ★ ★

# REGGIE MILLER
## Instant Offense

It wasn't particularly easy growing up as Reggie Miller. Though blessed with a basketball player's body and corresponding ability, Miller wasn't even the best player in his house as a young boy.

His older sister Cheryl was one of the greatest college basketball players in history.

Miller arrived in Indiana as the No. 11 pick overall in 1987. Since then, Miller has become one of the best all around shooters in the game. Despite averaging more than 300 three-point attempts a season, Miller has never shot below 47.9 percent from the floor. At the free-throw line he has connected on more than 87 percent of his attempts.

He averaged 24.6 points his third season and hasn't scored less than 19.2 points per game since 1989.

Miller also has the ability to play through injuries. Entering the 1993–94 season, he had started 339 consecutive games, the longest current streak in the league.

# LOS ANGELES CLIPPERS

# Still Striving For Success

No franchise has tried harder or struggled longer than the Los Angeles Clippers. Originally known as the Buffalo Braves, the team moved to San Diego and then Los Angeles. Once there the franchise was overshadowed by the brilliant Los Angeles Lakers teams led by Magic Johnson. For 12 straight seasons in the late 1970s and 1980s, the Clippers failed to register a winning season. Though things have changed lately, it's been a long process for Clippers fans.

When the Los Angeles Clippers moved from San Diego in 1984, some worried about the franchise having an identity crisis. After all, one of the league's most successful franchises, the Lakers, had long been a resident of Los Angeles.

Indeed, no team has suffered as much or as long as the Clippers in what seems to be a never ending quest for respectability.

Since they entered the league as the Buffalo Braves in 1970, the Los Angeles Clippers have won more than half their games just five times. They went 15 straight seasons without a playoff appearance from 1976 through 1991.

To make matters worse, the Clippers have had eight different coaches in 10 years, the latest being Bob Weiss, who took over prior to the 1993–94 campaign.

The franchise started its long climb as one of three expansion teams, along with Cleveland and Portland, added for the 1970–71 season. Thanks to wise drafting and Coach Jack Ramsay, Buffalo had a flashy young lineup loaded with potential by their fourth NBA season.

High scoring center/forward Bob McAdoo along with Randy Smith, Ernie DiGregorio, Jim McMillian, Garfield

**Ron Harper soars to the hoop for an easy basket**

Heard and veteran Jack Marin, led Buffalo into the Playoffs in 1974. McAdoo led the league in scoring, averaging more than 30 points a game, and Buffalo was the NBA's best offensive team.

The team won 49 games the following season and then 46, each followed by strong, yet limited playoff performances. But the future disintegrated just as it appeared to be taking shape.

## ROLL OF HONOR

| Conference/Division | Western/Pacific |
|---|---|
| First NBA year | 1970-71 |
| Home Arena details | LA Memorial Sports Arena (built 1959, capacity 16,005) |
| Former cities/nicknames | Buffalo Braves (1970-78), San Diego Clippers (1978-84) |
| NBA Championships | None |

| Playing Record | G | W | L | Pct |
|---|---|---|---|---|
| Regular Season | 1968 | 732 | 1236 | .372 |
| Playoffs (Series 1-5) | 32 | 13 | 19 | .406 |

Ramsay resigned to take over in Portland. McMillian and DiGregorio were traded and, in a move that disillusioned Buffalo fans, McAdoo was dealt along with future United States Congressman Tom McMillen to the New York Knicks for cash and journeyman center John Gianelli.

Those moves, coupled with disappointing results on the court, led to poor attendance and the franchise's eventual relocation to San Diego. With Coach Gene Shue now in charge, the Clippers posted a 43–39 record in 1978–79, their last winning mark in more than a decade.

Once again, a disastrous off-season trade undermined the franchise. This time Kermit Washington, Kevin Kunnert, a first-round pick and cash were shipped to Portland for the remarkable but often injured Bill Walton. Unfortunately, however, the trade only made things more difficult. Walton, a wondrously talented center, played just 14 games over the next three seasons and the Clippers went into a tail-spin.

Although poor seasons translated into great draft positions, the Clippers didn't reap any profits. From 1987 through 1989, the team used six first-round picks on Reggie Williams, Joe Wolf, Ken Norman, Danny Manning, Hersey Hawkins and Danny Ferry. Of that group, Manning was the only one still on the team entering the 1993–94 season. And he ended up being traded to Atlanta for high-scoring Dominique Wilkins.

The Clippers finally found a measure of success when Larry Brown took over as coach midway through the 1991–92 season. They finished 23–12 over their last 35 games and made the playoffs for the first time since 1976. The team made a return trip in 1993 before problems surfaced yet again.

Brown left to take over at Indiana and Norman, a talented forward, signed as a free agent with the Milwaukee Bucks. Once more, the Clippers appear to be searching for a future since Wilkins and Ron Harper, two of the league's most excit-

ing players, were headed for free agency following the 1993–94 season.

Exactly what the Clippers become in the immediate future remains to be seen.

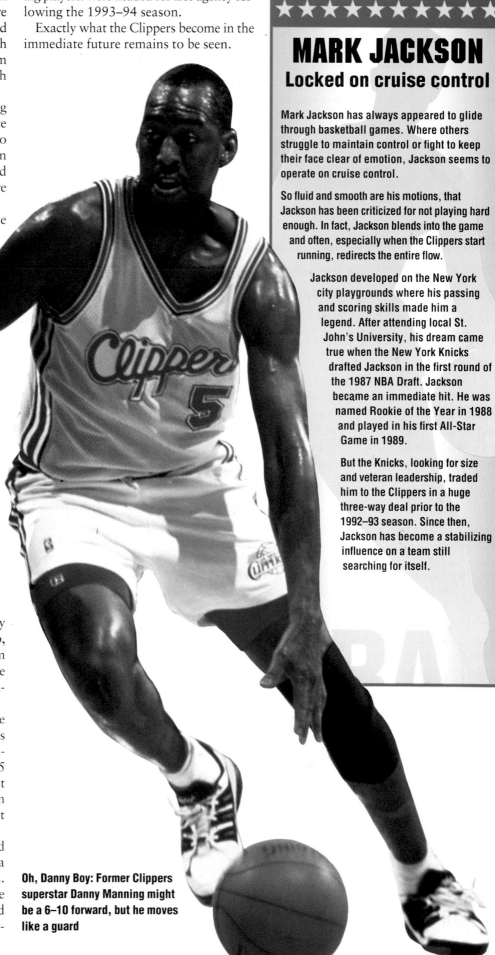

**Oh, Danny Boy: Former Clippers superstar Danny Manning might be a 6–10 forward, but he moves like a guard**

★★★★★★★★★★★

# MARK JACKSON
## Locked on cruise control

Mark Jackson has always appeared to glide through basketball games. Where others struggle to maintain control or fight to keep their face clear of emotion, Jackson seems to operate on cruise control.

So fluid and smooth are his motions, that Jackson has been criticized for not playing hard enough. In fact, Jackson blends into the game and often, especially when the Clippers start running, redirects the entire flow.

Jackson developed on the New York city playgrounds where his passing and scoring skills made him a legend. After attending local St. John's University, his dream came true when the New York Knicks drafted Jackson in the first round of the 1987 NBA Draft. Jackson became an immediate hit. He was named Rookie of the Year in 1988 and played in his first All-Star Game in 1989.

But the Knicks, looking for size and veteran leadership, traded him to the Clippers in a huge three-way deal prior to the 1992–93 season. Since then, Jackson has become a stabilizing influence on a team still searching for itself.

# The West's Winningest Team

**The names are some of the most famous in all of professional basketball. Players like George Mikan, Jerry West, Elgin Baylor, Wilt Chamberlain, Kareem Abdul-Jabbar and Magic Johnson all played on Lakers teams that won NBA championships. In the franchise's first 45 years, the team has failed to make the playoffs only three times. Not even the Boston Celtics can make that claim.**

The Lakers, who started out in Minneapolis, have won 11 Championships, 24 conference titles and own the second best winning percentage in NBA history (.611 entering the 1993–94 season). Only the Celtics, who had won 63.8 percent of their regular season games entering the 1993–94 season, have won more often.

The Lakers were named after Minnesota's claim as the "Land of 10,000 Lakes." They also earned their first championships there, mainly with George Mikan manning the middle. Mikan, basketball's first dominant big man, stood 6–10 and won three straight scoring titles

**Former Coach Pat Riley studies another victory**

after the Lakers became part of the NBA prior to the 1948–49 season.

Mikan played on seven championship teams in his first eight professional seasons, the first two for Chicago in the old National Basketball League. When that team disbanded, Mikan landed with the Minneapolis franchise in the NBA and helped that team to five titles in six years. Mikan's supporting cast included Slater Martin, Vern Mikkelsen, Jim Pollard and 1952 U.S. Olympic team hero Clyde Lovellette. When Mikan retired after the 1953–54 season, the Lakers last championship, the Lakers needed another star. They found one in 1958 when owner Bob Short signed University of Seattle star Elgin Baylor. Minneapolis reached the NBA Finals in 1959, but was quickly eliminated by Boston and Bill Russell. The Celtics were off and running toward eight straight titles while the Lakers were off to Los Angeles.

Despite a talented roster that included Baylor and Jerry West, the Lakers kept running into the Celtics. From 1961 through 1970, the Lakers won seven Western Division championships. Seven times they reached the NBA Finals and seven times they lost, six to the Celtics and once to the New York Knicks.

Los Angeles' NBA Finals frustration ended briefly in 1971–72, when an aging Wilt Chamberlain joined the team. In perhaps the greatest single season in NBA his-

tory, the Lakers set records with a 33-game winning streak and a 69–13 record. The team included Gail Goodrich and West at

## JERRY WEST
### All-Around Brilliance

Until Michael Jordan teamed with Magic Johnson on the Dream Team, the world had never seen a better backcourt than that of Jerry West and Oscar Robertson during the 1960 Rome Olympics.

In fact, until Jordan, West and Robertson were considered the two greatest shooting guards to ever play the game. Shorter at 6–2 and a more pure shooter and defender, West and the 6–5 Robertson went head-to-head through their entire NBA careers.

Despite leading the Lakers into the NBA Finals nine times, West's only championship came in 1972. But he knew how to win, as evidenced by a career that remains among the most successful in history.

West led the Lakers to the 1977 Pacific Division title in his first year as the team's head coach. Four years later, West moved to the front office and carefully constructed a Lakers team that would dominate the 1980s.

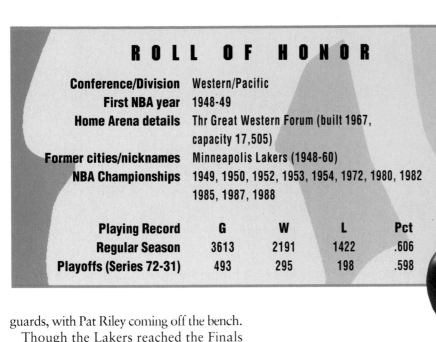

# ROLL OF HONOR

| | | | | |
|---|---|---|---|---|
| **Conference/Division** | Western/Pacific | | | |
| **First NBA year** | 1948-49 | | | |
| **Home Arena details** | Thr Great Western Forum (built 1967, capacity 17,505) | | | |
| **Former cities/nicknames** | Minneapolis Lakers (1948-60) | | | |
| **NBA Championships** | 1949, 1950, 1952, 1953, 1954, 1972, 1980, 1982 1985, 1987, 1988 | | | |

| Playing Record | G | W | L | Pct |
|---|---|---|---|---|
| **Regular Season** | 3613 | 2191 | 1422 | .606 |
| **Playoffs (Series 72-31)** | 493 | 295 | 198 | .598 |

guards, with Pat Riley coming off the bench.

Though the Lakers reached the Finals the following season, they didn't win another Championship until Magic Johnson arrived in 1979. That's when their luck changed. The team won a coin flip with the Chicago Bulls for the No. 1 pick in the 1979 Draft and chose Johnson.

The 6–9 guard teamed with another legendary big man, Kareem Abdul-Jabbar, and quickly helped the Lakers become the dominant team of the 1980s. Though the head-to-head matchups with Boston continued, this time the Lakers came out on top more often—winning twice in three NBA Finals meetings.

Los Angeles, with supporting players such as Jamaal Wilkes, James Worthy, Byron Scott, Norm Nixon and Michael Cooper, won five championships in Johnson's first nine seasons, four of those under the coaching of Riley.

Johnson and Bird, like Chamberlain and Russell before them, identified an entire decade. Indeed their battles might have been the greatest in league history given their respective skills. Fundamentally sound, they fought each other for control of the tempo.

As with Boston, however, those days have given way to another rebuilding process. For now the Lakers must to try claim the future with players such as Anthony Peeler, Doug Christie, Nick Van Exel and Elden Campbell. If their past is any indication, it's only a matter of time before the Lakers make another championship run.

**Extremely Worthy: James Worthy takes charge**

# A Dream Come True

Had it not been for injuries, the Miami Heat still might be climbing the NBA ladder. With a solid plan and front office patience, the Heat took just four seasons to reach the Playoffs after joining the NBA as an expansion franchise in 1988. Miami improved each of its first four seasons in the league before injuries slowed its progress. Now, with its players healthy and the roster full of young talent, the Heat could be warming up.

Few NBA expansion franchises have come together with the class and conviction of Miami.

While former NBA great Billy Cunningham dreamed of a team in Miami, a city that until 1988 had only one professional sports team in football's Miami Dolphins, critics wondered whether locals would gather regularly to watch basketball, particularly the NBA brand.

But Cunningham persevered. He lined

**Glen Rice gets a step on the defense**

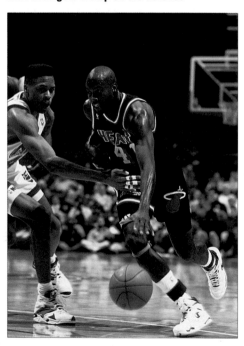

up investors such as Zev Bufman, a highly successful Broadway producer, Ted Arison, owner of the Carnival Cruise Lines, and long-time NBA executive Lewis Schaffel.

With indisputable credentials, Cunningham's group was awarded an NBA franchise in April, 1987. The team quickly became known as the "Heat" and Cunningham and Schaffel went to work on building a roster. A little over a year later, Miami played its first game, joining the expansion Minnesota Timberwolves for the 1988–89 season.

Two of Miami's primary building blocks were with the team on opening night. Center Rony Seikaly, a first-round pick in the 1988 Draft, and Grant Long, a hard-working forward, joined a group of veterans that included Jon Sunvold and Rory Sparrow.

Not surprisingly, the Heat stumbled badly, losing its first 17 NBA games and finishing just 15–67. Rookies Glen Rice and Sherman Douglas arrived for the 1989–90 season, but the young Heat continued to stumble and fall, this time to 66 losses.

By the third season, however, Miami had quietly assembled a nucleus of young talent. Though they were still learning on the job—Miami finished 24–58—the future was slowly coming into focus. That's when Cunningham turned to long-time friend and former teammate Kevin Loughery to assume the coaching reins.

## BILLY CUNNINGHAM
### A Basketball Mind

Billy Cunningham has never done things the easy way.

Cunningham followed a brilliant career at the University of North Carolina by joining the Philadelphia 76ers in 1965. Cunningham developed into a top forward and a key member of a Philadelphia franchise that made six straight playoff appearances and won the 1967 NBA title.

Cunningham followed his Hall of Fame playing career with an equally impressive head coaching stint in Philadelphia. In 1977, the 76ers finished 53–23 under Cunningham and started to roll. They reached the NBA Finals three times under Cunningham, winning the 1983 championship in a 4–0 triumph over the Los Angeles Lakers.

In just eight seasons, Cunningham won 69.8 percent of his regular season games.

In 1985, Cunningham formed a group to bring a team to Miami. The Heat started play in 1988 and have become one of the league's finest run organizations.

## ROLL OF HONOR

| Conference/Division | Eastern/Atlantic | | | |
|---|---|---|---|---|
| First NBA year | 1988-89 | | | |
| Home Arena details | Miami Arena (built 1988, capacity 15,200) | | | |
| Former cities/nicknames | None | | | |
| NBA Championships | None | | | |

| Playing Record | G | W | L | Pct |
|---|---|---|---|---|
| Regular Season | 492 | 173 | 319 | .352 |
| Playoffs (Series 0-2) | 8 | 2 | 6 | .250 |

Loughery's first team finished 38–44 and became the first of the four newest expansion teams to reach the playoffs. Rookie point guard Steve Smith proved to be even better than advertised, while Rice developed into one of the NBA's finest long-range shooters. Seikaly improved to 16.8 points and 11.8 rebounds a game and Miami appeared to be progressing ahead of even its own long-term schedule.

Then a rash of injuries jolted the franchise during the 1992–93 season. Despite adding flashy rookie Harold Miner and trading for former Detroit Pistons forward John Salley, Miami slipped to a 36–46 record and failed to reach the playoffs. The season, which started with high expectation, faded fast as injuries to Salley, Seikaly, Smith and Willie Burton took their toll. Salley missed 31 games, Smith 34, Burton 56 and Seikaly 10. Only two players on the entire roster appeared in more than 73 of the team's 82 games.

Still, there remained plenty of reason for optimism. With former Boston Celtics guard Brian Shaw coming off the bench and the injuries behind them, the team should be poised for a dramatic move toward the top of the Atlantic Division.

Cunningham's plan appears to have been effective. By building through the draft and filling the roster with young players instead of aging veterans, Miami could be well equipped for a long run at an NBA championship.

● ● ● ● ● ● ● ● ● ● ● ● ● ● ● ● ● ● ● ● ● ● ● ● ● ● ● ●

**All For One: Miami center Rony Seikaly runs the floor as well as any big man in the game. Here he glides in for an easy layup**

# Rebuilding for the Future

Although the Milwaukee Bucks reached the playoffs for 12 straight seasons from 1980 through 1991, they were never quite good enough to reach the NBA Finals. Now, with former Milwaukee player Mike Dunleavy as Coach and General Manager, the franchise is working on a new look. The roster is younger, the defense better and the future brighter.

Few will ever forget the one stroke of luck that turned an expansion franchise into an NBA champion in just three seasons.

Basketball history turned on the flip of a single coin in 1969. The Bucks had entered the NBA prior to the 1968–69 season and proceeded to lose 55 games. There were only two divisions in those days, and Phoenix, another expansion team, lost 66 games to finish last in the West. Since Milwaukee occupied the bottom spot in the East, a coin flip determined which team would have the No. 1 draft pick in 1969.

No game for either team had been as big as the coin flip. The winner would get 7–2 center Kareem Abdul-Jabbar (then known as Lew Alcindor), at the time the most accomplished center to leave the college ranks since Bill Russell and Wilt Chamberlain. In the minds of many, he

**Eric Murdock keys a Bucks fastbreak**

was potentially at least as good as either of those two legends.

And he didn't disappoint. Phoenix called heads, the coin came up tails and

Milwaukee became an instant contender. Abdul-Jabbar averaged 28.8 points and 14.5 rebounds as a rookie and the Bucks improved to 55 victories. Milwaukee then added aging superstar Oscar Robertson prior to the 1970–71 season to run the offense and take pressure off the young Abdul-Jabbar. The Bucks dominated the league, winning 66 games and cruising through the Playoffs. They finished one of the greatest seasons in NBA history by pounding Baltimore in the Finals, winning four straight games by an average of more than 12 points.

Though Abdul-Jabbar would lead the Bucks to an average of 61 victories over the next three seasons, Milwaukee reached the NBA Finals for the last time in 1974 where it lost a tough seven-game series to the Boston Celtics.

Injuries plagued Abdul-Jabbar's final season in Milwaukee and the team dipped to 38–44. With an aging roster, the Bucks decided to trade Abdul-Jabbar to the Los Angeles Lakers prior to the 1975–76 season. The legend, dealt with journeyman Walt Wesley, produced four young players in return including Elmore Smith, Brian Winters, Dave Meyers and Junior Bridgeman.

But it wasn't until Coach Don Nelson arrived early in the 1976–77 season that the franchise turned around. He built around

## ROLL OF HONOR

| | | | | |
|---|---|---|---|---|
| Conference/Division | Eastern/Central | | | |
| First NBA year | 1968-69 | | | |
| Home Arena details | Bradley Center (built 1988, capacity 18,633) | | | |
| Former cities/nicknames | None | | | |
| NBA Championships | 1971 | | | |

| Playing Record | G | W | L | Pct |
|---|---|---|---|---|
| Regular Season | 2132 | 1212 | 920 | .568 |
| Playoffs (Series 16-18) | 169 | 85 | 84 | .503 |

# SIDNEY MONCRIEF
## Quiet Superstar

The Milwaukee Bucks took Sidney Moncrief with the No. 5 pick in the 1979 Draft and never looked back.

By his third season, Moncrief had become one of the league's best end-to-end players. Defensively, he had few rivals at the guard spot. Although just 6–3 and weighing less than 185 pounds, Moncrief played as tough as any player in the league.

He made his first NBA All-Defensive team in 1982 and helped turn the Bucks into an Eastern Conference power. A year later, Moncrief was named NBA Defensive Player of the Year for the first of two consecutive seasons. He also became a terror at the other end of the court, averaging more than 20 points a game.

For five often brilliant seasons, Moncrief was among the league's finest all-around players. He rebounded, scored, defended and led the Bucks with a quiet toughness even opponents respected.

Though injuries would eventually limit Moncrief, Milwaukee had no regrets. Moncrief's 10 years with the Bucks produced 10 playoff appearances and the same number of winning seasons.

young players such as Bridgeman, Marques Johnson, Quinn Buckner and Sidney Moncrief. Later, veterans like Bob Lanier would help carry the Bucks through a period of seven straight seasons with 50 or more victories.

Although they continually ran into Julius Erving's Philadelphia 76ers and Larry Bird's Boston Celtics in the playoffs, Milwaukee remained one of the league's most successful franchises.

The only serious lapse since that first season started in 1991 and lingers on. Mike Dunleavy, a former Bucks player and highly successful head coach with the Los Angeles Lakers, took over the team's coaching and general manager duties in 1992 and immediately started to rebuild the franchise around younger players like Todd Day, Lee Mayberry, Eric Murdock, Blue Edwards and Ken Norman.

**Versatile Vin Baker goes up and over the Knicks**

# Those Howling Wolves

It took 29 years, but Minnesota finally found its way back into the NBA with the Timberwolves. The Minneapolis Lakers won five championships in that city before moving to Los Angeles in 1960. The void was filled when the Timberwolves joined the NBA as an expansion team in 1989. Now all the Timberwolves have to do is win enough to make locals forget about the Lakers.

After four losing seasons, three coaches and several front office changes, the Minnesota Timberwolves are still trying to find their trail to success in the NBA.

Minnesota has lost an average of over 60 games a season, hardly the kind of performance Timberwolves fans had expected in a city that produced one of the most successful franchises in NBA history.

In the 1940s and 1950s, Minneapolis was the home of the Lakers. With center George Mikan leading the charge, those Laker teams won five NBA titles in six years before eventually moving to Los Angeles in 1960.

So fans in Minneapolis, a group that includes Mikan, met their new team with a clear sense of expectation. Two local businessmen, Harvey Ratner and Marv

**Man In Motion: Micheal Williams sets off**

Wolfenson, were awarded the team in April, 1987.

What followed was a painstaking process of building the franchise. The team's executives, which included Bob Stein, spent hours discussing the particulars of the new venture. But some early decisions, particularly the hiring of one-time University of Minnesota Coach Bill Musselman, backfired. Musselman's teams won respectable totals of 22 and then 29 games, but he was criticized for failing to develop the Timberwolves' young talent. Musselman's desire for immediate results clashed with the long-term developmental philosophy of Minnesota's front office.

The team eventually dismissed Musselman in favor of former Boston Celtics Coach Jimmy Rodgers, who departed 29 games into his second season and was replaced by former Timberwolves player Sidney Lowe.

All-American Christian Laettner was drafted in 1992 and the 6–11 forward had an outstanding rookie season, averaging 18.2 points and 8.7 rebounds. For the first time, the Timberwolves appeared to have found the proper mix of young and old players to make a serious climb in the Midwest Division. Before the 1992–93 season, the team traded for sharp-shooting forward Chuck Person and lightening-quick point guard Micheal Williams.

Combined with shooting guard Doug West, the new Timberwolves were expect-

## ROLL OF HONOR

| Conference/Division | Western/Midwest | | | |
|---|---|---|---|---|
| First NBA year | 1989-90 | | | |
| Home Arena details | Target Center (built 1990, capacity 19,006) | | | |
| Former cities/nicknames | None | | | |
| NBA Championships | None | | | |
| **Playing Record** | **G** | **W** | **L** | **Pct** |
| Regular Season | 410 | 105 | 305 | .256 |
| Playoffs | Yet to qualify | | | |

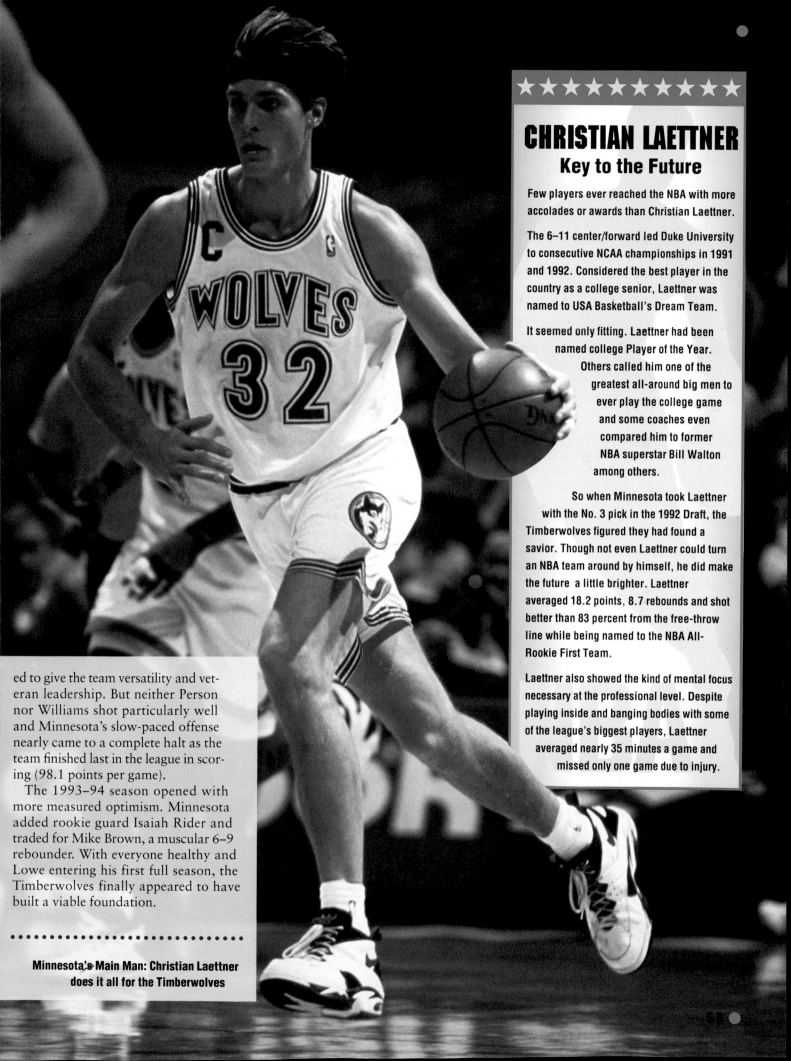

## CHRISTIAN LAETTNER
### Key to the Future

Few players ever reached the NBA with more accolades or awards than Christian Laettner.

The 6–11 center/forward led Duke University to consecutive NCAA championships in 1991 and 1992. Considered the best player in the country as a college senior, Laettner was named to USA Basketball's Dream Team.

It seemed only fitting. Laettner had been named college Player of the Year. Others called him one of the greatest all-around big men to ever play the college game and some coaches even compared him to former NBA superstar Bill Walton among others.

So when Minnesota took Laettner with the No. 3 pick in the 1992 Draft, the Timberwolves figured they had found a savior. Though not even Laettner could turn an NBA team around by himself, he did make the future a little brighter. Laettner averaged 18.2 points, 8.7 rebounds and shot better than 83 percent from the free-throw line while being named to the NBA All-Rookie First Team.

Laettner also showed the kind of mental focus necessary at the professional level. Despite playing inside and banging bodies with some of the league's biggest players, Laettner averaged nearly 35 minutes a game and missed only one game due to injury.

ed to give the team versatility and veteran leadership. But neither Person nor Williams shot particularly well and Minnesota's slow-paced offense nearly came to a complete halt as the team finished last in the league in scoring (98.1 points per game).

The 1993–94 season opened with more measured optimism. Minnesota added rookie guard Isaiah Rider and traded for Mike Brown, a muscular 6–9 rebounder. With everyone healthy and Lowe entering his first full season, the Timberwolves finally appeared to have built a viable foundation.

**Minnesota's Main Man: Christian Laettner does it all for the Timberwolves**

# Looking For Respect

The glory years came and went with Julius Erving and the old American Basketball Association. Since 1976, when the ABA merged with the NBA, the Nets have moved from New York to New Jersey, yet they have remained in the shadow of the New York Knicks. The Nets stopped a run of six straight losing seasons when Dream Team Coach Chuck Daly arrived in 1992–93.

They played their first games inside a dingy Armory just across the Hudson River from New York City's bright lights. And despite moving all around New York and New Jersey before finding a lasting home in the Meadowlands, the Nets survived, indeed thrived with a constantly changing roster that at one time or another has included some of the greatest players in basketball history.

The Nets were born out of the ABA's notion that no real sports league could survive without a strong franchise in the New York area. During the 1967–68 season,

**Preparing To Fire: Kenny Anderson sets to shoot**

the Nets had to forfeit one home game because of water on the Armory floor. Another game had to be moved to a high school gym because of scheduling conflicts with a circus.

Within a year, the Nets had moved to Commack Arena on Long Island where they nearly self-destructed. A 17–61 season sent the franchise in a spin that didn't stop until businessman Roy Boe stepped in and bought the team. He made three moves that turned the franchise around. Boe signed coach Lou Carneseca, moved the team to Island Garden Arena, also on Long Island, and traded a first-round draft pick and a bundle of cash to the struggling Virginia franchise for Rick Barry.

Barry, one of the greatest scorers in professional basketball history, became the franchise's first true superstar. Barry led the Nets to the 1972 ABA Finals before near disaster struck again. A federal judge ordered Barry back to his former NBA team, the Golden State Warriors, for whom Barry had originally signed out of college.

After yet another arena move, to the Nassau Coliseum, the Nets found salvation once more in the struggling Squires. One of the most lopsided deals in basketball history sent young Julius Erving to the Nets.

With former NBA player Kevin Loughery now coaching the team, Erving led the Nets to two ABA titles and helped

## DERRICK COLEMAN
### Coming Into His Own

The word hung on Derrick Coleman like an ugly coat.

Potential.

By the start of the 1992–93 season, Coleman had heard the word so often that he decided to make it go away. With Coach Chuck Daly leading the Nets and helping Coleman adjust to the role as franchise savior, Coleman took charge of his career.

The 1991 NBA Rookie of the Year silenced his doubters by producing by far the best season of his young career. Coleman averaged 20.7 points, a career-high 11.2 rebounds and blocked 243 shots, nearly three times the amount of either of his first two seasons. Coleman shot free throws better, had more steals and New Jersey finished above .500 (43–39).

Coleman was even better in the playoffs, averaging 26.8 points and 13.4 rebounds as the Nets extended Cleveland to Game 5 in a First Round match.

The potential had been realized.

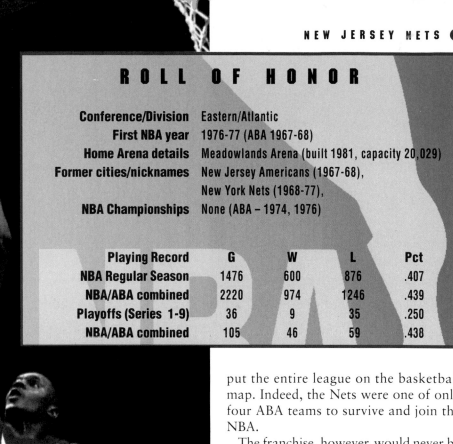

## ROLL OF HONOR

| | | | | |
|---|---|---|---|---|
| Conference/Division | Eastern/Atlantic | | | |
| First NBA year | 1976-77 (ABA 1967-68) | | | |
| Home Arena details | Meadowlands Arena (built 1981, capacity 20,029) | | | |
| Former cities/nicknames | New Jersey Americans (1967-68), New York Nets (1968-77), | | | |
| NBA Championships | None (ABA – 1974, 1976) | | | |

| Playing Record | G | W | L | Pct |
|---|---|---|---|---|
| NBA Regular Season | 1476 | 600 | 876 | .407 |
| NBA/ABA combined | 2220 | 974 | 1246 | .439 |
| Playoffs (Series 1-9) | 36 | 9 | 35 | .250 |
| NBA/ABA combined | 105 | 46 | 59 | .438 |

put the entire league on the basketball map. Indeed, the Nets were one of only four ABA teams to survive and join the NBA.

The franchise, however, would never be the same. A complicated and controversial deal landed Erving in Philadelphia and the Nets back at the drawing board. In 1977, after yet another arena switch, to Piscataway, N.J., on a temporary basis until the Meadowlands Arena was completed, the team became the New Jersey Nets.

But NBA success, which came during the 1992–93 season under the direction of former Coach Chuck Daly, was not without disappointment. The Nets finished 43–39 and came within a game of upsetting Cleveland in the First Round of the Playoffs.

But the optimism born out of that performance disappeared during the summer of 1993. Drazen Petrovic, who had become perhaps the finest shooter in the league, died tragically in an automobile accident. And a team that had been built around star forward Derrick Coleman, young point guard Kenny Anderson and Petrovic suddenly had a hole that would be tough to fill.

Once more the Nets' resiliency will be tested. Only this time it will be up to Coleman and Anderson to provide the strength.

• • • • • • • • • • • • • • • • • • • • • • • • •

**Derrick Dominates: Coleman controls another rebound against the Philadelphia 76ers**

# Another Garden Party

The Knicks won their first two NBA championships in 1970 and 1973, events that turned Madison Square Garden into one of the loudest arenas on earth. With former Lakers Coach Pat Riley now directing the show and superstar Patrick Ewing taking control, the Garden has started rocking again as the team looks for another championship.

It might have been the most intelligent basketball team ever to play the game, and after 48 professional seasons it's the one team New York Knicks fans have never forgotten.

A group of players that included a future United States Senator (Bill Bradley) and three NBA head coaches (Phil Jackson, Dave DeBusschere and Willis Reed) came together in the early 1970s to produce the only two championships for a franchise that played its first professional game in 1946.

With legendary Coach Red Holzman calling the shots, the Knicks destroyed opponents with a combination of skill, tenacity and discipline. They played team defense and spread the ball around an offense that had scorers at every position.

Bradley and DeBusschere manned the

**Charles Oakley leans in against Detroit**

forward spots, Reed played center and Walt Frazier, the flashy 6–4 guard, ran the show from out front. Jackson, who would win three NBA Championships as coach of the Chicago Bulls, was a defensive stopper off the bench and known for his unselfish play.

Cazzie Russell and Dick Barnett played key roles on the 1970 Championship team while Earl Monroe, a dazzling ballhandler and scorer, and Jerry Lucas came aboard for the 1973 title run. Those teams not only left a lasting impression on New Yorkers, but 20 years later Jackson applied many of Holzman's principles as coach of the Bulls.

Organized in 1946, the Knicks had a small but exciting lineup under another legendary coach, Joe Lapchick. Though the Knicks produced a string of solid seasons, they were no match for George Mikan and the Minneapolis Lakers. New York won three straight Eastern Division titles only to be defeated by Mikan's Lakers three times in the Finals.

After that, New York didn't win a single playoff game between 1957 and 1967. But when Holzman took over midway through the 1967–68 season, he quickly molded the Knicks into an Eastern power.

A championship roster came together as DeBusschere arrived via trade and Bradley returned after two years of study at Oxford. Reed had already established himself as a solid center and Frazier, only a

## ROLL OF HONOR

| | |
|---|---|
| Conference/Division | Eastern/Atlantic |
| First NBA year | 1946-47 |
| Home Arena details | Madison Square Garden (built 1968, capacity 19,763) |
| Former cities/nicknames | None |
| NBA Championships | 1970, 1973 |

| Playing Record | G | W | L | Pct |
|---|---|---|---|---|
| Regular Season | 3719 | 1877 | 1842 | .505 |
| Playoffs (Series 31-30) | 270 | 136 | 134 | .560 |

rookie on Holzman's first team, would soon become one of the NBA's greatest defensive players.

When Bill Russell retired after leading Boston to its 11th title in 13 years following the 1968–69 season, the Eastern Division became a wide open race with the Knicks perfectly positioned. They beat Wilt Chamberlain's Los Angeles Lakers for the 1970 Championship and then won again in 1973. But as the core players aged and injuries mounted, the Knicks headed into a period of inconsistency and almost constant change.

Between 1987 and 1992, New York had six head coaches in six seasons. Superstar center Patrick Ewing, the Knicks' No. 1 pick in the 1985 Draft, pushed the team to the brink of major playoff success in 1989 and 1990 only to see the franchise slip again.

But everyone seemed to know the Knicks were about to rise again. With Ewing, one of the most versatile centers ever to play the game, manning the middle, New York needed only to fill the edges. Before the Knicks front office worried about players, however, the team decided to find a master tactician.

This time the Knicks turned to another legendary coach in Pat Riley, whose Los Angeles Lakers had won four NBA titles during the 1980s. Riley came out of retirement and took control of a team led by Ewing, bruising power forward Charles Oakley and sharp-shooting guard John Starks.

With Michael Jordan retired, the Eastern Conference became wide open again. And just as they were in 1969, the Knicks again appear to be perfectly situated to take advantage of the opening.

**A solid defender, New York's John Starks is best known for his long-range shooting and sensational dunking**

★ ★ ★ ★ ★ ★ ★ ★ ★ ★ ★ ★

# WALT FRAZIER
## A Style All His Own

With long black sideburns and a thick mustache, Walt Frazier carried himself with a style that was his alone. No one dressed better than Frazier. No one had more shoes, "kicks" as he called them, or hats, known as "lids" to Frazier. His suits were colorful and among the finest made, as were his ties, ("knots").

On the floor, Frazier rarely changed expressions. His 6–4, 205-pound body seemed perfectly proportioned and always under control.

A first round draft pick in 1967 by the Knicks, Frazier had been an all-around star at Southern Illinois University. Frazier made the NBA All-Defensive first team seven straight seasons starting in 1969. By 1970, his third year in the league, Frazier had become one of the cornerstones to the NBA's best team.

Given Frazier's style, the title of his first book, *Rockin' Steady*, seemed only fitting.

# Orlando MAGIC

## The Shaq Attack

Orlando struggled through its first three seasons before Shaquille O'Neal came to the rescue. With O'Neal's arrival in 1992, the Magic improved by 20 games over the previous season. Now, with another young star on board in Anfernee Hardaway, Orlando could become one of the Eastern Conference's top teams.

Magic. The name fits. How else does an emerging franchise end up with two consecutive No. 1 Draft picks despite a lottery system which is weighted toward the league's worst teams?

A year after landing towering Shaquille O'Neal in the 1992 NBA Draft, Orlando won a franchise-record 41 games. But the Magic finished a game short of reaching the playoffs, which put them back into the Draft Lottery. Of the 11 lottery teams, Orlando easily had the best record which, given the nature of the lottery, made it a 1-in-66 long shot to end up with the top pick yet again.

Then it happened. After reaching the .500 mark for the first time, the Magic were rewarded with yet another No. 1 draft choice. That pick turned out to be Chris Webber, who was summarily dealt to Golden State in a wild draft-day deal that landed multi-talented guard Anfernee Hardaway in Orlando.

**Scott Skiles looks for a lefthanded layup**

It also led to a restructuring of the Lottery system, but not before the Magic had cashed in twice and, in the process, solidified the future.

All that was fine with front office dynamo Pat Williams, who had already provided the franchise with a solid foundation. One of the NBA's finest promoters, Williams arrived in Orlando after a nearly 20-year education that started with the Chicago Bulls in 1969.

Williams then moved on to the Philadelphia 76ers where his marketing skills and basketball knowledge helped revive a sagging franchise. In the mid-1980s, after a decade in Philadelphia, Williams departed to help bring a franchise to an Orlando community known primarily as the home to Disney World.

Williams' magic helped land one of four new expansion franchises and the team began play, along with Minnesota, in 1989. Not unexpectedly, Orlando struggled through a difficult first season, losing 64 games with aging veterans such as Reggie Theus, Sidney Green and Dave Corzine occupying roster spots.

The Magic improved quickly, however, behind young and talented players such as Dennis Scott and Nick Anderson. But a series of devastating injuries buried Orlando during the 1991–92 season and the team slipped to 61 losses and the NBA's second worst record.

The silver lining turned out to be the 1992 Draft which featured one of the most imposing young centers in years in O'Neal. Standing 7–1 and weighing more than 300 pounds, O'Neal had the ability and presence to redirect an entire franchise.

And that's exactly what he's done since landing in Orlando. O'Neal averaged 23. 4 points, 13.8 rebounds and blocked more

| ROLL OF HONOR | | | | |
|---|---|---|---|---|
| Conference/Division | Eastern/Atlantic | | | |
| First NBA year | 1989-90 | | | |
| Home Arena details | Orlando Arena (built 1989, capacity 15,291) | | | |
| Former cities/nicknames | None | | | |
| NBA Championships | None | | | |
| Playing Record | G | W | L | Pct |
| Regular Season | 410 | 161 | 249 | .393 |
| Playoffs (Series 0-1) | 3 | 0 | 3 | .000 |

# ANFERNEE HARDAWAY
## A Magic Penny

Anfernee Hardaway couldn't have ended up anywhere else. After spending his summers working out with Magic Johnson, another oversized point guard, Hardaway was a natural for Orlando.

The Magic felt the same way. Despite gaining the No. 1 pick in the 1993 Draft, team executives made a deal that could solidify the franchise for years to come. Orlando selected Chris Webber and then sent him to Golden State for Hardaway and three future No. 1 draft picks.

The deal, though stunning to some observers, worked perfectly for Orlando. Less than 48 hours before the draft, the team still wasn't sure which player it wanted. Webber had size, but the Magic already had 7–1 Shaquille O'Neal. So management summoned Hardaway to Orlando for one final workout.

At 6–7, Hardaway has the ballhandling skills of a point guard and the scoring ability of a shooting guard. By the end of the workout Orlando knew exactly who it wanted.

Hardaway, nicknamed "Penny", had a dazzling two-year career at Memphis State University. His size and skills, advanced well beyond his 21 years, reminded some of Johnson. Even Johnson, who helped Hardaway develop his ballhandling and shooting skills, figures Penny to be a steal.

than three shots a game in his first NBA season. He also helped make up for another season of injuries while carrying the Magic to within a single game of its first playoff appearance.

Hardaway, the eventual prize from 1993's lucky drawing, adds yet another dimension to a fast-rising franchise. With O'Neal dominating inside and Hardaway and Anderson operating on the perimeter, Orlando no longer needs magic.

• • • • • • • • • • • • • • • • • • • • • • • • • •

**A Penny From Heaven: Anfernee "Penny" Hardaway soars in for a slam**

# Looking For Another House Call

The Philadelphia 76ers rode Julius "Dr. J" Erving's brilliance to the 1983 NBA Championship. But after trading superstar Charles Barkley and revamping the roster from the bottom up, Philadelphia has turned the future over to 7–6 center Shawn Bradley and forward Clarence Weatherspoon. If the 76ers are going to rekindle title hopes, they'll have to do it with those two leading the way.

The "Spoon" dishes up a slam against Orlando

The Philadelphia 76ers have done just about everything at least once. From winning NBA championships to recording the single worst season in league history and trading away two of basketball's most accomplished players, Philadelphia has long been one of the NBA's more colorful creations.

The team started out as the Syracuse Nationals and didn't arrive in Philadelphia until 1963. Indeed, the 76ers were born out of the void created by the Philadelphia Warriors, who moved to San Francisco. In the 31 years since, the 76ers have usually been one of the league's foremost attractions for one reason or another.

The franchise is also largely responsible for the creation of the 24-second clock. In an intrasquad game prior to the 1954–55 season, Syracuse owner Danny Biasone improvised an early forerunner of the current shot clock. He decided on 24 seconds as an experimental time guide for offensive possessions. The experiment proved useful and the NBA adopted Biasone's idea as a league rule, which resulted in a faster, more high-scoring game.

Those early Syracuse teams also had two of the era's finest players in Dolph Schayes and Johnny "Red" Kerr. With the addition of rookie Earl Lloyd prior to the 1954–55 season, the Nationals won their only championship.

Once in Philadelphia, however, the franchise became a league-wide show. San Francisco grudgingly agreed to trade Wilt Chamberlain to the 76ers midway through the 1964–65 season. One year later, Philadelphia had a starting lineup loaded with talent. Chamberlain, Billy Cunningham, Chet Walker, Hal Greer and Wali Jones helped the 76ers to a brilliant 68–13 regular season record, second best in history.

With Chamberlain passing more than earlier in his career, Philadelphia ended Boston's string of eight straight NBA titles by eliminating the Celtics in the playoffs. The 76ers went on to beat San Francisco in the 1967 Finals for their first Philadelphia title.

## SHAWN BRADLEY
### Big On The Future

Shawn Bradley left Brigham Young University in 1991 following his only college season. He had established an NCAA record for blocked shots in a season and tied another when he swatted away 14 in a single game. But Bradley headed off to a two-year religious mission that took him to Sydney, Australia. Bradley's return became a matter of international interest. Would he go back to BYU? Would he try to play in the NBA?

At 7–6 and gifted with rare athletic skills for his size, Bradley intrigued just about every coach that had ever seen him play.

So when Bradley decided to end his college career and go directly into the NBA, the 76ers were waiting. In the 1993 Draft, Philadelphia took Bradley with the second pick.

Unlike past NBA giants, Bradley moves extremely well which should make the adjustment a little more smooth.

## ROLL OF HONOR

| | | | | |
|---|---|---|---|---|
| Conference/Division | Eastern/Atlantic | | | |
| First NBA year | 1949-50 | | | |
| Home Arena details | The Spectrum (built 1967, capacity 18,168) | | | |
| Former cities/nicknames | Syracuse Nationals (1949-63) | | | |
| NBA Championships | 1955, 1967, 1983 | | | |

| Playing Record | G | W | L | Pct |
|---|---|---|---|---|
| Regular Season | 3548 | 1993 | 1555 | .562 |
| Playoffs (Series 36-34) | 328 | 175 | 153 | .534 |

Less than two years later, however, Chamberlain was shipped off to the Los Angeles Lakers and the 76ers self-destructed. They lost a record 73 games during the 1972–73 season.

But within four years the team again had one of the most exciting rosters in the league with Julius Erving, George McGinnis, Doug Collins, Steve Mix and young Darryl Dawkins carrying Philadelphia into the 1977 NBA Finals.

Behind Erving's brilliant play and the coaching of Cunningham, the 76ers were one of the elite teams in the league along with the Los Angeles Lakers and Boston Celtics in the early 1980s. The era produced only a single title (in 1983), however, as the Lakers and Celtics started to dominate.

Charles Barkley arrived in 1984 and the 76ers remained a solid team capable of beating anyone. But Erving eventually slowed down and Philadelphia slowed with him.

Barkley was traded in 1992 and the 76ers lost 56 games in 1992–93, their worst record in 19 years.

The future, at least as far as owner Harold Katz was concerned, arrived prior to the 1993–94 season. Philadelphia used the No. 2 pick in the Draft to select 7–6 center Shawn Bradley, who was quickly given uniform No. 76. With young Clarence Weatherspoon alongside Bradley on the front line, the future suddenly has a little of that old Philadelphia color.

● ● ● ● ● ● ● ● ● ● ● ● ● ● ● ● ● ● ● ● ● ● ●

**Tower Of Power: 7–6 Shawn Bradley flips a hook shot over Houston's Matt Bullard**

**PHOENIX SUNS**

# Home Of The Rising Suns

For years the Phoenix Suns had been one of the Western Conference's top teams. They even made an appearance in the 1976 NBA Finals. But the Suns never won more than 57 regular season games until Charles Barkley rode into town prior to the 1992–93 season. The Suns won a franchise record 62 games and reached the 1993 Finals, this time losing to Chicago. The Suns have risen, but can they finally win a championship?

For years the first pick in the NBA Draft was determined by the simple toss of a coin. Representatives from the worst teams in the East and West conferences would gather for the annual coin flip.

As the Phoenix Suns can attest, being lucky usually translates into being good. The Suns entered the league along with Milwaukee in 1968. Both teams limped through difficult first seasons, Phoenix relying on sharp shooting guards Gail Goodrich and Dick Van Arsdale and not much else. Over in the East, the Bucks had similar problems.

As a result, Phoenix and Milwaukee ended up squaring off in the coin toss. This one, however, had historic implications that both franchises understood. The Suns won the right to call the toss and

**Thunder Dan: Majerle slams on the Trail Blazers**

## ROLL OF HONOR

| | | | | |
|---|---|---|---|---|
| Conference/Division | Western/Pacific | | | |
| First NBA year | 1968-69 | | | |
| Home Arena details | America West Arena (dedicated 1992, capacity 19,023) | | | |
| Former cities/nicknames | None | | | |
| NBA Championships | None | | | |
| **Playing Record** | **G** | **W** | **L** | **Pct** |
| **Regular Season** | 2132 | 1146 | 986 | .538 |
| **Playoffs (Series 19-16)** | 162 | 80 | 82 | .494 |

called heads. The coin came up tails, Lew Alcindor (now Kareem Abdul-Jabbar) went to Milwaukee and within two seasons the Bucks had an NBA title.

What about the Suns? It has been a struggle often frustrated by stinging

**Passing Fancy: One of the NBA's greatest point guards, Kevin Johnson keys the Suns attack**

losses in the playoffs.

Just one year after that inaugural season, Phoenix extended the Los Angeles Lakers to seven games in the Western Division Semifinals, a remarkable turnaround aided by playground legend Connie Hawkins.

Although it would be six years before Phoenix reached the playoffs again, the building process remained impressive. By 1976 the team had assembled the best team in the West with young stars such as Paul Westphal, the current Suns coach, Alvan Adams, Garfield Heard and Curtis Perry along with veterans like Van Arsdale and Keith Erickson.

A 42–40 regular season finish set up a dramatic postseason that included what many think is the best playoff game in NBA history. Phoenix beat Seattle in the Western Conference Semifinals and then upset defending champion Golden State to reach the Finals. And that's when the real drama began. Matched against the powerful Boston Celtics, the Suns won two of the first four games to set up a crucial Game 5 at Boston. The contest took three overtime periods and rolled along at a numbing pace. It took Heard's incredible, high-arching jump shot with one second left in the second overtime to force yet a third extra period. Ultimately, Boston's deep bench and veteran cool prevailed and the Celtics went on to close out the title in six games.

But the Suns had established themselves under Coach John MacLeod. Players such as Westphal, Adams and Walter Davis would help make Phoenix one of the West's top teams for years. However, the Suns wouldn't make a return trip to the Finals until Charles Barkley arrived prior the 1992–93 season.

With Westphal assuming the coaching reins and Barkley taking over the scoring and rebounding, Phoenix rolled through the 1992–93 season. And this time no one stopped them until Chicago and Michael Jordan in the NBA Finals.

The Suns have built perhaps the best roster, man-for-man, in the league. Phoenix President Jerry Colangelo's dealing has produced veteran shooter Danny Ainge and young talented frontcourt players such as Oliver Miller.

These days the Suns don't need luck. They are already good.

# BLAZERS™

# One Brief Shining Moment

It happened in 1977 when center Bill Walton found the strength and physical good fortune to last an entire season. The Trail Blazers won the only championship in franchise history, an improbable romp past the Philadelphia 76ers. Since then, however, near misses on and off the court have left Portland looking for yet another chance.

Despite years of success and two recent trips to the NBA Finals, the Portland franchise is marked by two events that came seven years apart.

The first happened in 1977 when a Trail Blazers team led by legendary center Bill Walton and bruising forward Maurice Lucas marched through an unlikely, yet

**The Buck Stops Here: Buck Williams clears off another rebound**

brilliant postseason en route to the franchise's only NBA Championship.

The team had joined the NBA in 1971 along with Buffalo and Cleveland. Lenny Wilkens took over the coaching duties in 1974, which was also his last season as a player.

Wilkens lasted two seasons before management turned the team over to Jack Ramsay. A great coach in his own right, Ramsay received the gift of his career when Walton stayed healthy enough to last through the 1976–77 season.

Teamed with Lucas and a collection of hard-working players, Walton turned the Trail Blazers into champions. Walton led the league in rebounding (14.4) and blocked shots (3.25) and his passing helped ignite the league's third best offense.

But after breezing through the first three rounds of the 1976 Playoffs, Portland ran hard into Julius Erving and the Philadelphia 76ers in the Finals. Philadelphia took a quick 2–0 lead and as the series shifted to Portland, many thought the Trail Blazers were simply overmatched.

That's when Portland exploded, winning the next two games by 22 and 32 points and forever shifting the momentum. The Trail Blazers went on to win four straight games and claim their first and only NBA title. The championship run not only shocked the rest of the league, but it made a folk hero out of Walton.

## BILL WALTON
### Two Feet Short

The pain in Bill Walton's feet could be felt throughout the entire NBA. One of the greatest college players in the history of basketball, Walton figured to be at least that good as a professional.

He could shoot, defend, run the floor and pass as well as any big man in the game. So when Portland acquired Walton in the 1974 Draft, the league took notice.

Though Walton's performance never disappointed, his body failed miserably. Foot injuries limited him to 35 games as a rookie and just 51 games his second season. Walton stayed healthy enough to play 65 games during the 1976–77 season, however, and then carried on through the playoffs.

Walton averaged 18.2 points, 15.2 rebounds, blocked more than three shots a game and helped direct the Portland offense. The Trail Blazers overcame Philadelphia to win the 1977 NBA Championship.

Although Walton's career would continue to be marked by injuries, he did win another NBA title with Boston in 1986.

**Cliff Note: Robinson registers another rejection**

Able to defend, pass and score as well as any big man in the league, Walton appeared to be the kind of player that could carry an entire franchise. Once considered a solid but thin team, Portland was now seen as a team on the rise with a potentially dominating player leading the ascension.

Portland was even better the following season, but Walton's foot problems ended any chance of another title. His season ended two games into the playoffs and eventually, so did his career in Portland. Walton missed the entire 1978–79 season and a year later was shipped off to the San Diego Clippers.

Portland had a chance to take another giant leap forward in 1984. A previous trade had given Portland, 48–34 during the 1983–84 season, the No. 2 pick in the 1984 Draft.

But with it came a decision that will forever haunt the franchise. After Houston selected Hakeem Olajuwon with the first choice, Portland decided to gamble on 7–1 center Sam Bowie. Chicago then used the third pick to grab Michael Jordan.

With a young Clyde Drexler set to take over the shooting guard spot and Kiki Vandeweghe the team's leading scorer at small forward, Portland lacked only a solid big man in the middle.

But Bowie had missed two entire seasons during college at the University of Kentucky with leg problems. Though no one figured Jordan would become the game's brightest star, everyone knew about

Bowie's medical problems. And Portland paid dearly for what turned out to be a horrible mistake. Bowie missed 44 games in his second season, 77 in his third and then didn't play at all in his fourth year in the league.

As with Walton, however, Portland survived Bowie's injuries. Indeed, the franchise corrected itself quickly and entered the 1990s as the West's dominant team.

The Trail Blazers, led by Drexler, Terry Porter, Jerome Kersey and Buck Williams, reached the NBA Finals in 1990 and 1992 only to lose hard-fought championship rounds against Detroit and then Chicago.

Whether the current team gets another title shot remains to be seen, but one thing is certain: It will take more than a visit to the NBA Finals to make fans forget about Walton and Bowie.

• • • • • • • • • • • • • • • • • • • • • • • • • • • • •

**Terry Porter sets up for a jumper**

## ROLL OF HONOR

| | |
|---|---|
| Conference/Division | Western/Pacific |
| First NBA year | 1970-71 |
| Home Arena details | Memorial Coliseum (built 1960, capacity 12,888) |
| Former cities/nicknames | None |
| NBA Championships | 1977 |

| Playing Record | G | W | L | Pct |
|---|---|---|---|---|
| Regular Season | 1968 | 1041 | 927 | .529 |
| Playoffs (Series 14-16) | 136 | 67 | 69 | .493 |

# The Traveling Kings

They have moved across the country with stops in Rochester, Cincinnati, Kansas City and finally Sacramento, but the Kings still haven't found the road to the NBA Finals. But since settling in Sacramento in 1985, the Kings have started to assemble a roster capable of making a run at the playoffs.

Consider the cross-country odyssey that landed the Kings in Sacramento. It does provide perspective. The Sacramento Kings used to be the Kansas City Kings who used to be the Kansas City-Omaha Kings who used to be the Cincinnati Royals who were originally the Rochester Royals. There was even a brief life before that in the Midwest.

If that's not enough, consider the disparate group of players on that first team. Future pro football Hall of Fame quarterback Otto Graham, eventual television star Chuck Connors, future New York Knicks Coach Red Holzman and long-

time major league baseball player Del Rice were all members of the 1946 team that won the National Basketball League title. Not surprisingly, the team was located elsewhere, in Sheboygan, Wisconsin, during that championship season.

Rochester joined the NBA in 1948 and immediately became one of the league's strongest franchises. By their third season, the Royals were playing for the NBA title thanks to players such as Arnie Risen and Bob Davies.

The Royals, and later the Kings, would never reach another championship series. That might have changed had the career of Maurice Stokes not been cut short by tragedy. Stokes arrived in the 1955 Draft and was developing into a top player when he contracted a crippling brain disease called encephalitis.

A year earlier, in 1957, the team had moved to Cincinnati in part because management wanted to claim the great Oscar Robertson with a territorial pick in the 1960 Draft. Two horrible seasons followed the move, but the gamble paid off.

Robertson, star of the U.S. men's team in the 1960 Rome Olympics, joined the team for the 1960–61 season and he was even better than anyone expected. Robertson averaged an incredible 30.8 points, 12.3 rebounds and 11.5 assists per game during the 1961–62 season. No player

**King Of Kings: Lionel Simmons glides toward the basket**

## MITCH RICHMOND
### King Of The Kings

Everybody wanted to know which opponent Michael Jordan considered the toughest to play against.

To the surprise of many, Jordan usually answered Mitch Richmond.

"He's almost as big (6–5, 215 pounds) as me, he's strong and he can do many of the things I can do," said Jordan. "He's also one of the few guys that plays both ends of the court like me."

The No. 5 pick in the 1988 NBA Draft, Richmond was picked by Golden State. Then, after a brilliant season in 1990–91, Golden State gambled and sent Richmond to Sacramento for rookie Billy Owens.

Richmond never missed a beat, leading the Kings in scoring in each of his first two seasons. He went into the 1993–94 season with a 22.5 points per game career scoring average and remained one of the best pure shooting guards the league has ever seen. And he finally made his All-Star debut in the 1994 game in Minneapolis.

has even come close to averaging double figures in any three statistical categories, much less a player that stood only 6–5 and played guard.

But not even Robertson could carry the Royals past Bill Russell's Boston Celtics. Cincinnati did come close, extending the eventual champion Celtics seven games in the 1963 Eastern Division Finals.

From there, however, the franchise lapsed into a 26-year period marked by moves and mediocrity. It moved West and became the Kansas City-Omaha Kings and, four years later, the Kansas City Kings.

The team's only real playoff success came unexpectedly following the 1980–81 season. With Otis Birdsong, Scott Wedman and Phil Ford doing all the scoring, the Kings just made the playoffs with a 40–42 regular season record.

But after knocking off Portland in the First Round, the Kings shocked Pacific Division champion Phoenix in a rousing seven-game series. They were eventually eliminated by the Houston Rockets in the Western Conference Finals and the franchise hasn't seen a playoff victory since.

By 1985 the Kings were on the move again, this time landing in Sacramento.

The Kings appeared headed out of their dark age until injuries beat them down again. Still, with young talent like Mitch Richmond, Walt Williams, Bobby Hurley and Lionel Simmons, Sacramento has the tools to improve.

· · · · · · · · · · · · · · · · · · · · · · · · ·

**Chairmen Of The Boards: Three Kings control the paint as the Lakers' Vlade Divac fights for space**

## ROLL OF HONOR

| | | | | |
|---|---|---|---|---|
| **Conference/Division** | Western/Pacific | | | |
| **First NBA year** | 1948-49 | | | |
| **Home Arena details** | ARCO Arena (built 1988, capacity 17,317) | | | |
| **Former cities/nicknames** | Rochester Royals (1948-57), Cincinnati Royals (1957-72), Kansas-City-Omaha Kings (1972-75) | | | |
| **NBA Championships** | 1951 | | | |

| **Playing Record** | G | W | L | Pct |
|---|---|---|---|---|
| **Regular Season** | 3613 | 1653 | 1960 | .458 |
| **Playoffs (Series 9-19)** | 114 | 45 | 69 | .395 |

# A Tale Of Two Players

Few teams won more creatively than the San Antonio Spurs of the late 1970s and early 1980s. They led the league in scoring by connecting from just about anywhere on the court. But they never reached a single championship series. Now the responsibility for carrying the franchise rests with 7–1 center David Robinson, a former Naval officer nicknamed "the Admiral".

They will be remembered as the greatest two players in San Antonio history. Unfortunately for the Spurs, by the time David Robinson and George Gervin ended on the same bench, one was playing while the other coached.

Look back to the league's most dominant championship teams and all of them had an inside-outside attack.

Unfortunately for Robinson and Gervin, the two championship components never intersected. Gervin ended a brilliant 12-year career in San Antonio four years before Robinson arrived and so far, neither has an NBA title to show for all their wondrous talents.

The Spurs started out as the Dallas Chaparrals in the ABA. Though Dallas had immediate success on the court, winning 46 games its first season, the franchise was a box office disaster. The team eventually became the Texas Chaparrals and alternated home games between Dallas, Fort Worth and Lubbock.

Then, in 1973, San Antonio businessman Red McCombs bought the franchise, moved it to his home town and renamed it the Spurs. Prior to the 1973–74 season, McCombs also spent more than $500,000, an enormous sum then, to buy Gervin and center Swen Nater from Virginia.

Gervin, a slender 6–7 scoring machine, had a dazzling array of hooks, scoops, jumpers and dunks. By the time San

**Dennis Rodman controls yet another rebound**

Antonio joined the NBA in 1976, Gervin had four professional seasons behind him and a fully-developed offensive arsenal.

With Gervin winning four scoring titles in five years, the Spurs became one of the most explosive teams in history. But without an impact player at center, Gervin's heroics weren't enough. San Antonio reached the Western Conference Finals under Coach Stan Albeck in 1982 and 1983 but couldn't get past the Los Angeles Lakers.

San Antonio didn't return to form until Robinson arrived out of the Naval Academy in 1989. The Spurs had used the

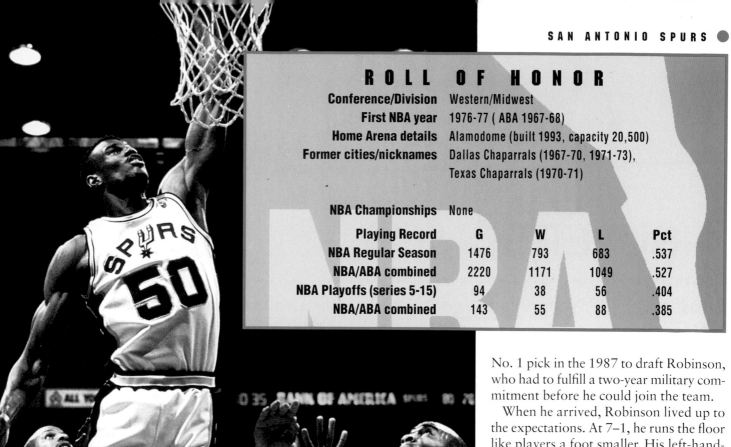

## ROLL OF HONOR

| | | | | |
|---|---|---|---|---|
| Conference/Division | Western/Midwest | | | |
| First NBA year | 1976-77 ( ABA 1967-68) | | | |
| Home Arena details | Alamodome (built 1993, capacity 20,500) | | | |
| Former cities/nicknames | Dallas Chaparrals (1967-70, 1971-73), | | | |
| | Texas Chaparrals (1970-71) | | | |
| | | | | |
| NBA Championships | None | | | |
| Playing Record | G | W | L | Pct |
| NBA Regular Season | 1476 | 793 | 683 | .537 |
| NBA/ABA combined | 2220 | 1171 | 1049 | .527 |
| NBA Playoffs (series 5-15) | 94 | 38 | 56 | .404 |
| NBA/ABA combined | 143 | 55 | 88 | .385 |

No. 1 pick in the 1987 to draft Robinson, who had to fulfill a two-year military commitment before he could join the team.

When he arrived, Robinson lived up to the expectations. At 7–1, he runs the floor like players a foot smaller. His left-handed shooting touch extends to the free-throw line and his rebounding and defensive skills make him one of the NBA's most complete players.

Robinson not only helped San Antonio improve from 21 to 56 victories in his first season, but the Spurs narrowly missed the Western Conference Finals. Portland needed two overtime victories, the second in a grueling Game 7, to eliminate San Antonio in the 1990 Western Conference Semifinals.

The Spurs, however, haven't been as good since. Injuries to starters Terry Cummings and Willie Anderson stunted the team's progress. Then numerous coaching changes sent the franchise spinning until former player John Lucas took over 21 games into the 1992–93 campaign.

Lucas immediately turned to Robinson, who carried San Antonio back into the Conference Semifinals. The team added Dennis Rodman prior to the 1993–94 season and Cummings and Anderson appeared recovered from their injuries.

Still, locals wonder what might have been. Gervin now sits on the Spurs bench as an assistant coach while Robinson tries to reclaim the glory Gervin once helped create.

• • • • • • • • • • • • • • • • • • • • • • • • • •

**The Admiral Takes Command: David Robinson throws down a lefthanded slam on the Bucks**

# SEATTLE SUPERSONICS

# Blasting Off Again

It had been nearly 15 years since the SuperSonics put together a postseason run like the one in 1992–93. That surge ran out of gas when Seattle came up against Phoenix and Charles Barkley. But with young stars like Shawn Kemp and Kendall Gill on board, the Sonics could be headed for another boom.

When the SuperSonics charged into the Western Conference Finals in 1993, they might have been following a familiar pattern. Though Seattle ended up a game short of the NBA Finals, the lesson, as it had been back in 1979, might prove to have been invaluable.

Indeed, Coach George Karl can only hope the experience pays off like it did for Lenny Wilkens' squad. Wilkens, who had been a player/coach for Seattle in the early 1970s, returned to the bench early in the 1977–78 season. Wilkens immediately transformed the franchise into a winner.

Seattle had come into the league in 1967, but had only limited success until Wilkens' arrival in 1969. As the Sonics' point guard, he led the team to 47 victories during the 1971–72 season but, incredibly, Seattle failed to make the playoffs.

Former Boston Celtics great Bill Russell coached the team for four seasons and led Seattle to its first playoff appearance in 1975. But Russell's hard-edged approach didn't wear well. Before long, owner Sam Schulman was digging in his files for another leader.

That's where he found Wilkens, who had since retired as a player. Wilkens returned to his former team and quickly molded players Gus Williams, Dennis Johnson, rookie Jack Sikma, reserve Freddie Brown and Marvin Webster into a title contender.

The SuperSonics rolled through the early rounds of the playoffs before meeting Washington. A seven-game championship battle ended with the Bullets taking the 1978 championship on Seattle's home court, something no one forgot when the two teams met again a year later.

Sonic Boom: the SuperSonics crowd the basket

Although Webster, a towering center, left the team for New York following the Finals, the SuperSonics never missed a beat. They received bulky Lonnie Shelton from the Knicks as compensation for Webster and turned the center spot over to Sikma.

By the time the SuperSonics returned to the Finals in 1979 not even the Bullets had

a chance. Seattle eliminated Washington in a quick five-game series for the franchise's first championship.

The team remained solid through the next 12 seasons, but never quite as good as it was under Wilkens. Players such as Tom Chambers, Xavier McDaniel and Dale Ellis helped keep the team competitive. Then, midway through the 1991–92 season, Coach George Karl took over and the SuperSonics' roster came together.

Combining veterans Eddie Johnson and Ricky Pierce with youngsters Shawn Kemp, Derrick McKey and Gary Payton, Karl turned the SuperSonics into an end-to-end menace.

Seattle then traded for veteran center Sam Perkins just after the 1993 All-Star break. Suddenly, the SuperSonics were ready to make their run. Kemp, one of the NBA's rising superstars, averaged 17.8 points and more than 10 rebounds a game. But it was defense that keyed the Seattle charge as they became the only team in the league to finish among the top five in both scoring and defense.

The SuperSonics knocked off Western Conference rivals Utah and Houston before extending Phoenix to Game 7 in the 1993 Western Conference Finals.

If the SupersSonics learned anything it was that the team needed just a little more help, particularly in the starting lineup. In two quick, if not brilliant moves, Seattle added 6–5 guard Kendall Gill in a trade with Charlotte and then 6–10 forward Detlef Schrempf in a trade with Indiana.

Schrempf provided veteran leadership on the frontline, his outside shooting ability matched by a rugged inside game. Gill, among the league's most versatile guards, added yet another dimension out front. Both became perfect additions to the kind of full-court attack that has turned Seattle into one of the league's new powers.

Lesson learned, it's now time for another title run.

**Home Grown Sonic: A former college star in Washington, Detlef Schrempf returned home in 1993 to bolster Seattle's title hopes**

## RICKY PIERCE
### Seattle's Hired Gun

When Ricky Pierce landed in Seattle midway through the 1990–91 season, his reputation had preceded him.

In 1987 and 1990 he was named Sixth Man of the Year for his heroics off the bench in Milwaukee. Talented enough to be a full-time starter for most teams, Pierce, just 6–4, settled into the role of hired gun. When the Bucks needed help, Pierce came to the rescue.

A brilliant shooter capable of scoring points in bunches, Pierce was exactly the player Seattle needed. He averaged 21.7 points in just 34 minutes a game during the 1991–92 season while hitting 91.6 percent of his free throws. A year later, Pierce became even more efficient. He had a career-high 100 steals and averaged 18.2 points despite playing only 28.8 minutes a game.

Few players have ever been able to impact a game off the bench like Pierce.

# UTAH JAZZ
## The Jazz Age

The name belongs to another city, but the results are Utah's alone. Riding the remarkable talents of superstars John Stockton and Karl Malone, the Jazz haven't missed the playoffs since 1983. But if Utah hopes to map out a championship run it's going to need more than a dynamic duo to get the job done.

In a city best known for the Mormon Tabernacle, the nickname of the state's only major professional sports franchise doesn't fit. Then again, no one figured the New Orleans Jazz would one day be situated in Salt Lake City, Utah.

When the team became the NBA's 18th franchise in 1974 it was situated in New Orleans, a city known for its music at its 24-hour clubs. Given the sensibilities of the respective communities, the Jazz couldn't have endured a greater culture shock when the franchise moved to Utah in 1979.

But it had been a rocky start in New Orleans, where the team had five coaches in its first five seasons. Management had also gambled heavily on local legend "Pistol" Pete Maravich, one of the greatest showmen the game has ever known.

**The Jazz surround San Antonio's David Robinson**

Maravich had been a college basketball legend at Louisiana State University and management, banking on Maravich's drawing power, wanted him back home. The Jazz put together an elaborate package of players and draft picks to obtain Maravich from the Atlanta Hawks for New Orleans' first season.

After a difficult debut, the Jazz quickly became respectable thanks in large part to Maravich. The 6–5 guard, who handled the ball as well as any player in his-

## ROLL OF HONOR

| Conference/Division | Western/Midwest | | | |
|---|---|---|---|---|
| First NBA year | 1974-75 | | | |
| Home Arena details | Delta Center (built 1991, capacity 19,911) | | | |
| Former cities/nicknames | New Orleans Jazz (1974-79) | | | |
| NBA Championships | None | | | |
| Playing Record | G | W | L | Pct |
| Regular Season | 1640 | 802 | 838 | .489 |
| Playoffs (Series 8-11) | 94 | 43 | 51 | .457 |

tory, was twice named to the All-NBA First Team during his five seasons with the Jazz. Maravich led the league in scoring in 1976–77 and once drilled the New York Knicks for 68 points in a single game. But the Pistol wasn't enough to keep the franchise from moving west. It wasn't until Frank Layden assumed control in 1981 that the Jazz started making some noise, and in the 1983–84 season when the team reached the Playoffs for the first time.

With virtually total control of the roster, Layden went to work molding exactly the kind of team he wanted. Starting with a nucleus that included Adrian Dantley, Darrell Griffith and Danny Schayes, Layden pushed and pulled the team to its first winning season. By 1984, he had added Thurl Bailey and 7–4 Mark Eaton, who had been discovered by a UCLA assistant coach while Eaton was working as an automobile mechanic.

With a Midwest Division title also coming that season, the Jazz had arrived. Staying among the elite, however, proved difficult until Utah made the two most important draft choices in franchise history.

The Jazz used a first-round pick to select point guard John Stockton in 1984 and a year later used another for 6–9 forward Karl Malone. Since Malone's arrival, Utah went into the 1993–94 season without a single losing season.

Indeed, Malone and Stockton have developed into an ideal inside-outside combination. Although the Jazz have operated without the benefit of a top-flight center, Malone has held Utah together under the basket. Out front, Stockton has developed into the greatest assist man of his era. Stockton's passes, fundamentally sound and almost always on the mark, have helped Malone become one of the highest scoring power forwards in history.

With the team up and running, Layden turned over the coaching duties to former Chicago Bulls star Jerry Sloan. Sloan had learned the ropes as Layden's assistant. As a player, Sloan was known as one of the toughest players in the league, twice being named to the NBA All-Defensive First Team, and he brought that competitive fire to the bench.

The Jazz might have sounded better in New Orleans, but they look a lot better in Utah.

• • • • • • • • • • • • • • • • • • • • • • • •

**All That Jazz: Karl Malone hits a high note**

## JERRY SLOAN
### Master Jazzman

Ask about the crooked nose and Jerry Sloan will tell you he can't remember how many times it was broken.

"I think I broke it about seven or eight times," he says with a shrug.

Sloan made up for limited skills with determination and grit. Though just 6–5 and 200 pounds, Sloan feared no one. He directed the Bulls defense like a general directing an army and refused to give an inch, even in practice.

He made the NBA All-Defensive First Team four times and led Chicago to a string of 50-win seasons in the early 1970s. A two-time All-Star, Sloan retired in 1975 and became a coach.

When Sloan moved into the head job with the Jazz, the team responded immediately. Utah averaged more than 50 victories a season in Sloan's first four full seasons. The Jazz also won two Midwest Division titles and 17 playoff games.

Other than Sloan's nose, there's no longer anything out of line in Utah.

# Bullets™
## Looking To Reload

Coach Wes Unseld was the last link to a glorious past as Washington tried to reload for another attack on the Eastern Conference powers. But the rebuilding process has dragged on, and for now Washington remains under construction, the winning past a distant memory.

One way or another Chicago has usually played a key role in the success of the Bullets.

The franchise originated in 1961, in what the NBA brass considered a perfect market. Chicago had spawned the Harlem Globetrotters and some of the best college basketball of the era.

So when the league decided to add a ninth team, Chicago became the logical choice. But the Packers, as they were known that first season, didn't come close to capturing the hearts of locals. A year later the franchise changed its name to the Zephyrs, but the impact, on and off the court, was minimal. Though stars such as Walt Bellamy, a hulking 6–11 center, and Terry Dischinger provided a solid foundation, the team was a disaster at the box office. And after two years, the experiment was abandoned with the team moving to Baltimore where it assumed yet another nickname, the Bullets.

**Former Washington head coach, Wes Unseld**

A new location did little to improve performance until 1968. With Earl "the Pearl" Monroe operating on the outside and Wes Unseld, a muscular 245-pound center, taking care of things under the bas-

ket, Baltimore won 57 games. Unseld was named Rookie of the Year and Most Valuable Player after grabbing 18.2 rebounds a game in his first season.

Two years later, in 1971, the Bullets reached the NBA Finals for the first time, only to be quickly eliminated by Kareem Abdul-Jabbar's Milwaukee Bucks. Former Boston Celtics great K.C. Jones eventually took over the coaching duties and promptly guided the Bullets back into the Finals.

With Unseld, Elvin Hayes, Phil Chenier and Mike Riordan, the Bullets knocked off Boston in the Eastern Conference Finals and met Golden State for the 1975 Championship. Now known as the Washington Bullets following a move from Baltimore, the team won a franchise-record 60 regular-season games. But Golden State, led by superstar Rick Barry, made quick work of Washington, winning the title in four straight games.

Jones lasted one more season until management went back to Chicago for its next savior. Coach Dick Motta had turned a young Chicago Bulls franchise into an Eastern Conference power. But Motta wanted a new challenge and the Bullets, still blessed with a solid roster, looked like the perfect opportunity.

Within two years the Bullets were back in the NBA Finals, and this time there were no disappointments. With Hayes, Bobby Dandridge, Mitch Kupchak and Unseld, Washington had one of the most rugged frontlines in the league. The Bullets breezed

| ROLL OF HONOR | | | | |
|---|---|---|---|---|
| Conference/Division | Eastern/Atlantic | | | |
| First NBA year | 1961-62 | | | |
| Home Arena details | USAir Arena (built 1973, capacity 18,756) | | | |
| Former cities/nicknames | Chicago: Packers (1961-62), Zephyrs (1962-63), Baltimore: Bullets (1963-73), Capital Bullets (1973-74) | | | |
| NBA Championships | 1978 | | | |
| Playing Record | G | W | L | Pct |
| Regular Season | 2613 | 1250 | 1363 | .478 |
| Playoffs (Series 13-19) | 163 | 69 | 94 | .423 |

★★★★★★★★★★★

# EARL MONROE
## A Pearl Bullet

There are players who have scored more points and passed out more assists, but few ever did either with the flash and flair of Earl "the Pearl" Monroe.

The Baltimore Bullets made Monroe, from Winston-Salem University in North Carolina, the No. 2 pick in the 1967 Draft. He became an instant sensation.

Monroe averaged 24.3 points per game his first season and was named Rookie of the Year. He improved to 25.8 points a game during the 1968–69 season and was named to the Eastern Division All-Star team. His ballhandling and scoring skills amazed even veterans, many of whom could only watch as Monroe performed his magic.

Monroe, along with Wes Unseld, led the Bullets to the 1971 NBA Finals. Monroe, however, landed in New York a year later in a lopsided deal that helped the Knicks to the 1973 Championship.

Monroe was elected to the Hall of Fame in 1989.

through the first three rounds of the 1978 NBA Playoffs and beat Seattle in seven games for the NBA title.

Though the Bullets had a league best 54–28 record in 1978–79, the championship rematch went to the SuperSonics. That loss ended an era as Motta moved on a year later and the team faded with the retirement of Unseld and the trade of Hayes. Since that championship, the Bullets have had just three winning records in 14 seasons. Despite Unseld's return as head coach, Washington hasn't reached the playoffs since 1988.

Although young players like Tom Gugliotta and Calbert Cheaney, the Bullets' No. 1 pick in 1993, have shown promise, the Bullets know they have a long climb ahead.

● ● ● ● ● ● ● ● ● ● ● ● ● ● ● ● ● ● ● ● ● ●

**Washington's Bullet: Rex Chapman flies over the Milwaukee Bucks**

# THE PLAYOFFS
## The NBA's Second Season

For six months 27 teams battle each other for 16 precious playoff spots. The best teams jockey for home-court advantage while the up-and-coming fight each other for one of the last playoff openings. As the 82-game schedule moves toward conclusion in late April, the games become more important and the skirmishes more fierce. When it's over, eight teams from each conference embark on a second season defined by its intensity and celebrated for its opportunity. After a two-month process of elimination, only the strongest is left standing.

The goal never changes. By the time the first ball is tossed into the air in the first game of every season, NBA players and coaches already have looked down the road. For most teams, success is measured by the playoffs.

"Nothing else matters," says Chicago Bulls forward Scottie Pippen. "You can get all kinds of individual honors during the regular season, but when it comes to real accomplishment, that happens in the playoffs. That's the way it's always been for this team and I'm sure that's the way it's always been for teams that win championships."

During the 82-game war that is the regular season, teams fight each other for playoff position. For some teams, merely becoming one of the 16 teams that qualify for the postseason tournament is enough. For others, getting home-court advantage and going on to the championship round is the sole measure of success. And for a few teams like Chicago, New York and Phoenix, anything short of an NBA title represents failure.

"When I was playing, we played for championships," says former Boston Celtics guard K.C. Jones. "That's all we

thought about. We knew we'd make the playoffs. We were looking at another title."

## HOW THE SYSTEM WORKS

The process, though long, is relatively simple. Eight teams from the Western Conference and eight teams from the Eastern Conference qualify for the playoffs. Regular season champions from the four divisions — Midwest, Pacific, Central and Atlantic — become the top two seeds in each conference.

The team with the best record in each conference is assured of home-court advantage through the Conference Finals. The team with the best record in the league is guaranteed home-court advantage throughout the entire playoffs.

"Home-court advantage wasn't that important to us," recalled former Chicago Bulls star Michael Jordan, a three-time Finals MVP. "But for some teams that was the only way they had a chance. Winning playoff games on the road is one of the hardest things to do as a team.

**Los Angeles guard Walt Hazzard fires off a pass to launch another quick break**

"Don't get me wrong. We wanted home-court advantage. Although we learned how to win on the road, we were just like every other team. We wanted to play as much as possible."

The eight teams from each conference are seeded according to their regular-season record and division finish. There are four First Round best-of-5 playoff series in each conference with the No. 1 team playing the No. 8 team, the No. 2 team meeting the No. 7 team and so on.

Winners of the First Round move into the Conference Semifinals. There the series become best-of-7. Once again, the team with the best regular-season record has home-court advantage, or four of the seven games on its floor.

The site of the series goes back and forth in a 2–2–1–1–1 format. In other words, the first two games are played in one city followed by two games in the other. After that the teams alternate until a winner is determined.

The Conference Finals are set up the same way as the Conference Semifinals.

The format changes slightly in the NBA Finals, where the Western Conference champion meets the Eastern Conference champ. Again, the team with the best regular-season record gets home-court advantage in the seven-game series. But this time, the series is set up in a 2–3–2 format, a change that was instituted in 1985 to lessen the burden of travel on the participants.

● ● ● ● ● ● ● ● ● ● ● ● ● ● ● ● ● ● ● ● ● ● ●

**K.C. Jones of the Boston Celtics makes like the Leaning Tower of Pisa as the L.A. Lakers' Rudy LaRusso snags a rebound**

# 1969

## Boston vs. Los Angeles

Time had taken its toll on the Boston Celtics, winners of 10 championships in the previous 12 years, and no one, including player/coach Bill Russell, knew for sure whether the Celtics had yet another championship in them. The Boston regulars averaged 31 years of age with Sam Jones, 35, playing in his final series and Russell, 35, right behind him. To go out on top, however, Russell would have to eliminate his legendary nemesis, Wilt Chamberlain and the Los Angeles Lakers.

The regular season had been a rough one for the tiring Boston Celtics. Known for its balanced scoring attack, the Celtics had been forced to rely on John Havlicek to carry the load.

Legendary players like Sam Jones and Bill Russell were clearly fighting through the accumulated fatigue of 12 and 13 seasons, respectively. And the league appeared to have finally caught up with the Celtic mystique. With Russell averaging nearly 43 minutes a game and also coaching the team, Boston finished fourth in the Eastern Division.

But that was during the regular season. Once the playoffs started, Boston, as it had done for more than a decade, found a way to get through. The Celtics knocked off Philadelphia 4–1 in the division semifinals and then got past New York, 4–2, in the finals to set up a meeting with Wilt Chamberlain's Los Angeles Lakers.

Man-for-man, the Lakers appeared to have the edge. Superstars Elgin Baylor, Jerry West and Chamberlain gave Los Angeles three 20-point scorers. And that appeared to be more than enough as the Lakers took a quick 2–0 lead in the best-of-7 series thanks to West's brilliant scoring. The All-Star guard bombed Boston for 53 points in the opener and then 41 in Game 2.

Back in Boston Garden, the Celtics fought back. They won two straight, the second on Jones' dramatic jumper at the buzzer. Though they would fall behind again after another loss in Los Angeles, Boston, despite nagging injuries, would not be denied.

Havlicek played the last four games of the series with a black eye and a sore leg. But Boston marched on thanks to reserves Don Nelson and Larry Siegfried. The Celtics evened the series 3–3 with a victory at home and then traveled back out to Los Angeles.

For the Lakers, it was the sixth time they had been to the Finals since moving from Minneapolis. And for the sixth time they would fail. Boston held off a furious fourth-quarter rally and escaped with its 11th championship in 13 years.

The Russell years ended just as they had started: with an NBA title.

| GAME | 1969 NBA FINALS | | |
|---|---|---|---|
| 1 | Los Angeles | 120–118 | Boston |
| 2 | Los Angeles | 118–112 | Boston |
| 3 | Boston | 111–105 | Los Angeles |
| 4 | Boston | 89–88 | Los Angeles |
| 5 | Los Angeles | 117–104 | Boston |
| 6 | Boston | 99–90 | Los Angeles |
| 7 | Boston | 108–106 | Los Angeles |

Russell and Chamberlain (13) battle for a rebound

# 1970

# New York vs. Los Angeles

The Los Angeles Lakers should have been one of the greatest dynasties in all of basketball. For the seventh time in nine years, Los Angeles reached the NBA Finals. But not once in the previous six trips had the Lakers come away with a championship. With Bill Russell gone and Boston no longer the East's dominant team, the New York Knicks emerged with undersized center Willis Reed leading the charge. Would it stop in Los Angeles?

**Take That: Chamberlain nearly takes the head off of an unsuspecting New York Knicks player**

The timing couldn't have been better for New York. Just as Boston dropped out of the playoff picture, the young Knicks came together.

The team even resembled those legendary Celtics squads. No one player dominated the scoring and all of them, particularly superstar guard Walt Frazier, played exceptional defense.

Still there were questions. After playing without 7–1 center Wilt Chamberlain for 70 games, the Lakers clearly were better than their 46–36 record suggested. With him back and matched against New York's 6–9 center Willis Reed, some wondered whether the Knicks could survive a long seven-game series.

They almost didn't.

Though Reed outplayed Chamberlain and the Knicks won the opener, Jerry West connected on two free throws with 46 seconds to play in Game 2 and the Lakers evened the series.

That's when the match turned into a battle for the ages. New York came back to win in overtime in Game 3 as Reed had 38 points and 17 rebounds. In Game 4, the Lakers returned the favor by coming back to tie the series with another thrilling victory, this one also in overtime.

After fighting through tough series just to reach the Finals, both teams appeared worn down. West played with a jammed thumb and Reed played despite a sore knee. But as the series turned back to New York, Reed's medical situation became more serious.

He was knocked out of Game 5 in the first quarter with a bruised muscle in his right leg. The Knicks still rallied to a 107–100 victory, but the Lakers were more than ready to exploit the injury.

Back in Los Angeles, Reed couldn't play and the Lakers evened the series at 3–3 with an easy victory.

That set up one of the most dramatic final games in playoff history. Reed, limping badly, started Game 7 and spent the game trying to neutralize Chamberlain. Though limited to 27 minutes, Reed was successful. He also scored the game's first two baskets and proved inspirational as the Knicks blasted Los Angeles to gain the first title in franchise history.

| GAME | | 1970 NBA FINALS | | |
|------|-------------|---------|------------------|
| 1 | New York | 124–112 | Los Angeles |
| 2 | Los Angeles | 105–103 | New York |
| 3 | New York | 111–108 | Los Angeles (OT) |
| 4 | Los Angeles | 121–115 | New York (OT) |
| 5 | New York | 107–100 | Los Angeles |
| 6 | Los Angeles | 135–113 | New York |
| 7 | New York | 113–99 | Los Angeles |

# 1980

# Los Angeles vs. Philadelphia

● ● ● ● ● ● ● ● ● ● ● ● ● ● ● ● ● ● ● ● ● ● ● ● ● ● ● ● ● ● ● ● ● ● ● ● ● ●

**Legendary center Kareem Abdul-Jabbar had arrived in a 1975 trade  many figured would turn the Los Angeles Lakers into a dynasty. By 1979, however, it hadn't happened. Though competitive, the Lakers hadn't won a single title in the Abdul-Jabbar era. The game changed when a smiling rookie named Earvin "Magic" Johnson arrived.  But was it enough to offset the brilliance of Philadelphia's Julius "Dr. J" Erving and effusive center Darryl Dawkins?**

● ● ● ● ● ● ● ● ● ● ● ● ● ● ● ● ● ● ● ● ● ● ● ● ● ● ● ● ● ● ● ● ● ● ● ● ● ●

The regular season had pointed to a showdown between two of the most entertaining teams in NBA history. The Los Angeles Lakers won 60 games and rolled through the Western Conference playoff field.

Over in the East, Philadelphia reeled off 59 victories and buried Boston 4–1 in the Conference Finals.

The scene had been set. Could the Lakers, running behind 6–9 rookie guard Magic Johnson and the dominating center play of Kareem Abdul-Jabbar, fight off a 76ers attack led by Julius "Dr. J" Erving, massive center Darryl Dawkins and a deep Philadelphia roster?

By Game 6, the Lakers had proved their place. But they also needed a miracle.

They found Magic instead.

Through the first five games of the series the balance of power shifted back and forth. By Game 5, the Lakers appeared to

have finally gained a measure of momentum, as well as a 3–2 lead in the series.

Abdul-Jabbar had been spectacular, averaging 33.4 points and 13.6 rebounds. Johnson, clearly not intimidated by his first title run, had averaged an equally impressive 17.4 points, 10.2 rebounds and 9.0 assists.

Then lightening struck. Abdul-Jabbar hobbled through the fourth quarter of Game 5 with a badly sprained left ankle. A day later, he could barely walk. As the Lakers headed to Philadelphia for Game 6, Abdul-Jabbar, the team's only real center, remained back in Los Angeles.

That's when Magic took over. Johnson moved to the center position for Game 6 and one of the most incredible individual performances in championship series history followed.

Johnson led both teams with 42 points and 15 rebounds. He was so dominant that the Lakers won by the largest margin of the series, 123–107.

A new era had dawned in Los Angeles. And it was Magic.

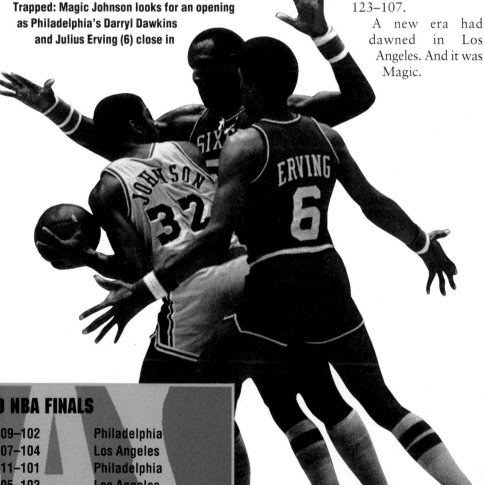

**Trapped: Magic Johnson looks for an opening as Philadelphia's Darryl Dawkins and Julius Erving (6) close in**

| GAME | 1980 NBA FINALS | | |
|------|-----------------|--|--|
| 1 | Los Angeles | 109–102 | Philadelphia |
| 2 | Philadelphia | 107–104 | Los Angeles |
| 3 | Los Angeles | 111–101 | Philadelphia |
| 4 | Philadelphia | 105–102 | Los Angeles |
| 5 | Los Angeles | 108–103 | Philadelphia |
| 6 | Los Angeles | 123–107 | Philadelphia |

# 1984

# Boston vs. Los Angeles

● ● ● ● ● ● ● ● ● ● ● ● ● ● ● ● ● ● ● ● ● ● ● ● ● ● ● ● ● ● ● ● ● ● ● ● ● ● ●

While Magic Johnson and Kareem Abdul-Jabbar dominated the West, Red Auerbach had done it again in the East. The Boston Celtics, one of basketball's greatest franchises, were loaded. Auerbach had drafted Larry Bird and Kevin McHale and traded for Robert Parish and Dennis Johnson. The talent extended throughout the Celtics' roster. The same, however, could be said of the Lakers. But could Boston shut down a Lakers attack now called "Showtime?"

● ● ● ● ● ● ● ● ● ● ● ● ● ● ● ● ● ● ● ● ● ● ● ● ● ● ● ● ● ● ● ● ● ● ● ● ● ● ●

Larry Bird and Magic Johnson had passed this way before. As college players at Indiana State and Michigan State, respectively, Bird and Johnson had led their teams into the national championship game.

But Johnson, with a much better supporting cast, stole the show. Though Bird played valiantly, he wasn't enough by himself and Michigan State won the NCAA title. When the two joined the NBA they ended up at opposite ends of the country on the league's two most storied franchises.

The rematch, however, didn't take place until 1984. The Lakers had a roster full of talent with players such as Johnson, Kareem Abdul-Jabbar, James Worthy, Byron Scott, Michael Cooper, Bob McAdoo and

**Boston's Robert Parish battles the Lakers**

Jamaal Wilkes. The Celtics countered with Bird, Parish, McHale, Dennis Johnson, Quinn Buckner, Cedric Maxwell and Scott Wedman.

Through the early skirmishes and leading into Game 4, Boston appeared to be outgunned. The Lakers' fast break had produced a 2–1 advantage with Game 4 in Los Angeles.

But the Celtics refused to go quietly. By the time Game 4 ended in overtime, Boston had redirected the momentum. The Celtics had rallied from a 10-point halftime deficit and held on during a wild five-minute overtime period.

So as the Finals shifted back to Boston, so too did the Celtics' prospects for victory. Bird's brilliant 34-point, 17-rebound performance, which included 15-of-20 shooting from the floor, keyed an easy Boston victory and gave the Celtics a 3–2 lead.

Back in Los Angeles it took a furious fourth-quarter rally before the Lakers evened the series again. But Boston, playing inside fabled Boston Garden in Game 7, seemed to sense success.

Playing before another sellout in the old arena, Boston dominated. The Celtics, led by Bird and Parish, controlled the rebounds and shut down the Lakers' fast-break in a 111–102 win.

For Bird, the first rematch was his to cherish.

| GAME | 1984 NBA FINALS | | |
|---|---|---|---|
| 1 | Los Angeles | 115–109 | Boston |
| 2 | Boston | 124–121 | Los Angeles (OT) |
| 3 | Los Angeles | 137–104 | Boston |
| 4 | Boston | 129–125 | Los Angeles (OT) |
| 5 | Boston | 121–103 | Los Angeles |
| 6 | Los Angeles | 119–108 | Boston |
| 7 | Boston | 111–102 | Los Angeles |

# 1993
## Chicago vs. Phoenix

• • • • • • • • • • • • • • • • • • • • • • • • • • • • • • • • • • • • • • • • • •

**Prior to the 1992–93 season, Michael Jordan knew there was only one way to distance himself from the legacies of Magic Johnson and Larry Bird. They had won more titles, but neither had won as many as three in a row. The Phoenix Suns, however, had other ideas. In one of the biggest trades in league history, Charles Barkley had moved to Phoenix from Philadelphia. Now surrounded by talented scorers, Barkley figured his championship season had come.**

• • • • • • • • • • • • • • • • • • • • • • • • • • • • • • • • • • • • • • • • • •

The season had been the longest of Michael Jordan's career. Fresh off Chicago's second straight championship in 1992, Jordan had joined Dream Team workouts for the Barcelona Olympics.

But Jordan, like the rest of the Bulls, understood the mission as the 1992–93 season unfolded. No team since the 1966 Boston Celtics had won as many as three straight titles.

"We're here to make history," he announced. "It's all about history now."

Though beaten and bruised after a grueling Eastern Conference final series against New York, the Bulls knew exactly how to handle the Finals pressure. For Phoenix, everything was new.

Including defeat.

Chicago, behind Jordan and brilliant defense, blasted Phoenix from the opening taps of Games 1 and 2. As they headed back

to Chicago, a sweep had become possible. Indeed, most fans, even those in Phoenix, figured the Suns had simply run up against a better team.

Though Phoenix took Game 3 with an incredible triple-overtime victory, the performance seemed only to stun the Bulls momentarily.

Three days later, Jordan helped Chicago regain control of the momentum with an equally incredible performance of his own. He bombed the Suns for 55 points in Game 4, giving the Bulls a commanding 3–1 lead. Convinced that Chicago would finish off the series at home, local politicians made plans for a victory parade.

But the Suns had other ideas. They stunned the entire city of Chicago by winning Game 5 and sending the series back to Phoenix.

And it took the spectacular to make sure the Bulls ended it there. Chicago blew a six-point, fourth-quarter lead in Game 6

**Chicago swarms the Phoenix Suns**

as the Suns rallied. But with 3.9 seconds left and Chicago trailing by two points, John Paxson, who had missed much of the season with knee problems, hit a three-point basket that gave the Bulls a third consecutive title.

For Jordan, that was enough. Three months later he announced his retirement at age 30.

| GAME | 1993 NBA FINALS | | |
|---|---|---|---|
| 1 | Chicago | 100–92 | Phoenix |
| 2 | Chicago | 111–108 | Phoenix |
| 3 | Phoenix | 129–121 | Chicago |
| 4 | Chicago | 111–105 | Phoenix |
| 5 | Phoenix | 108–98 | Chicago |
| 6 | Chicago | 99–98 | Phoenix |

# SUPERSTARS OF THE NBA

They have turned the NBA into one of the greatest shows on and off earth by combining speed, strength, style and substance. And the brightest of them are known as Superstars.

The game has always revolved around its greatest players, constantly evolving with each new talent and turning on the brilliance of each era's stars. In the early days, George Mikan dominated with a rare combination of size and skill. It was Mikan who set the stage for later star centers such as Bill Russell, Wilt Chamberlain and Kareem Abdul-Jabbar by dominating at both ends of the court.

So gifted were the early giants that rules were actually changed to keep them from twisting the entire game toward themselves. The introduction of the 24-second clock to limit offensive possession time and thus speed up the game opened the floor to another group of players. All-round stars such as Oscar Robertson showed how smaller players with multiple talents could dominate just as much as the era's big men.

But then the game took off for good on the wings of players such as Julius "Dr. J" Erving. His high-flying style and all-around brilliance created a whole new level. Dominique Wilkins, Hakeem Olajuwon, Patrick Ewing, David Robinson, and Michael Jordan, players who combined size, speed and remarkable leaping ability, became some of the game's greatest scorers. Others such as Magic Johnson and Larry Bird, with near-perfect fundamentals and an innate understanding of the game, lifted the NBA game into one of the most popular team sports in the world.

**Air Jordan in mid flight against the New York Knicks**

# KAREEM ABDUL-JABBAR
## Master Of The Sky Hook

Bill Russell may have played better defense and Wilt Chamberlain scored more points. But no one has ever played center with the grace, eloquence and all around brilliance of Kareem Abdul-Jabbar.

He was known as Lew Alcindor during his college career at UCLA and early years in the NBA. And at 7–2 he seemed to almost glide around the basket. He led UCLA to three straight NCAA championships and was largely responsible for the dunk being outlawed briefly in the college ranks.

**Unstoppable: Kareem Abdul-Jabbar scores again**

Abdul-Jabbar landed in Milwaukee for the 1969–70 season. With exceptionally long arms and an equally long frame, he had one of the greatest rookie seasons in history. He averaged 28.8 points, grabbed 14.5 rebounds a game and turned the Bucks into an instant power.

Just one year after his arrival, Milwaukee won its first and only NBA championship as Abdul-Jabbar led the league in scoring for the first of two consecutive seasons. But it was the total package, offense, defense and even passing, that made Abdul-Jabbar a true wonder.

## CAREER RECORD

**PERSONAL**

| | |
|---|---|
| **Birthplace/Date** | New York, NY/4.16.47 (formerly known as Lew Alcindor) |
| **Height /Weight** | 7-2/267 |

**AWARDS**

| | |
|---|---|
| **MVP** | 1971, 1972, 1974, 1976, 1977, 1980 |
| **All-Star Selections** | 1970-77 (did not play 1973), 1979-89 |
| **Finals MVP** | 1971, 1985 |

**CAREER**

| | |
|---|---|
| **University** | UCLA (1965-69) |
| **Pro. Career** | 20 seasons, Milwaukee Bucks (1969-75) Los Angeles Lakers (1975-89) |

| PLAYING RECORD | G | FG | Pct | FT | Pct | Reb | Ast | Stl* | Bl* | Pts | ppg |
|---|---|---|---|---|---|---|---|---|---|---|---|
| **Regular Season** | 1560 | 15,837 | .559 | 6712 | .721 | 17,440 | 5660 | 1160 | 3189 | 38,387 | 24.6 |
| **Playoffs** | 237 | 2,356 | .553 | 1040 | .740 | 2,481 | 767 | 189 | 476 | 5,762 | 24.3 |
| **All-Star** | 18 | 105 | .493 | 41 | .820 | 149 | 51 | 6 | 31 | 251 | 13.9 |

*Steals and blocks only recognized from 1973-74 season

> ## "HE WAS THE BEST BIG MAN I EVER SAW. I THINK EVEN BETTER THAN WILT."
> Guy Rodgers, a former NBA guard.

"He had a hidden flair for passing and the ability to keep everyone on his team alert and involved in the offense," says Guy Rodgers, a former NBA guard.

No one stayed near the top of their game longer than Abdul-Jabbar, who played a record 20 NBA seasons and set numerous career marks. Six times he was named Most Valuable Player, the last in 1980, 10 years after his first game. He helped the Los Angeles Lakers to five championships after arriving there in a 1975 trade.

"Kareem had that one incredible offensive weapon—the sky-hook," said Artis Gilmore, a 7–2 center who was often no match for Abdul-Jabbar. "It was totally unstoppable."

"As far as the sky-hook, that may have been the greatest offensive weapon in the history of basketball," says former Boston great Larry Bird. "How could anyone stop it?"

No one could. Abdul-Jabbar would back in toward the basket, then turn and with either hand hook the ball toward the basket. Defenders couldn't come close to blocking the shot and Abdul-Jabbar rarely missed.

A remarkably conditioned athlete, Abdul-Jabbar was named Most Valuable Player of the 1985 NBA Finals three months after his 38th birthday. And he didn't retire for another four seasons, all the while a starter and key contributor to the Lakers' dominating run in the 1980s.

"Even when he was a rookie, you could see that Abdul-Jabbar was going to put a lot of people into retirement," said Johnny Kerr, a former NBA coach and player. "He had so many offensive abilities, so many defensive moves. And he could pass. He always did so many things so great."

And he probably did all of them combined better than anyone else before or since.

**Kareem shuts down the middle against Boston's Gerald Henderson**

# CHARLES BARKLEY

## They Call Him Sir Charles

Charles Barkley didn't look like a basketball player as a boy growing up in tiny Leeds, Alabama. His legs were heavy, his body short and wide. Coaches didn't think he was tall enough to play inside or fast enough to play guard.

So Charles went to work. He spent hours jumping back and forth over the fence behind his family's small house. By the time he entered Auburn University, Barkley's huge frame was supported by equally strong legs. Before long, nobody cared much about Barkley's relatively short stature. The Philadelphia 76ers, then one of the league's top teams with Moses Malone and Julius Erving, made Barkley the No. 5 pick in the 1984 NBA Draft.

Almost immediately Barkley, who was nicknamed "The Round Mound of Rebound," proved to be an even better player in the NBA. With the game played more freely, Barkley used his strength and speed to punish players a half foot taller. He used his bulk to hold his ground under the basket for rebounds and his lightning quick jumping ability to go up and over taller opponents.

But he could also score from anywhere on the court. In his first nine NBA seasons, Barkley never shot less than 52 per-

**Call Me Sir: Charles Barkley sails in for another score**

## CAREER RECORD

| PERSONAL | | | | | | | | | | | |
|---|---|---|---|---|---|---|---|---|---|---|---|
| Birthplace/Date | Leeds, Alabama/2.20.63 | | | | | | | | | | |
| Height /Weight | 6-6/252 | | | | | | | | | | |
| **AWARDS** | | | | | | | | | | | |
| MVP | 1993 | | | | | | | | | | |
| All-Star Selection | 1987-94 (did not play 1994) | | | | | | | | | | |
| Finals MVP | None | | | | | | | | | | |
| **CAREER** | | | | | | | | | | | |
| University | Auburn (1981-84) | | | | | | | | | | |
| Pro. Career | 10 seasons, Philadelphia 76ers (1984-92), Phoenix Suns (1992-94) | | | | | | | | | | |

| PLAYING RECORD | G | FG | Pct | FT | Pct | Reb | Ast | Stl | Bl | Pts | ppg |
|---|---|---|---|---|---|---|---|---|---|---|---|
| Regular Season | 751 | 6259 | .562 | 4683 | .734 | 8734 | 2957 | 1227 | 717 | 17,530 | 23.3 |
| Playoffs | 85 | 753 | .615 | 513 | .707 | 1126 | 362 | 146 | 84 | 2,058 | 24.2 |
| All-Star | 7 | 34 | .466 | 20 | .625 | 51 | 13 | 10 | 4 | 90 | 12.9 |

> **"CHARLES IS A TOTALLY DOMINANT PLAYER. GUYS WHO ARE 6–4 OR 6–5 JUST AREN'T SUPPOSED TO BE ABLE TO DO THAT IN THE NBA."**
>
> Larry Bird

**The Round Mound Of Rebound: Barkley lives up to his nickname against the Chicago Bulls**

cent from the floor. He could hit short jump shots, long three-pointers and slam as well as any player in history.

Like Los Angeles Lakers legend Magic Johnson, Barkley also had one of the most engaging personalities in the league. Though he played with emotion that sometimes boiled over, Barkley became a favorite of fans and teammates.

"With the Sixers, even when he was new, Charles got us awake at times," says former Philadelphia guard Maurice Cheeks. "Sometimes we got on too low a flame, but then Charles would come along and slam the ball or something and we'd remember

**Charles In Charge: Barkley became the Suns main man the moment he arrived in 1992**

what we were out there for. And we had better know because you didn't want Charles mad at you."

Barkley, who became known as "Sir Charles," was named to the All-NBA First Team four straight years in Philadelphia starting in 1988. In a game against New York and 7-foot center Patrick Ewing in 1987, Barkley set NBA records with 11 offensive rebounds in one quarter and 13 in one half. He also became one of the shortest players to ever lead the league in rebounding when he averaged 14.6 a game during the 1986–87 season.

But his greatest success didn't come until the 76ers shipped him to Phoenix in a blockbuster four-player trade in 1992. After performing with USA Basketball's "Dream Team", Barkley turned the Suns into a title contender, leading the team to the 1993 NBA Finals. Though Phoenix lost to Michael Jordan's Chicago Bulls, Barkley earned his first Most Valuable Player award.

Larry Bird bombs away against the Pistons

# LARRY BIRD

## Known In Boston As 'Larry Legend'

Individually, the physical elements were never very special. Larry Bird, though 6–9, didn't jump exceptionally well, run particularly fast or move as quickly as others.

But none of that mattered. Bird spent countless hours developing one of the greatest jump shots in the league. And that, combined with a brilliant basketball mind, were all Bird needed to become one of the greatest players in NBA history.

As with Bill Russell more than 20 years earlier, Arnold "Red" Auerbach saw the future of the Boston Celtics when he watched Bird perform for Indiana State University. Auerbach drafted Bird under an old rule and had to wait an entire season

OPPOSITE LEFT **Bird Man takes off for two points**

before Bird became eligible to join the team.

Once with the Celtics, however, he turned a previously pitiful Boston roster into a championship-caliber team. His passing helped make average players into major contributors.

As a rookie, Bird started a string of nine straight seasons on the All-NBA First Team. He won three straight Most Valuable Player awards starting in 1984. He was twice named Most Valuable Player in the NBA Finals and still holds the career record for most defensive rebounds in the Playoffs.

### CAREER RECORD

**PERSONAL**

**Birthplace/Date**   West Baden, Indiana/12.7.56

**Height /Weight**   6-9/220

**AWARDS**

**MVP**   1984, 1985, 1986

**All Star Selection**   1980-88, 1990-92 (did not play 1991 and 1992, injured)

**Finals MVP**   1984, 1986

**CAREER**

**University**   Indiana (1974, did not play), Indiana State (1975-79 – ineligible 1975)

**Pro. Career**   13 seasons, Boston Celtics (1979-92),

| PLAYING RECORD | G | FG | Pct | FT | Pct | Reb | Ast | Stl | Bl | Pts | ppg |
|---|---|---|---|---|---|---|---|---|---|---|---|
| Regular Season | 897 | 8591 | .496 | 3960 | .890 | 8974 | 5695 | 1556 | 755 | 21,791 | 24.3 |
| Playoffs | 164 | 1458 | .472 | 901 | .890 | 1683 | 1062 | 296 | 145 | 3,897 | 23.8 |
| All-Star | 10 | 52 | .423 | 27 | .844 | 79 | 41 | 23 | 3 | 134 | 13.4 |

"Larry Bird was one of the most totally prepared basketball players I ever saw," says former Lakers center Kareem Abdul-Jabbar. "His mind was always 100 percent in the game 100 percent of the time. He always knew where he should be on the court and he was always there. A truly phenomenal, hard-working basketball player."

Bird's practice habits were as legendary as his game performances. He would often arrive as much as three hours before a game to work on his shooting. And it showed. Bird was a career 49.6 percent shooter from the floor despite taking more than 1,700 shots from beyond the three-point line. But shooting was only part of Bird's attack. He could pick apart defenses with pin-point passes and almost always made those around him better.

"He showed a court savvy that I had never seen before," says Auerbach. "Maybe guys like John Havlicek or Jerry West had some of it and Bill Russell was a better defender, but in terms of incorporating the five main components of the game—scoring, rebounding, passing, defending and running—into one player, Bird was as good as there has ever been."

## "AN ABSOLUTE BASKETBALL GENIUS."

**Pat Riley, New York Knicks Coach.**

Bird led the Celtics to three NBA Championships and played on USA Basketball's 1992 "Dream Team". Had it not been for a persistent back injury that led to his retirement in 1992, the Celtics might still be winning championships. No one knows that more than Pat Riley, who coached all those Lakers teams during a decade of battles with Bird's Celtics.

"He never quit and was never beaten, never admitted defeat," said Riley, now Coach of the New York Knicks. "That's why he was responsible for some of the most dramatic comebacks in the history of the game. He never lost his concentration on the court."

**Larry keeps his eyes on the prize**

# WILT CHAMBERLAIN

## Basketball's Greatest Scorer

The "Big Dipper" was the complete player

Everything that you will ever need to know about Wilt Chamberlain's impact on basketball can be found by flipping through the NBA's record book.

Known as Wilt "the Stilt" and the "Big Dipper," Chamberlain stood 7-1 and carried 275 pounds of muscle on his angular frame. If he had merely been tall, opposing teams might have figured a way to defend Chamberlain. But he was much more than that. Chamberlain could jump as well as any player in the league and he might have been the game's fastest player as well.

The combination made for remarkable feats. Chamberlain played two college seasons at Kansas before turning professional and doing a tour of duty with the entertaining Harlem Globetrotters barnstorming exhibition team.

Chamberlain eventually started his NBA career with the Philadelphia Warriors in 1959. He immediately became the most dynamic scoring machine the game has ever known. Chamberlain averaged 37.6 points as a rookie and led the league in scoring in each of his first seven seasons. But he also was a dominating rebounder, leading the league 11 times including four straight at the start of his career.

He averaged an astounding 50.4 points per game during the 1961–62 season to go with 25.7 rebounds a contest. He also played virtually every minute of every game and, as he would do eight times, led the league in minutes played.

The crowning moment, however, came March 2, 1962 before just 4,124 fans in

Hershey, Pennsylvania. Chamberlain, a poor free-throw shooter through his career, made 28-of-32 from the line en route to an amazing 100-point game. Chamberlain scored 59 of those points in the second half alone and the Warriors beat the New York Knicks 169-147.

Though Chamberlain proved capable of doing anything on the court—he even led the league in assists one year with the Los Angeles Lakers—Russell gained more accolades because of all the Celtics' championships. Critics, however, sometimes

chastised Chamberlain for not winning more. Chamberlain, inducted in the Hall of Fame 1978, played for three teams during his 14 seasons. Two of those won NBA Championships.

But the head-to-head battles with Russell were among the most fierce in league history. And while Chamberlain usually won the statistical battle, it was Russell's Celtics which usually came away with the victory.

"I have thought a lot about Russell versus Chamberlain and it almost comes

## CAREER RECORD

| PERSONAL | |
|---|---|
| Birthplace/Date | Philadelphia, Pennsylvania/8.21.36 |
| Height/Weight | 7-1/275 |
| **AWARDS** | |
| MVP | 1960, 1966, 1967, 1968 |
| All-Star Selection | 1960-69, 1971-73 |
| Finals MVP | 1972 |
| **CAREER** | |
| University | Kansas (1955-58, did not play in 1955, freshman ineligible) |
| Pro. Career | 14 seasons, Philadelphia/San Francisco Warriors (1959-65), Philadelphia 76ers 1965-68, Los Angeles Lakers (1968-73) |

| PLAYING RECORD | G | FG | Pct | FT | Pct | Reb | Ast | Pts | ppg |
|---|---|---|---|---|---|---|---|---|---|
| Regular Season | 1045 | 12,681 | .540 | 6057 | .511 | 23,924 | 4643 | 31,419 | 30.1 |
| Playoffs | 160 | 1,425 | .522 | 757 | .465 | 3,913 | 673 | 3,913 | 22.5 |
| All-Star | 13 | 72 | .590 | 47 | .500 | 197 | 36 | 191 | 14.7 |

down to a matter of taste," says Bob Pettit, a Hall of Fame forward. "No one has ever scored like Wilt, no one has ever played defense like Russell. They weren't just the giants of their time, but of all time. I look at the guys today and nothing comes close to the battles they had."

It's possible no one will ever come close to Chamberlain's scoring records either.

**Wilt The Stilt: Chamberlain was not only the biggest player of his era, but also the strongest and some say even the fastest**

**"NO ONE, INCLUDING BILL RUSSELL, COULD STOP WILT CHAMBERLAIN IF HE DECIDED TO SCORE. WILT WAS A MAN AMONG BOYS."**

Johnny "Red" Kerr, former NBA center.

# CLYDE DREXLER

## They Call Him 'The Glide'

Watching Clyde Drexler float through the air, the ball usually held high overhead in his right hand, it's hard to believe he was once a chubby child who was always picked last on the Houston, Texas, playgrounds of his youth.

With a slender 6–7 frame and angular features, Drexler now looks as if he were built to be a basketball player. A remarkable leaper, Drexler once dunked on an 11-foot basket, a foot higher than the regulation NBA rim. In fact, at the University of Houston, Drexler, Hakeem Olajuwon and Larry Micheaux keyed one of the most acrobatic college basketball teams in history. The trio dunked so often with such exuberance they formed a fictional fraternity called "Phi Slamma Jamma."

The Portland Trail Blazers made him the team's first-round pick in 1983 and then watched him slowly develop into an NBA superstar. They thought so much of Drexler's abilities in those early years that the team passed on Michael Jordan in the 1984 NBA Draft and chose center Sam Bowie instead.

One way or another, Drexler ended up lost in Jordan's shadow for much of the next nine years. Playing in the Northwest

**Gently Does It: Clyde Drexler floats a finger roll toward the basket**

## CAREER RECORD

**PERSONAL**

| | |
|---|---|
| Birthplace/Date | New Orleans, Louisiana/6.22.62 |
| Height /Weight | 6-7/222 |

**AWARDS**

| | |
|---|---|
| MVP | None |
| All-Star Selection | 1986-94 |
| Finals MVP | None |

**CAREER**

| | |
|---|---|
| University | Houston (1980-83) |
| Pro. Career | 11 seasons, Portland Trail Blazers (1983-94), |

| PLAYING RECORD | G | FG | Pct | FT | Pct | Reb | Ast | Stl | Bl | Pts | ppg |
|---|---|---|---|---|---|---|---|---|---|---|---|
| Regular Season | 826 | 6584 | .480 | 3591 | .786 | 5105 | 4725 | 1721 | 572 | 17,186 | 20.8 |
| Playoffs | 94 | 746 | .450 | 464 | .792 | 1699 | 651 | 626 | 184 | 2,015 | 21.4 |
| All-Star | 8 | 35 | .493 | 12 | 1.000 | 42 | 20 | 9 | 6 | 85 | 10.6 |

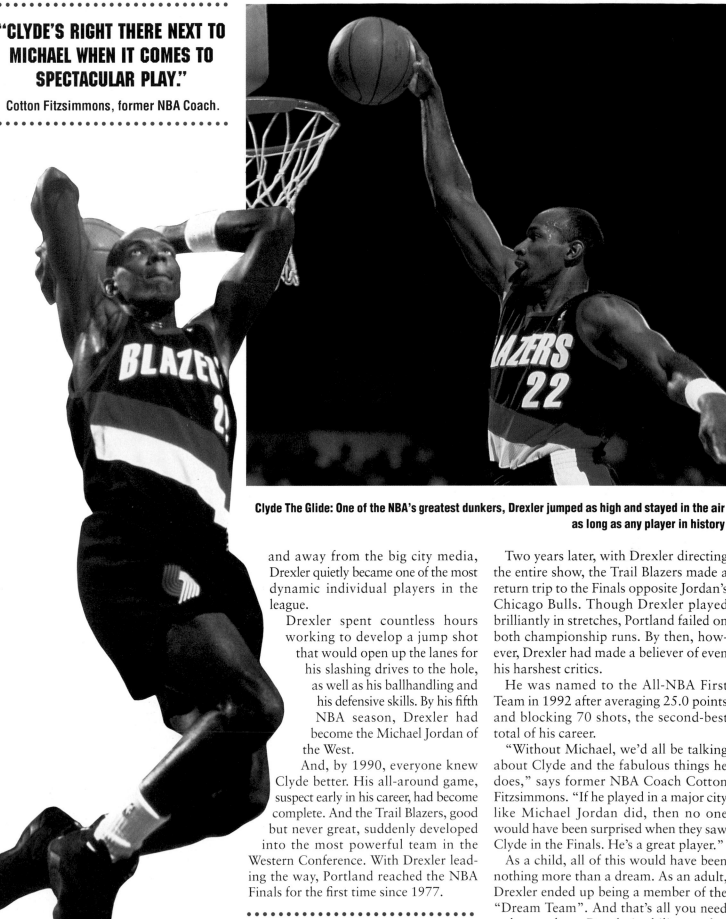

**Clyde The Glide: One of the NBA's greatest dunkers, Drexler jumped as high and stayed in the air as long as any player in history**

and away from the big city media, Drexler quietly became one of the most dynamic individual players in the league.

Drexler spent countless hours working to develop a jump shot that would open up the lanes for his slashing drives to the hole, as well as his ballhandling and his defensive skills. By his fifth NBA season, Drexler had become the Michael Jordan of the West.

And, by 1990, everyone knew Clyde better. His all-around game, suspect early in his career, had become complete. And the Trail Blazers, good but never great, suddenly developed into the most powerful team in the Western Conference. With Drexler leading the way, Portland reached the NBA Finals for the first time since 1977.

**Drexler floats in for a two-handed slam**

Two years later, with Drexler directing the entire show, the Trail Blazers made a return trip to the Finals opposite Jordan's Chicago Bulls. Though Drexler played brilliantly in stretches, Portland failed on both championship runs. By then, however, Drexler had made a believer of even his harshest critics.

He was named to the All-NBA First Team in 1992 after averaging 25.0 points and blocking 70 shots, the second-best total of his career.

"Without Michael, we'd all be talking about Clyde and the fabulous things he does," says former NBA Coach Cotton Fitzsimmons. "If he played in a major city like Michael Jordan did, then no one would have been surprised when they saw Clyde in the Finals. He's a great player."

As a child, all of this would have been nothing more than a dream. As an adult, Drexler ended up being a member of the "Dream Team". And that's all you need to know about Drexler's ability to play the game.

# JULIUS ERVING

## An Artist Called Dr. J

With a flair and grace unlike anything the game had known, Julius Erving changed the game forever when he descended upon the old American Basketball Association in 1971.

Erving spent five spectacular seasons with two ABA teams before the league folded and he joined the NBA prior to the 1976–77 season.

"Dr. J" joined the Philadelphia 76ers and became an immediate sensation. He seemed to soar through the air and hang until just the right moment before throwing down any one of a variety of slam dunks. Indeed, Erving redefined the art of dunking during his 11-year NBA career.

Then again, he had already established the dunking standard during a dunk competition at the 1976 ABA All-Star Game in Denver. With long loping strides, Erving headed for the free throw line where he took off and floated toward the basket and dunked. Fans and players alike were shocked by the exhibition which only furthered the legend of Dr. J.

"He was absolutely phenomenal," recalls Kevin Loughery, who coached

**The Doctor Makes A House Call: A classic Erving slam**

## CAREER RECORD

**PERSONAL**

| | |
|---|---|
| Birthplace/Date | Roosevelt, NY/2.22.50 |
| Height /Weight | 6-7/210 |

**AWARDS**

| | |
|---|---|
| MVP | 1974 (ABA), 1975 (ABA, co-MVP), 1976 (ABA), 1981 |
| All-Star selections | 1972-76 (ABA), 1977-87 |
| Finals MVP | 1974 (ABA), 1976 (ABA) |

**CAREER**

| | |
|---|---|
| University | Massachusetts (1968-71) |
| Pro. Career | 16 seasons, Virginia Squires (ABA – 1971-73), New York Nets (ABA – 1973-76) Philadelphia 76ers (1976-87) |

| PLAYING RECORD | G | FG | Pct | FT | Pct | Reb | Ast | Stl | Bl | Pts | ppg |
|---|---|---|---|---|---|---|---|---|---|---|---|
| Regular Season | 1243 | 11,828 | .506 | 6256 | .777 | 10,525 | 5,176 | 1508 | 1293 | 30,026 | 24.2 |
| Playoffs | 189 | 1,769 | .496 | 1025 | .733 | 1,611 | 841 | 235 | 239 | 4,580 | 24.2 |
| All-Star | 16 | 123 | .494 | 73 | .793 | 106 | 59 | 18 | 11 | 321 | 20.1 |

(Combined record for ABA-NBA, except shotblocking and steals statistics not available for ABA)

**Erving often seemed to float through the air**

Erving during those early years in the ABA. "Michael Jordan was from the same cut, but Doc seemed more of a pure artist."

Erving's most memorable moments often came around the basket where his creativity was unmatched. He could take off toward the hole, change hands to avoid a defender and still have enough flight to finish the play in spectacular fashion.

"Julius had this motion where he just hung up there and levitated up and down, up and down," says former NBA center Billy Paultz. "I know that it just couldn't be, but I swear it is what he did. Talk about hang time."

Erving's brilliance helped elevate Philadelphia as well. With Erving being named to the All-NBA First Team five times between 1978 and 1983, the 76ers became one of the league's dominant teams. Despite the presence of Larry Bird's Boston Celtics, Philadelphia won the 1983 NBA Championship and reached the Finals four times during the Erving era.

"You never wanted to be embarrassed and your only consolation if you were was that it was because of Julius Erving," says Bird. "His first step was explosive and once he was in the air, you sometimes wished you could see the replay of what he had just created."

Erving impacted the game on the court and off. With an easy-going demeanor, Erving became the NBA's first true goodwill ambassador. Opponents often liked Erving as much as his own teammates, as evidenced by an almost universal respect.

Erving was twice named Most Valuable Player in All-Star Games and in 1981 was named MVP of the league. But everyone will remember the unique grace with which Erving glided through the game, on and off the court.

• • • • • • • • • • • • • • • • • • • • • • • • • • • •

**"I THINK HIS STYLE WAS MORE OF THAT OF A VIRTUOSO, AN INDIVIDUAL PERFORMER. HE PROBABLY BROUGHT BASKETBALL AS CLOSE TO BALLET AS IT'S EVER BEEN."**

**Magic Johnson**

• • • • • • • • • • • • • • • • • • • • • • • • • • • •

# PATRICK EWING

## New York's Tower Of Power

Quiet and soft-spoken, with a gentle smile and manner,
Patrick Ewing seems nothing like the menacing shot blocker
that he is on the basketball court.

Watch Ewing long enough and it's hard to believe that he started playing basketball late in his youth. Watch him rally the New York Knicks past another opponent, or slap away a shot attempt, and it seems unlikely Ewing ever lacked confidence or consistency. Look over Ewing's resume, which includes an NCAA championship at Georgetown University and Olympic gold medals in 1984 and 1992, and it's hard to think of him as anything less than the dominant big man he has become.

"Very early on, Patrick had to learn, had to be convinced, how good he really was,

how good he could be," says Georgetown Coach and former NBA center John Thompson. "Defensively, to help him with both his confidence and his consistency, I told him to go up and block every shot and take his chances on being called for goaltending. The guy on the other team would remember that."

Whatever the lesson, it worked. Ewing developed into a college star at Georgetown before graduating to the New York Knicks as the first pick in the 1985 NBA Draft. Though injuries slowed Ewing in his first two NBA seasons, the marvelous

**Patrick Ewing goes up and over everyone**

## CAREER RECORD

| PERSONAL | |
|---|---|
| Birthplace/Date | Kingston, Jamaica/8.5.62 |
| Height /Weight | 7-0/240 |
| **AWARDS** | |
| MVP | None |
| All- Star Selections | 1986 (did not play, injured), 1988-94 |
| Finals MVP | None |
| **CAREER** | |
| University | Georgetown (1981-85) |
| Pro. Career | 9 seasons, New York Knicks (1985-94) |

| PLAYING RECORD | G | FG | Pct | FT | Pct | Reb | Ast | Stl | Bl | Pts | ppg |
|---|---|---|---|---|---|---|---|---|---|---|---|
| Regular Season | 680 | 6386 | .522 | 3412 | .741 | 7006 | 1431 | 774 | 1984 | 16,231 | 23.9 |
| Playoffs | 78 | 714 | .434 | 365 | .750 | 866 | 195 | 85 | 194 | 1,799 | 23.1 |
| All-Star | 7 | 37 | .544 | 14 | .636 | 54 | 5 | 7 | 15 | 88 | 12.6 |

**Young And Old: Ewing teaches young Alonzo Mourning about position**

talents were obvious to everyone, particularly opposing players.

Ewing was named NBA Rookie of the Year despite missing 32 games his first season. By 1988, Ewing made his first All-NBA team and, for the first time, an NBA All-Defensive team as well.

But it wasn't until the 1989–90 season that Ewing's abilities came together for one entire season. He averaged 28.6 points while scoring from virtually anywhere on the court. He slammed down rim-rattling dunks, lofted soft fall away jumpers and, when teams forced him outside, dropped long-range jump shots. He also averaged nearly 11 rebounds a game and blocked a career-high 327 shots in 82 games.

Two years later, with former Los Angeles Lakers Coach Pat Riley taking over on the bench, Ewing's Knicks had become one of the NBA's most devastating teams. New York, led by Ewing's relentless defensive play, took the eventual champion Chicago Bulls

to the Eastern Conference Finals in 1993, narrowly missing a shot at the championship round. The reason was simple:

Patrick Ewing. At 7-foot and more than 240 pounds, Ewing had turned a once slender frame into a mass of muscle. His workouts are now legendary around the Knicks team. As a result, Ewing had missed just four games in the six seasons prior to the 1993–94 campaign.

**Strong And Agile: Ewing dunks as hard as any player in history**

. . . . . . . . . . . . . . . . . . . . . . . . .

**"HE MADE ME FEEL LIKE AN OLD MAN IN A YOUNG MAN'S GAME WHEN HE CAME INTO THE LEAGUE. WHEN HE IS ON HIS GAME, ALL YOU CAN DO IS KEEP PUSHING HIM AND HOPE FOR THE BEST. WITH EXPERIENCE HE HAS BECOME AN AMAZING PLAYER."**

**Moses Malone**

. . . . . . . . . . . . . . . . . . . . . . . . .

# LARRY JOHNSON

## Charlotte's Toughest Hornet

............................................................

**Larry Johnson had played only two NBA seasons when his star became one of the brightest in the league.**

............................................................

With an infectious smile and an easy manner off the court, Johnson led the Charlotte Hornets into the big time. As "Grandmama" in his Converse shoe commercials, Johnson had become a marketing sensation. Though Michael Jordan's uniform No. 23 was the all-time best seller, Johnson's No. 2 Hornets jersey was second. And while the Chicago Bulls led all teams in the sale of NBA merchandise, Charlotte ranked just behind them thanks in large part to Johnson.

If the league was looking for another star, it didn't have to look any further than Charlotte. Even while the Hornets were losing games during their first few seasons in the league, Johnson made them a show worth watching.

A boxer during his childhood days in Texas, Johnson developed into a massive basketball player with enormous potential. At 6–7 and weighing 250 pounds, Johnson cut a striking figure during his two seasons at the University of Nevada-Las Vegas. He helped make the team one of college basketball's most dominant by scoring points, blocking shots and rebounding.

By the time he reached the NBA as the No. 1 pick in the 1991 Draft, no one doubted his star power. And Johnson certainly didn't disappoint.

**Make no mistake, Larry Johnson is the No.1 man in Charlotte**

## CAREER RECORD

| PERSONAL | | | | | | | | | | | |
|---|---|---|---|---|---|---|---|---|---|---|---|
| **Birthplace/Date** | Tyler, Texas/3.14.69 | | | | | | | | | | |
| **Height /Weight** | 6-7/250 | | | | | | | | | | |
| **AWARDS** | | | | | | | | | | | |
| **MVP** | None | | | | | | | | | | |
| **All-Star Selection** | 1993 | | | | | | | | | | |
| **Finals MVP** | None | | | | | | | | | | |
| **CAREER** | | | | | | | | | | | |
| **University** | Odessa Junior College (1987-89), Nevada-Las Vegas (1989-91) | | | | | | | | | | |
| **Pro. Career** | 3 seasons, Charlotte Hornets (1991-94), | | | | | | | | | | |

| PLAYING RECORD | G | FG | Pct | FT | Pct | Reb | Ast | Stl | Bl | Pts | ppg |
|---|---|---|---|---|---|---|---|---|---|---|---|
| **Regular Season** | 215 | 1690 | .510 | 812 | .778 | 2211 | 829 | 163 | 92 | 4220 | 19.6 |
| **Playoffs** | 9 | 68 | .557 | 41 | .788 | 62 | 30 | 5 | 2 | 178 | 19.8 |
| **All-Star** | 1 | 2 | .333 | 0 | 0 | 4 | 0 | 0 | 0 | 4 | 4.0 |

**See You Later: Johnson accelerates past New Jersey's Derrick Coleman**

He was named NBA Rookie of the Year following the 1991–92 season after averaging 19.2 points and 11.0 rebounds despite often being matched against taller players at the power forward spot.

His superior strength, the result of tireless offseason workouts, and the amazing quickness for his size, make Johnson virtually unstoppable near the basket. But if teams force Johnson outside, which is often the preferred way of defending against him, Johnson calmly drops in jump shots.

"Larry is strong, quick and very aggressive," says former Celtics star Larry Bird. "He's also a great team player. He gets better position than anyone in the league. And he's so powerful that when he does get the ball he can jump over anybody. He's just a great player."

"He is a terrific player with tremendous upper body strength," says former NBA Coach Bob Hill.

As good as Johnson was his rookie season, he got even better the second time around. During the 1992–93 season, Johnson led the league in minutes played and hit 52.6 percent of his shots, all while averaging 22.1 points and 10.5 rebounds.

Teamed with Alonzo Mourning, the Hornets' young center, Johnson carried Charlotte into the NBA Playoffs for the first time in franchise history, where they defeated the Boston Celtics in a spirited First Round series. Though they were eliminated by New York in the Eastern Conference Semifinals, the Hornets put a scare into the Knicks and Patrick Ewing before going down.

. . . . . . . . . . . . . . . . . . . . . . . . . . . .

**"HE DOES ALL THE LITTLE THINGS YOU LIKE TO SEE AS A COACH. SOMETHING GOOD IS GOING TO HAPPEN TO THE HORNETS WITH JOHNSON ON THEIR SIDE."**

Bob Hill, former NBA Coach.

. . . . . . . . . . . . . . . . . . . . . . . . . . . .

# MAGIC JOHNSON

## Basketball's True Magician

• • • • • • • • • • • • • • • • • • • • • • • • • • • •

**Few nicknames in NBA history have been more fitting than the one hung on Earvin Johnson.**

• • • • • • • • • • • • • • • • • • • • • • • • • • • •

Johnson was only a high school player when a local sportswriter noticed the remarkable ballhandling and passing skills. "Magic", thought the writer. Indeed, it often looked as if Johnson's wizardry could be nothing else.

By the time he left Michigan State University after just two seasons, one of the greatest rivalries in NBA history had been set. Johnson's Michigan State team defeated Larry Bird's Indiana State University squad for the 1979 NCAA championship. A year later, Johnson had landed with the Los Angeles Lakers and Bird with the Boston Celtics.

The two would go head-to-head for an entire decade, with Johnson leading the Lakers to five NBA Championships, two of those against Bird's Celtics. But all the victories were only part of the legend Johnson created during his 13-year career.

Johnson showed the world just how dominant a 6–9 guard can be when he took over at center in Game 6 of the 1980 NBA Finals. With Kareem Abdul-Jabbar injured and unable to play, Johnson played opposite Philadelphia's 7-foot, 255-pound Darryl Dawkins. Johnson dominated the

**Another Magic Show: Johnson rises up and over the defense**

## CAREER RECORD

| PERSONAL | |
|---|---|
| Birthplace/Date | Lansing, Michigan/8.14.59 |
| Height /Weight | 6-9/225 |
| **AWARDS** | |
| MVP | 1987, 1989, 1990 |
| All-Star Selections | 1980, 1982-92 (did not play 1989, injured) |
| Finals MVP | 1980, 1982, 1987 |
| **CAREER** | |
| University | Michigan State (1977-79) |
| Pro. Career | 12 seasons, Los Angeles Lakers (1979-91) |

| PLAYING RECORD | G | FG | Pct | FT | Pct | Reb | Ast | Stl | Bl | Pts | ppg |
|---|---|---|---|---|---|---|---|---|---|---|---|
| Regular Season | 874 | 6074 | .521 | 4788 | .848 | 6376 | 9921 | 1698 | 361 | 17,239 | 19.7 |
| Playoffs | 186 | 1276 | .508 | 1040 | .838 | 1431 | 2320 | 358 | 64 | 3,640 | 19.6 |
| All-Star | 11 | 64 | .489 | 38 | .905 | 57 | 127 | 21 | 7 | 191 | 16.0 |

**The Eyes Have It:** With remarkable court vision and an even more stunning ability to find openings, Johnson became one of the greatest passers in history

game by scoring 42 points while the Lakers rolled to their first championship of the Magic era.

He would go on to win three Most Valuable Player awards and make the All-NBA First Team nine straight years starting in 1983. But it was Johnson's exuberance and dazzling play making that led writers to name the Lakers attack "Showtime."

Despite his size, Johnson could handle the ball as well as any player in history. He could drive, dunk and even had a soft outside jump shot. It was Johnson who kept a team full of stars happy by setting them up for wide open shots.

"He wanted the fans and his teammates to enjoy every success on the court, says Abdul-Jabbar, a teammate for 10 years. "The quintessential Earvin experience didn't start until he passed his man and started for an easy layup. Then, just as he had to deal with a last second attempt to block his shot, the Magic Show would really begin. Doing what he did under the pressure of competition was one of the greatest continuous athletic feats ever."

Johnson's infectious smile and easy-going personality made him a one-man show on or off the court.

"Before Michael Jordan," says Larry Bird, "Magic was the only player that I'd pay money to see. He always played the game the way I thought it should be played."

"When he came to the Lakers it was like a brand new product," said former Lakers Coach Pat Riley. "Nobody knew what was going on. Then, bam! Six trips to the Finals in eight years. He's probably the greatest team showman the game has ever seen."

Such was the magic of Earvin Johnson.

• • • • • • • • • • • • • • • • • • • • • • •

## "MAGIC RAN THE GAME LIKE A DISC JOCKEY RUNNING A DISCO."

**Kareem Abdul-Jabbar, Johnson's teammate for 10 years.**

• • • • • • • • • • • • • • • • • • • • • • •

# MICHAEL JORDAN

## Rare Air

**According to Michael Jordan, it all started with "The Shot".**

Just a freshman at the University of North Carolina, Jordan hit the first game-winning shot of what would become an illustrious career. With the clock winding down, Jordan drained a medium-range jump shot that propelled North Carolina to the national championship and a 63–62 victory over rival Georgetown.

"That's where I think my career really began," says Jordan, who retired prior to the 1993–94 season after nine brilliant years with the Chicago Bulls. "I proved to myself that I could deliver in a pressure situation."

And Jordan never stopped delivering. He led the U.S. men's basketball team to the gold medal in the 1984 Los Angeles Olympics before starting his professional career in Chicago.

Jordan averaged 28.2 points per game while leading the team in rebounds, assists and steals and was named NBA Rookie of the Year in 1985. Ironically, it was Jordan's second season that left a lasting impression. After missing 64 regular season games with a broken foot, Jordan returned in time for the playoffs against the eventual champion Boston Celtics.

Jordan scored 49 points in Game 1 at Boston and then, in perhaps the greatest Playoff performance of all time, bombed Celtics defensive whiz Dennis Johnson for a record 63 points in Game 2. It took two overtimes before the heavily favored Celtics escaped and eventually ended the Bulls' charge.

**Look Out Below: Air Jordan lifts off against Philadelphia**

## CAREER RECORD

**PERSONAL**

| | |
|---|---|
| Birthplace/Date | Brooklyn, NY/2.17.63 |
| Height /Weight | 6-6/198 |

**AWARDS**

| | |
|---|---|
| MVP | 1988, 1991, 1992 |
| All-Star Selections | 1985-93 (did not play 1986, injured) |
| Finals MVP | 1991, 1992, 1993 |

**CAREER**

| | |
|---|---|
| University | North Carolina (1981-84) |
| Pro. Career | 9 seasons, Chicago Bulls (1984-93), |

| PLAYING RECORD | G | FG | Pct | FT | Pct | Reb | Ast | Stl | Bl | Pts | ppg |
|---|---|---|---|---|---|---|---|---|---|---|---|
| Regular Season | 667 | 8079 | .516 | 5096 | .846 | 4219 | 3935 | 1815 | 684 | 21,541 | 32.3 |
| Playoffs | 111 | 1411 | .501 | 942 | .834 | 741 | 738 | 258 | 109 | 3,850 | 34.7 |
| All-Star | 8 | 74 | .493 | 27 | .750 | 31 | 29 | 27 | 6 | 177 | 22.1 |

Tongue Tied: That's how Jordan's quickness often left opponents, including New York's John Starks

"He just flat out came down and let us know what he was going to do and for the most part, he did it," said Boston superstar Larry Bird later. "He was a completely different player from anything I've seen. He's literally on a different level."

And Jordan remained there throughout an often dramatic career. He won seven straight scoring titles, matching a record set by 7–2 Wilt Chamberlain, and became the league's best defensive guard.

In one of the most remarkable individual seasons in league history, Jordan was named Most Valuable Player and Defensive Player of the Year while leading the league in scoring and steals. He

also won his second Gatorade Slam-Dunk Championship.

He proved capable of taking over entire games by himself. With a competitive streak that amazed even his coaches, Jordan often left opponents stunned and fans standing in amazement.

Jordan's performances were so electrifying that his popularity actually transcended the sport. Thanks to the "Air Jordan" line, Nike became the world's biggest athletic shoe company. And thanks to his personality, Jordan's endorsement deals generated as much as $30 million a year.

On the court, Jordan carried Chicago to three consecutive NBA Championships. He also became the first player to be

named MVP in three straight NBA Finals.

"He was the ultimate superstar of the game," said Chuck Daly, who coached Jordan on the USA Basketball "Dream Team" in the 1992 Barcelona Olympics. "There might never be another one like him."

●●●●●●●●●●●●●●●●●●●●●●●●●●●●●

**"MAYBE IT'S GOD DISGUISED AS MICHAEL JORDAN."**

Larry Bird, former Boston superstar.

●●●●●●●●●●●●●●●●●●●●●●●●●●●●●

# SHAWN KEMP

## A SuperSonic Star In the Making

Just 19 years old, Shawn Kemp hadn't played a minute of college basketball in the year since he left high school when the Seattle SuperSonics called. A brilliant player throughout his youth, Kemp's 6–10 frame was as agile and quick as those of players six inches shorter.

So when he enrolled at the University of Kentucky, coaches there thought Kemp could develop into one of the greatest college players in history. But a dispute ended Kemp's stay quickly and suddenly he was without a team, and to some extent, a future as well. He transferred to a junior college and sat out the

**Get Ready 'Cos Here I Come: Shawn Kemp shapes up for another slam**

basketball season.

On the playgrounds, Kemp was a legend. According to a cousin, Kemp once dunked so hard on an outdoor rim that "sparks flew off" as the ball blew through. NBA executives had heard these stories, too.

But when Kemp entered the 1989 Draft without a single year of college basketball behind him, the skeptics shook their head. Although Moses Malone, Darryl Dawkins and Bill Willoughby had gone from high school directly into the pros, times had changed. No player, especially one as unpolished as Kemp, could make the transition these days.

## CAREER RECORD

| PERSONAL | |
| --- | --- |
| **Birthplace/Date** | Elkhart, Indiana/11.26.69 |
| **Height /Weight** | 6-10/245 |
| **AWARDS** | |
| **MVP** | None |
| **All-Star selections** | 1993, 1994 |
| **Finals MVP** | None |
| **CAREER** | |
| **University** | Kentucky (did not play – left school before season) |
| **Pro. Career** | 5 seasons, Seattle SuperSonics (1989-94) |

| PLAYING RECORD | G | FG | Pct | FT | Pct | Reb | Ast | Stl | Bl | Pts | ppg |
| --- | --- | --- | --- | --- | --- | --- | --- | --- | --- | --- | --- |
| **Regular Season** | 383 | 2075 | .508 | 1397 | .716 | 3374 | 618 | 455 | 629 | 5552 | 14.5 |
| **Playoffs** | 38 | 206 | .465 | 198 | .776 | 385 | 76 | 47 | 70 | 610 | 16.1 |
| **All-Star** | 2 | 3 | .273 | 0 | .0 | 14 | 4 | 0 | 3 | 6 | 3.0 |

Seattle thought otherwise. The Super-Sonics selected Kemp with the 17th pick overall in 1989. Kemp quickly developed into a power player at both ends of the court. He could dunk as well as any player in the league, his jumping ability stunning for a man his size. He also blocked shots with a vengeance.

In his second NBA season, Kemp averaged 15.0 points and 8.4 rebounds. He also had become the foundation for a SuperSonics team on the rise.

"The things that Shawn has going for him all along with his skills are his love for the game and his work ethic," says former SuperSonics coach K.C. Jones. "That's at the core of what is making him a great player.

"The only thing that ever really concerned me as far as his quick move into the pros was how he would react to the way that the fans react to the NBA-style player. A part of you must become a performer as much as a player, and you could see that he was a little slow to become accustomed to the oohs and aahs of the fans at his spectacular play."

Kemp became one of the most dynamic one-man shows in basketball with a dazzling array of dunks and slams. But he also developed into a complete player, propelling Seattle into the 1993 Western Conference Finals. .

At least one thing is known: Kemp will be a member of USA Basketball's "Dream Team II" at the 1994 World Championship of Basketball in Canada.

"Shawn," says teammate Nate McMillan, "has become the elite player we have been waiting for."

........................................

**"SHAWN HAS THAT GREAT COMBINATION OF SKILL AND CREATIVITY. HE IS VERY SIMILAR TO THE WAY I WAS WHEN I WAS YOUNGER."**

Michael Jordan

........................................

**Boom Boom, Shake The Room: Shawn Kemp slams so hard that opposing players sometimes appear to duck out of his line of fire**

# KARL MALONE

## This Mailman Delivers

Off the court, Karl Malone doesn't look much like a professional basketball player.

D uring the summer he operates an 18-wheel custom-made truck that hauls a variety of products to stores throughout the West. He owns a ranch in Louisiana, usually drives a pick-up truck to Utah Jazz games and would rather wear a 10-gallon hat and cowboy boots than gold chains and Gucci loafers.

But once on the court, Malone plays like a man possessed. When he isn't operating his trucking company or overseeing his ranch, Malone spends his summers lifting weights and fine-tuning his body. And no one knows that more than opposing power forwards. Not only is Malone one of the strongest players in the league, but at 6–9 and 256 pounds, he might be one of the best

conditioned athletes on the planet.

"The guy is relentless," says former NBA center Dave Corzine. "He never stops working. It's almost as if he gets stronger as the game goes on. He's a machine."

Utah drafted Malone out of Louisiana Tech University, a small school tucked deep into the Louisiana countryside. Nicknamed "the Mailman" because, according to supporters, "he always delivered," Malone went to work on his game. A poor free-throw shooter as a rookie, Malone was hitting more than 70 percent two years later. An average scorer at first, Malone became the highest scoring power forward

**The Mailman Delivers: Malone lifts off for another two points**

## CAREER RECORD

| PERSONAL | | | | | | | | | | | |
|---|---|---|---|---|---|---|---|---|---|---|---|
| Birthplace/Date | Summerfield, Louisiana/7.24.63 | | | | | | | | | | |
| Height /Weight | 6-9/256 | | | | | | | | | | |
| AWARDS | | | | | | | | | | | |
| MVP | None | | | | | | | | | | |
| All- Star Selections | 1988-94 (did not play 1990, injured) | | | | | | | | | | |
| Finals MVP | None | | | | | | | | | | |
| CAREER | | | | | | | | | | | |
| University | Louisiana Tech (1981-85) | | | | | | | | | | |
| Pro. Career | 9 seasons, Utah Jazz (1985-94) | | | | | | | | | | |
| PLAYING RECORD | G | FG | Pct | FT | Pct | Reb | Ast | Stl | Bl | Pts | ppg |
| Regular Season | 734 | 6977 | .520 | 4956 | .719 | 8058 | 2185 | 1037 | 615 | 19,050 | 26.0 |
| Playoffs | 74 | 880 | .581 | 573 | .764 | 859 | 177 | 106 | 62 | 2,018 | 27.3 |
| All-Star | 6 | 46 | .575 | 19 | .679 | 54 | 14 | 8 | 4 | 111 | 18.5 |

the league. Which is exactly why Malone has been a member of the Western Conference All-Star team every year since 1988.

"There's only one way I know how to play the game," says Malone, "and that's all out. If you're not going to go at it like I do, then find someplace else to play."

"IF YOU DON'T COME READY TO PLAY, KARL WILL CHEW YOU UP AND SPIT YOU OUT."

Dave Corzine, former NBA center.

in the NBA. A sometimes disinterested defensive player, Malone became one of the best end-to-end players in the game.

And despite playing perhaps the toughest position in the league, Malone missed just four games his first eight seasons. That's one reason Malone has been a member of the All-NBA First Team for five consecutive years going into the 1993–94 season. He also was a member of USA Basketball's "Dream Team" in 1992 and had led the Jazz in scoring and rebounding for seven straight seasons.

"They don't come any tougher than Karl," says Chicago's John Paxson. "He runs the court like a guard, blocks shots like a center and rebounds like no one I've ever seen. There really isn't anything he can't do which is scary for someone as big as he is."

Few players have ever done as much at both ends of the court as Malone. He hasn't averaged less than 27.7 points a game since his second season. Overall, Malone has averaged an astounding 26.1 points and 10.9 rebounds since he entered

Jazz Man: As strong as any player in the league and driven to succeed, Malone takes control at both ends of the court; (TOP) Karl comes up with some magic tricks of his own

# MOSES MALONE

## A Long Running Show

Moses Malone was 19 years old and fresh out of Petersburg High School in Virginia when the Utah Stars of the old American Basketball Association made him an offer he couldn't refuse.

Although every college and university in the country wanted him, Malone decided to move right into the professional ranks. And so he did. Malone, a skinny 6–10 center, became an instant hit with the Stars, averaging 18.8 points and making the 1975 ABA All-Star team. However, the league folded a year later.

By 1978, Malone was playing for the NBA's Houston Rockets. Now 23 years old, Malone's frame had become stronger and his moves more varied. He averaged 24.8 points, a league-leading 17.6 rebounds while playing a league-high 41 minutes a night.

**Holy Moses: Malone as a member of Atlanta Hawks**

## CAREER RECORD

**PERSONAL**

| | |
|---|---|
| **Birthplace/Date** | Petersburg, Virginia/3.23.55 |
| **Height /Weight** | 6-10/255 |

**AWARDS**

| | |
|---|---|
| **MVP** | 1979, 1982, 1983 |
| **All-Star Selections** | 1975 (ABA) 1978-89 (did not play 1984, injured) |
| **Finals MVP** | 1983 |

**CAREER**

| | |
|---|---|
| **University** | Did not attend university |
| **Pro. Career** | 20 seasons, Utah Stars (ABA – 1974-5), Spirits of St. Louis (ABA – 1975-76), Buffalo Braves (1976), Houston Rockets (1976-82), Philadelphia 76ers (1982-86), Washington Bullets (1986-88), Atlanta Hawks (1988-91), Milwaukee Bucks (1991-93), Philadelphia 76ers (1993-94) |

| PLAYING RECORD | G | FG | Pct | FT | Pct | Reb | Ast | Stl | Bl | Pts | ppg |
|---|---|---|---|---|---|---|---|---|---|---|---|
| **Regular Season** | 1438 | 10,264 | .495 | 8996 | .760 | 17,788 | 1930 | 1087 | 1730 | 29,531 | 20.5 |
| **Playoffs** | 100 | 801 | .487 | 610 | .756 | 1,400 | 145 | 85 | 151 | 2,213 | 22.1 |
| **All-Star** | 12 | 46 | .455 | 42 | .583 | 118 | 15 | 9 | 6 | 134 | 11.2 |

(Combined record for ABA-NBA, except shotblocking and steals statistics not available for ABA)

Malone the superstar had arrived.

"When he developed his moves and shot away from the basket, he became one of the greatest inside forces in the history of offensive basketball," says former NBA and ABA Coach Tom Nissalke.

Malone became a little of everything. With a no-nonsense approach, Malone quietly became one of the greatest rebounders in history. Starting with the 1978–79 season, Malone led the league in rebounding five times in seven years. He led the league in minutes played twice, rarely missing a game, and still managed to be one of the best scoring centers of his era. He also won three Most Valuable Player awards and four times was named to the All-NBA First Team.

In 1981, Malone led an average Houston team all the way into the NBA Finals before the Rockets were eliminated. Two years later, after signing with Philadelphia, Malone carried the 76ers into the NBA Finals opposite the Los Angeles Lakers and Kareem Abdul-Jabbar.

This time, Malone wouldn't be denied. He averaged 26.0 points and 15.8 rebounds during Philadelphia's title run and was named Most Valuable Player of the series.

"We never would have won a championship in Philadelphia without Moses," says Julius Erving, a member of that title team. "He was the hardest working player in the league and just supreme in the middle. With his size, strength and work ethic, I don't think there have been many players who could truly anchor a team in the most literal sense of the word as Moses could."

Malone, 38 years old when the 1993–94 season began, returned to Philadelphia after stints in Washington, Atlanta and Milwaukee. He entered the season ranked among the top 10 on the all-time lists in minutes played, games played, field goals made and attempted, free throws made and attempted and rebounds. And despite playing inside and banging bodies with the biggest players in basketball, Malone hadn't fouled out of a game in 15 years.

Old Hand: Moses Malone, 38, works against the next generation, Orlando's Shaquille O'Neal, 22, during the 1993–94 season

**"HE WAS A CLASSIC PICTURE OF CONCENTRATION. JUST SITTING ON THE BENCH AND WATCHING HIM PLAY MEANT MORE THAN ONE THOUSAND HOURS OF PRACTICE."**

Dwight Jones, former NBA center.

# GEORGE MIKAN

## An Era Unto Himself

He marked an entire era by himself, George Mikan's incredible size and ability bringing national attention to a league that had formed just two years earlier.

Mikan played his first NBA game for the Minneapolis Lakers in 1948 after a brilliant college career at De Paul University and two professional seasons in the old Midwest-based National Basketball League.

Until Mikan, only three players had ever averaged as many as 20 points a game over an entire season and none more than 23. Mikan, who was big at 6–10 and surprisingly agile at 245-pounds, changed all that.

He averaged 28.3 points and finished second in the league in field-goal percentage during the 1948–49 season for Minneapolis. Opponents tried everything, including using two and sometimes three players to surround Mikan down near the basket. But Mikan, as he would do throughout a brilliant professional career, dominated.

With Mikan in the middle, Minneapolis won five NBA championships in six years, including three straight from 1952 through 1954. Thanks to Mikan, the Lakers finished among the top five in scoring and defense for six consecutive years.

"What Mikan showed more than anything

**George Mikan readies for a hook**

## CAREER RECORD

| PERSONAL | |
|---|---|
| Birthplace/Date | Joliet, Illinois/6.18.24 |
| Height /Weight | 6-10/245 |
| **AWARDS** | |
| MVP | None |
| All-Star Selections | 1951-54 |
| Finals MVP | None |
| **CAREER** | |
| University | DePaul (1941-46) |
| Pro. Career | 9 seasons, Chicago Stags (NBL – 1946-7), Minneapolis Lakers (NBL – 1947-8, BAA – 1948-9, NBA – 1949-54, 1955-56) |

| PLAYING RECORD | G | FG | Pct | FT | Pct | Reb | Ast | Pts | PPG |
|---|---|---|---|---|---|---|---|---|---|
| Regular Season | 520 | 4097 | * | 3570 | .778 | * | * | 11,764 | 22.6 |
| Playoffs | 91 | 723 | * | 695 | .767 | * | * | 2,141 | 23.5 |
| All-Star | 4 | 28 | .350 | 22 | .815 | 51 | 7 | 78 | 19.5 |

*Statistics not kept for these categories in part of his career. NBL/BAA/NBA combined

else was what size could mean to a basketball team," says Johnny Kerr, a former NBA center and coach. "The fact that he was more than big, that he had some coordination and a few moves, enabled him to become the first dominant center in NBA history."

And Mikan did dominate. He won six straight scoring titles in his first six professional seasons and did just about anything he wanted on offense or defense. Even the greatest teams of the era were no match for the Lakers as long as Mikan was around. Indeed, Mikan played on seven championship teams in his first eight professional seasons.

"You had to be alive during Mikan's day to realize what a phenomenon he was," said Slater Martin, a teammate with the Lakers. "He was a big man for his era with remarkable tenacity and strength. He had the agility to pursue his own rebound and no one could keep him off the boards."

Mikan was the league's first truly dominant player and the first big man capable of carrying an entire team. Though Bill Russell, Wilt Chamberlain, Kareem Abdul-Jabbar and others would follow, Mikan remains one of the most dominating players in league history.

"In my lifetime I've seen only two centers who could just take charge of a game, who could put so much fear in the other players that they stayed away from the middle," said former NBA player Jim Pollard. "One was Bill Russell. The other, and he was even more dominant, was George Mikan."

Enough said.

••••••••••••••••••••••••••••••••

**"PRO BASKETBALL WAS RULED BY GEORGE MIKAN. AT 6–10, AND WITH ONLY A SIX-FOOT LANE, HE DETERMINED HOW THE GAME WAS PLAYED. IF YOU WERE GOING TO WIN ANYTHING YOU HAD TO OVERCOME MIKAN."**

Arnold "Red" Auerbach

••••••••••••••••••••••••••••••••

**Mikan's all-around play helped Minneapolis dominate the early 1950s**

# CHRIS MULLIN

## Golden State's Shooting Star

• • • • • • • • • • • • • • • • • • • • • • • • • • • • • • • • • • • • • •

Chris Mullin started hearing the criticisms in grade school. Some said he was too slow. Others claimed Mullin couldn't jump. And still others wondered if he'd ever be quick enough to become a productive player at any level.

• • • • • • • • • • • • • • • • • • • • • • • • • • • • • • • • • • • • • •

"I heard it all," says Mullin. "I guess I've just gotten used to all those things. I've been hearing it all my life."

Not anymore. After four solid seasons at St. John's University, Mullin took one of the game's greatest jump shots to the NBA. Mullin had learned to cover all he lacked in physical talent with an almost fundamentally perfect game. In four college sea-

**Mullin's jumper is among the most fundamentally sound in all of professional basketball**

sons Mullin never shot less than 52 percent from the floor, a stunning number for a player who spent most of his time taking jump shots.

Then again, given Mullin's eye for detail and perfection, it's not surprising. He spent countless hours turning his left-handed shot into a deadly weapon from anywhere on the court. It was Mullin's shooting, along with Michael Jordan's acrobatics and Patrick Ewing's shot blocking, that made the 1984 U.S. men's Olympic basketball team one of the country's greatest.

## CAREER RECORD

| PERSONAL | | | | | | | | | | | |
|---|---|---|---|---|---|---|---|---|---|---|---|
| **Birthplace/Date** | New York, N.Y/7.30.63 | | | | | | | | | | |
| **Height /Weight** | 6-7/215 | | | | | | | | | | |
| **AWARDS** | | | | | | | | | | | |
| **MVP** | None | | | | | | | | | | |
| **All-Star Selections** | 1989-93 (did not play 1993, injured) | | | | | | | | | | |
| **Finals MVP** | None | | | | | | | | | | |
| **CAREER** | | | | | | | | | | | |
| **University** | St. John's (1981-85) | | | | | | | | | | |
| **Pro. Career** | 9 seasons, Golden State Warriors (1985-94), | | | | | | | | | | |

| PLAYING RECORD | G | FG | Pct | FT | Pct | Reb | Ast | Stl | Bl | Pts | ppg |
|---|---|---|---|---|---|---|---|---|---|---|---|
| **Regular Season** | 628 | 5237 | .513 | 2906 | .861 | 2917 | 2486 | 1101 | 492 | 13,767 | 21.9 |
| **Playoffs** | 33 | 263 | .520 | 136 | .861 | 146 | 105 | 43 | 32 | 685 | 20.8 |
| **All-Star** | 4 | 12 | .500 | 7 | .875 | 8 | 8 | 4 | 1 | 33 | 8.3 |

And the three would do it again eight years later on the 1992 "Dream Team".

By the time he reached the NBA as Golden State's first-round pick in 1985, Mullin had legions of believers.

Mullin became the Warriors' leader during the 1988–89 season. Despite taking 100 shots from beyond the three-point line, Mullin hit 50.9 percent of his shots and averaged a career-best 26.5 points. Mullin also made the first of five consecutive appearances on the Western Conference All-Star team. For his part, Mullin only got better. He hit 53.6 percent of his shots two years straight, even while taking significantly more three-pointers. His defense, suspect early in his career, improved dramatically and Mullin rarely made a mental error.

"I see Chris go into a certain mental zone and he just locks in," says Golden State Coach Don Nelson. "You can see it when he steps up to the free-throw line. It doesn't matter what is going on around him, it's just him and the basket. Guys like Magic Johnson, Michael Jordan, Larry Bird and Chris—they have that higher level of concentration that just kicks in. They thrive on it. They develop a taste for it. You are born with that."

What might have been Mullin's best season ended prematurely due to injury. In the first 46 games of the 1992–93 season, Mullin hit a remarkable 45.1 percent of his three-point attempts and was averaging less than one turnover a game.

"Chris steadies all of us," says Golden State's Chris Webber. "He plays with a quiet confidence that lifts us. He always reminded me of Larry Bird. He's our Larry Bird."

What more could you ask?

. . . . . . . . . . . . . . . . . . . . . . . .

**My Aim Is True: Whether bombing away from three-point land or driving the lane, Chris rarely misses**

. . . . . . . . . . . . . . . . . . . . . . . .

**"WHEN GOD MADE BASKETBALL HE JUST CARVED CHRIS MULLIN OUT AND SAID, 'THIS IS A BASKETBALL PLAYER'."**

Magic Johnson.

. . . . . . . . . . . . . . . . . . . . . . . .

# HAKEEM OLAJUWON

## The Dream Comes True

For most of his youth, Hakeem Olajuwon figured he'd be a soccer player. No one played basketball much in Lagos, Nigeria, while he was growing up, so he became the goal-keeper on a soccer team.

Nowadays Olajuwon, who changed his name from Akeem to Hakeem in 1991, credits the defensive skills he learned playing soccer with helping make him a defensive giant in the NBA. Then again, the fact Olajuwon even made it to America, much less the greatest basketball league in the world, once seemed like a long-shot.

He arrived at the University of Houston in 1980 with only basic basketball skills, but daunting physical gifts. Standing 7 feet tall and able to move like a much smaller man, Olajuwon caught onto the game quickly thanks to summer work-outs with NBA star Moses Malone.

After three college seasons, Olajuwon had become a dominant player capable of turning an entire game around almost entirely by himself.

Hakeem readies a jump hook

## CAREER RECORD

**PERSONAL**

| | |
|---|---|
| Birthplace/Date | Lagos, Nigeria/1.21.63 |
| Height /Weight | 7-0/255 |

**AWARDS**

| | |
|---|---|
| MVP | 1994 |
| All-Star selections | 1985-90, 1992-94 |
| Finals MVP | 1994 |

**CAREER**

| | |
|---|---|
| University | Houston (1980-84) |
| Pro. Career | 10 seasons, Houston Rockets (1984-94) |

| PLAYING RECORD | G | FG | Pct | FT | Pct | Reb | Ast | Stl | Bl | Pts | ppg |
|---|---|---|---|---|---|---|---|---|---|---|---|
| Regular Season | 756 | 7107 | .517 | 3675 | .705 | 9464 | 1880 | 1448 | 2741 | 17,899 | 23.7 |
| Playoffs | 85 | 902 | .531 | 492 | .724 | 1045 | 259 | 154 | 329 | 2,298 | 27.1 |
| All-Star | 9 | 32 | .395 | 25 | .543 | 77 | 15 | 13 | 20 | 89 | 9.9 |

With the No. 1 pick in the 1984 Draft, the Houston Rockets merely had to look across town to find their savior. Olajuwon, who had improved dramatically during college, developed even faster once in the NBA, leading the league in offensive rebounds and averaging 20.6 points and 11.9 rebounds, incredible numbers considering his background.

Olajuwon and 7–4 Ralph Sampson became known as the "Twin Towers" and Houston became one of the league's forces. In just two seasons, the Rockets went from 29 victories and one of the league's worst records, to the 1986 NBA Finals against Larry Bird's Boston Celtics. Just as quickly, Olajuwon became a dominant center with a variety of defensive and offensive skills.

"I never felt anyone could play Hakeem one-on-one," says former NBA coach and player K.C. Jones. "To defense him you either had to deny him the ball, or bump him, and collapse players around him to force him to give up the ball."

"When he's on, which is most of the time, Hakeem is unstoppable," says New York Knicks Coach Pat Riley. "We always told our defenders, 'Don't let him touch the ball'."

By the time Olajuwon did touch the ball it was usually too late for defenders to do anything but hope he missed. His spin moves to the basket often leave defenders stuck in their tracks. His ability to get into the air quickly makes him capable of dunking anything in close to the basket. But it's Olajuwon's fadeaway jump shot, like Kareem Abdul-Jabbar's sky-hook, that has become the most unstoppable shot in the league.

"Olajuwon is blessed with grace, ability and quickness," says former NBA superstar Rick Barry. "To a large extent, his edge is his ability to beat his opponents physically. He also outworks them. His relentlessness, his second and third jumps on the offensive glass, is unparalleled in the NBA."

That's why he's now known as "the Dream."

**"IN TERMS OF RAW ATHLETIC ABILITY, HAKEEM IS THE BEST I HAVE EVER SEEN."**

Magic Johnson

**No Shaq Attack Here: Olajuwon prepares to slap away a shot from Shaquille O'Neal**

Olajuwon's ballhandling skills have helped him develop into one of the best all around centers ever to play the game

# SHAQUILLE O'NEAL
## The Shaq Attack

The stories preceded Shaquille O'Neal.

More than once during his college career at Louisiana State University, O'Neal tore a basket clean off the backboard while executing a dunk. His strength and size reminded some of Wilt Chamberlain. His ability to block shots recalled the Bill Russell era. Some even wondered if O'Neal might be the best of both of them, a huge player with enough athletic ability to lift an entire team.

O'Neal arrived in Orlando following the 1992 Draft, and coaches and players were still wondering just how good the 7–1, 301-pound center might become.

O'Neal was just 20 years old when the Magic played its first game with him in the middle. And no one, not even veteran centers such as Patrick Ewing, David Robinson and Hakeem Olajuwon, seemed to make much of an impression on O'Neal. Instead of feeling his way through the league, O'Neal attacked.

He averaged 23.4 points despite constant double-teaming and grabbed an impressive 13.8 rebounds a game. He also blocked shots, 286 of them in his first 81 professional games to become the easy choice as NBA Rookie of the Year.

"Shaq is much more athletic than I ever thought he would be," says former

**Nothing magic about this Shaq Attack**

## CAREER RECORD

| PERSONAL | | | | | | | | | | | |
|---|---|---|---|---|---|---|---|---|---|---|---|
| **Birthplace/Date** | Newark, NJ/3.6.72 | | | | | | | | | | |
| **Height /Weight** | 7-1/301 | | | | | | | | | | |
| **AWARDS** | | | | | | | | | | | |
| **MVP** | None | | | | | | | | | | |
| **All- Star Selections** | 1993-94 | | | | | | | | | | |
| **Finals MVP** | None | | | | | | | | | | |
| **CAREER** | | | | | | | | | | | |
| **University** | Louisiana State (1989-92) | | | | | | | | | | |
| **Pro. Career** | 2 seasons, Orlando Magic (1992-94) | | | | | | | | | | |

| PLAYING RECORD | G | FG | Pct | FT | Pct | Reb | Ast | Stl | Bl | Pts | ppg |
|---|---|---|---|---|---|---|---|---|---|---|---|
| **Regular Season** | 162 | 1686 | .582 | 898 | .572 | 2194 | 347 | 136 | 517 | 4270 | 26.4 |
| **Playoffs** | 3 | 23 | .511 | 16 | .461 | 40 | 7 | 2 | 9 | 62 | 20.7 |
| **All-Star** | 2 | 6 | .286 | 10 | .500 | 17 | 0 | 1 | 4 | 22 | 11.0 |

Orlando Coach Matt Goukas. "I played with and against Wilt Chamberlain and Shaq has the same kind of presence on the court. He's the type of force that opposing players always want to be aware of where he is and what he may try to do next. And he can do an awful lot."

O'Neal is so powerful, in fact, that he actually moved an entire basket support on one dunk.

Off the court, O'Neal has become the same kind of marketing phenomenon as Michael Jordan. He endorses a wide array of products and already has appeared in a major motion picture. If that's not enough, O'Neal is a rap artist with a growing singing career. O'Neal's first album—*Shaq Diesel*—gained critical acclaim and started climbing the record charts from the day it was released.

For now, however, O'Neal remains a basketball player first and foremost. The Magic improved from 21 to 41 victories during O'Neal's first season despite a thin bench and injuries to key players such as Dennis Scott.

In addition to making the All-Rookie Team, O'Neal topped off his first season by being named to the Eastern Conference All-Star Team. And that came as no surprise to players such as Chicago's Horace Grant.

"He's so big and strong that when you go over to help out on O'Neal you're taking your life into your hands," says Grant. "Shaquille's strength and your knowledge of what it can do is an intimidating offensive factor for Orlando."

So far, no one would disagree.

O'Neal's incredible size is matched only by his all-around ability which extends to every corner of the game

# SCOTTIE PIPPEN
## Out of the Shadows

There were days growing up in the tiny community of Hamburg, Arkansas, that Scottie Pippen couldn't even play basketball.

It wasn't that there weren't plenty of games going on. It's just that Pippen was considered too small and certainly not good enough to run with his older brothers. So he would stand along the sidelines watching the others play while dribbling a ball and wondering if his time would ever come.

Even as a high school senior, Pippen was a starting guard with a limited future. He stood only 6–1 and not a single college scout came around to watch him play. His high school coach eventually convinced a small local college—Central Arkansas—to give Pippen a job helping out with the team which in turn would help him pay school expenses.

"I was actually a water boy, a manager on my first college team," says Pippen. "No one thought I could play. Then a couple guys quit the team and I think the coach was tired of hearing me beg for an opportunity. He finally gave me a spot on the team."

Four years later, Pippen had grown to 6–7 and every NBA executive wanted Pippen playing for them. Chicago was one of the first teams to catch Pippen's college

**With Jordan gone, Pippen is No.1 in Chicago**

## CAREER RECORD

**PERSONAL**

| | |
|---|---|
| Birthplace/Date | Hamburg, Arkansas/9.25.65 |
| Height /Weight | 6-7/225 |

**AWARDS**

| | |
|---|---|
| MVP | None |
| All-Star Selections | 1990, 1992-94 |
| Finals MVP | None |

**CAREER**

| | |
|---|---|
| University | Central Arkansas (1983-87) |
| Pro. Career | 7 seasons, Chicago Bulls (1987-94) |

| PLAYING RECORD | G | FG | Pct | FT | Pct | Reb | Ast | Stl | Bl | Pts | ppg |
|---|---|---|---|---|---|---|---|---|---|---|---|
| Regular Season | 551 | 3778 | .491 | 1571 | .683 | 3765 | 2862 | 1173 | 531 | 9302 | 16.9 |
| Playoffs | 110 | 765 | .472 | 472 | .812 | 848 | 573 | 210 | 107 | 2016 | 18.3 |

act. By the time the 1987 NBA Draft rolled around, the Bulls wheeled and dealed to land Pippen.

After a slow start, Pippen developed into one of the league's most versatile players. He could play small forward, substitute for Michael Jordan at shooting guard and, when the Bulls needed a big team on the floor, move over to the point.

By the beginning of the 1990–91 season, Pippen had also developed into one of the league's best defenders. With long arms, unusual quickness, incredible jumping ability and an innate ability to read offenses, Pippen became a defensive force.

"There were times when I felt that Scottie had an even greater potential than Michael," says Bulls assistant coach Tex Winter. "Michael wouldn't agree with that, but Pippen has those long arms and great reaction and he can jump over the moon. Michael could do those things too, but Pippen was a little bigger."

As Pippen developed into a star, the Bulls developed into champions. Pippen was named to the NBA All-Defensive First Team in 1992 and 1993 while averaging more than 18 points a game and playing a variety of positions. He also joined Jordan as a member of USA Basketball's 1992 "Dream Team'.

"For all those years playing with Michael, Scottie Pippen had to accept that in the public's eye no matter how well he might have played, he'd never be better than the second-best player in the league," says Bill Walton, a former NBA star. "Now, with Michael gone, who's better—who does more things? Maybe no one."

**"NOW, WITH MICHAEL (JORDAN) GONE, WHO'S BETTER—WHO DOES MORE THINGS? MAYBE NO ONE."**
Former All-Star center Bill Walton

**Why the black wrist band? To keep Pippen's elbow from hitting the rim on slams like this**

# OSCAR ROBERTSON

## "The Big O"

**The legend of Oscar Robertson started long before he became a national hero while attending the University of Cincinnati.**

According to Wayne Embry, who was an early teammate, Robertson dominated every level he ever played.

"When Oscar Robertson walked into the ninth grade, he was a great player—not just for junior high, but for anywhere," says Embry, a long-time front office operative for the Cleveland Cavaliers. "The thing to remember about Oscar was that he was always great. As a freshman in college, he was once challenged to a game of one-on-one by Jack Twyman, who was in the NBA at the time. Oscar won 21-0.

"People still don't appreciate Oscar as a player, though. They talk about triple doubles (double figures in three statistical categories in the same game). He averaged them. He outrebounded centers."

And Robertson made it all look easy. The "Big O", as he was known, had one of the greatest careers in the history of college sports before leading the U.S. men's basketball team to a gold medal in the 1960 Rome Olympics.

Robertson led the nation in scoring three

## CAREER RECORD

| PERSONAL | | | | | | | | | |
|---|---|---|---|---|---|---|---|---|---|
| **Birthplace/Date** | Charlotte, Tennessee/11.24.38 | | | | | | | | |
| **Height /Weight** | 6-5/220 | | | | | | | | |
| **AWARDS** | | | | | | | | | |
| **MVP** | 1964 | | | | | | | | |
| **All-Star Selections** | 1961-72 | | | | | | | | |
| **Finals MVP** | None | | | | | | | | |
| **CAREER** | | | | | | | | | |
| **University** | Cincinnati (1956-60) | | | | | | | | |
| **Pro. Career** | 14 seasons, Cincinnati Royals (1960-70), Milwaukee Bucks (1970-74) | | | | | | | | |
| **PLAYING RECORD** | G | FG | Pct | FT | Pct | Reb | Ast | Pts | ppg |
| **Regular Season** | 1040 | 9508 | .485 | 7694 | .838 | 7804 | 9887 | 26,710 | 25.7 |
| **Playoffs** | 86 | 675 | .460 | 560 | .855 | 578 | 769 | 1,910 | 22.2 |
| **All-Star** | 12 | 88 | .512 | 79 | .714 | 69 | 81 | 246 | 20.5 |

ABOVE **The Big O helped Milwaukee become No.1 in 1971**

RIGHT **Triple Threat: Oscar Robertson averaged a triple-double during the 1961–62 season**

straight years at Cincinnati with a rare combination of exceptional skill and relentless determination. By the time Robertson's college career ended everyone knew exactly what to expect.

And they weren't disappointed. He joined the Cincinnati Royals in 1960 and immediately impacted the NBA. He averaged a stunning 30.5 points and more than 10 rebounds a game as a rookie, remarkable numbers for a 6–5 guard.

No one has ever been more complete than Robertson was during the 1961–62 season, his second in the league. He averaged 30.8 points, 12.5 rebounds and 11.4 assists, a feat that no player has even come close to matching in the history of the NBA.

To put Robertson's accomplishment in perspective, former Chicago Bulls great Michael Jordan had a total of 27 triple-doubles in his entire nine-year career. The Big O actually came close to averaging a triple-double for his entire career!

"Oscar was great from Day 1 in the NBA," says Jerry West, himself one of the league's greatest guards. "He was the most advanced player I had ever seen at such an early stage in his career. His greatness was his simplicity. He made every play in the simplest way because his skill level was enormous."

Robertson made the All-NBA First Team nine straight seasons, including his first. He led the league in assists six times even while scoring more than 25 points a game during his career. An 11-time All-Star and three times that game's Most Valuable Player, Robertson won his only NBA championship in 1971 after being traded to the Milwaukee Bucks and teaming with a young Kareem Abdul-Jabbar.

. . . . . . . . . . . . . . . . . . . . . . . .

**"THERE WAS NO POINT IN TRYING TO DESCRIBE THE MAN. YOU COULD WATCH HIM, YOU COULD ENJOY HIM, YOU COULD APPRECIATE HIM, BUT YOU COULDN'T ADEQUATELY DESCRIBE HIM."**

**Jack Twyman, former NBA star.**

. . . . . . . . . . . . . . . . . . . . . . . .

# DAVID ROBINSON

## The Admiral's In Charge

Nicknamed "the Admiral", David Robinson became an All-America center during his four years at the U.S. Naval Academy.

With extraordinary quickness and finesse for a player his size, the 7-1 Robinson reminded NBA coaches of past greats like Wilt Chamberlain and Bill Russell. In fact, some thought Robinson might eventually be the best of both, combining remarkable defensive skills with an offensive game that included everything from dunks to jump shots.

But San Antonio had to wait two years after using the No. 1 pick in the 1987 NBA Draft to select Robinson. Although his height kept Robinson from many military jobs, he was required to fulfill two years of active duty following his final year of school. Robinson was allowed to play in the 1988 Olympics where he led the men's basketball team to a bronze medal.

"We knew what we were getting," says Bob Bass, who drafted Robinson for San Antonio. "We knew what kind of impact he would make on our ballclub. All you had to do was watch him play. There wasn't anything he couldn't do on a basketball floor."

Even after two years off, Robinson became an instant star. He averaged 24.3

## CAREER RECORD

| PERSONAL | | | | | | | | | | | |
|---|---|---|---|---|---|---|---|---|---|---|---|
| **Birthplace/Date** | Key West, Florida/8.6.65 | | | | | | | | | | |
| **Height /Weight** | 7-1/235 | | | | | | | | | | |
| **AWARDS** | | | | | | | | | | | |
| **MVP** | None | | | | | | | | | | |
| **All-Star Selections** | 1990-94 | | | | | | | | | | |
| **Finals MVP** | None | | | | | | | | | | |
| **CAREER** | | | | | | | | | | | |
| **University** | Navy (1983-87) | | | | | | | | | | |
| **Pro. Career** | 5 seasons, San Antonio Spurs (1989-94 – in military service 1987-89), | | | | | | | | | | |

| PLAYING RECORD | G | FG | Pct | FT | Pct | Reb | Ast | Stl | Bl | Pts | ppg |
|---|---|---|---|---|---|---|---|---|---|---|---|
| **Regular Season** | 394 | 3552 | .527 | 2852 | .738 | 3585 | 1235 | 689 | 1473 | 9971 | 25.3 |
| **Playoffs** | 28 | 233 | .505 | 191 | .705 | 340 | 85 | 30 | 101 | 657 | 23.5 |
| **All-Star** | 4 | 27 | .614 | 17 | .630 | 31 | 4 | 7 | 6 | 71 | 23.80 |

The Admiral: Former U.S. Naval officer David Robinson now directs a floor show in San Antonio; (OPPOSITE) Jump shots are just part of the repertoire

points, 12 rebounds and blocked nearly four shots a game while directing one of the most impressive single-season turnarounds in NBA history. San Antonio finished 21-61 the year before Robinson arrived. With the Admiral in the middle, the Spurs improved to 56-26 and extended Portland to the seventh game of the Western Conference Semifinals, a game the Trail Blazers won in overtime.

"You look at David Robinson and what is there that he can't do?" says former Chicago star Michael Jordan. "He's as fast as any big man in the game, he can block shots better than any player in the league and he can score. If he ever develops a sky-hook like Kareem Abdul-Jabbar did, David Robinson will be unstoppable."

Though the Spurs have bobbed and weaved since that first season, Robinson has remained a tower of power. He has never averaged less than 23 points or 11 rebounds during the season. And he has never hit less than 50 percent of his shots from the floor.

Defensively, Robinson has been a force since his first NBA game. Twice he has led the league in blocked shots. In 1992, Robinson also was named NBA Defensive Player of the Year. During the 1990-91 and 1991-92 seasons, Robinson was a member of the All-NBA First Team and NBA All-Defensive First Team.

And in 1992, Robinson finally got the Olympic gold medal that had eluded the United States in 1988. Robinson was a key member of USA Basketball's "Dream Team."

> **"DAVID ROBINSON CAN BE AS GOOD AS HE WANTS TO BE IN THIS GAME. HE HAS EVERYTHING IT TAKES TO BECOME ONE OF THE GREATEST CENTERS TO EVER PLAY THE GAME."**
>
> Chuck Daly, "Dream Team" coach.

# BILL RUSSELL

## The Game's Greatest Defender

He didn't shoot that well and he wasn't a 7-footer. But by the time Bill Russell's NBA playing career ended, many thought the game had never seen a better player.

A 1980 poll by the Professional Basketball Writers Association of America made it official, voting Russell the greatest individual player in NBA history, a label that legendary Boston Celtics Coach Arnold "Red" Auerbach had long since given Russell.

Indeed, no player won more often at every level than Russell. It started at the University of San Francisco where Russell's incredible rebounding and shot blocking translated into consecutive NCAA titles in 1955 and 1956. Then, before joining the Celtics in a stunning Draft Day deal, Russell led the U.S. men's basketball team to the gold medal in the 1956 Rome Olympics.

Russell arrived in Boston for the 1956–57 season and the Celtics quickly became the most dominating franchise in the history of team sports in America. Russell led the league in rebounding in two of his first three years and averaged an amazing 24.7 a game during the 1963–64 season.

In just his second NBA season, Russell set the first of many NBA records by collecting 32 rebounds in one half in a game

**Russell could score when he had to**

## CAREER RECORD

**PERSONAL**

| | |
|---|---|
| **Birthplace/Date** | Monroe, Louisiana/2.12.34 |
| **Height /Weight** | 6-10/220 |

**AWARDS**

| | |
|---|---|
| **MVP** | 1958, 1961, 1962, 1963, 1965 |
| **All-Star selections** | 1958-69 |
| **Finals MVP** | None |

**CAREER**

| | |
|---|---|
| **University** | San Francisco (1952-56) |
| **Pro. Career** | 13 seasons, Boston Celtics (1956-69) |

| PLAYING RECORD | G | FG | Pct | FT | Pct | Reb | Ast | Pts | ppg |
|---|---|---|---|---|---|---|---|---|---|
| **Regular Season** | 963 | 5687 | .440 | 3149 | .561 | 21,620 | 4100 | 14,522 | 15.1 |
| **Playoffs** | 165 | 1003 | .430 | 667 | .603 | 4,104 | 770 | 2,673 | 16.2 |
| **All-Star** | 12 | 51 | .459 | 18 | .529 | 139 | 39 | 120 | 10.0 |

4,104 and five times was voted the NBA's Most Valuable Player.

Russell even won two NBA Championships as a player/coach for Boston. When Auerbach left coaching for the front office following the Celtics' eighth straight championship in 1966, he made Russell the league's first black head coach.

Russell promptly led the Celtics to consecutive NBA Championships in 1968 and 1969, beating Chamberlain's Los Angeles Lakers for the 1969 title in what proved to be his final game.

"We all knew that the Celtics revolved around Russell," said former teammate Tom "Satch" Sanders. "We knew he made us better. We knew he brought out the best in our individual skills. He was the reason we won and why all those championship banners hang at Boston Garden."

. . . . . . . . . . . . . . . . . . . . . . . . . . . .

## "RUSSELL WAS THE GREATEST PLAYER EVER TO PLAY BASKETBALL. BILL COULD PLAY A WHOLE TEAM DEFENSIVELY."

Arnold "Red" Auerbach, former Celtics coach.

. . . . . . . . . . . . . . . . . . . . . . . . . . . .

against Philadelphia. As a rookie, he led the Celtics to the first of 11 NBA titles, a string that included eight straight during the 1960s.

Russell became the first, and perhaps the only, player able to dominate a game at the defensive end. He played with a cold, calculating intensity. Even when matched against 7–2 Wilt Chamberlain, it was Russell's Celtics that usually came away the victors.

"Bill could hold any one player scoreless, but he was more interested in stopping all five," says Auerbach. "No other big man had his perfect timing when it came to blocking shots."

Russell was elected to the Hall of Fame in 1974. He has also been voted to the NBA 25th Anniversary All-Time Team (1970) and the 35th Anniversary All-Time Team (1980). Russell also holds the career record for rebounds in the playoffs with

**Many still consider Russell the greatest defender in NBA history**

**Russell played with a quiet intensity that often intimidated opponents**

# JOHN STOCKTON

## No Passing Fancy

John Stockton has never understood all the fuss. As a high school sophomore, Stockton stood 5–4 and weighed just 115 pounds. That he often destroyed players bigger and stronger on neighborhood basketball courts surprised everyone but Stockton.

Somehow John Stockton knew exactly where he was going. More than anyone else, Stockton knew nothing would get in his way, including the pint-size body that housed the spirit of a fighter. But even when the Utah Jazz made Stockton their No. 1 pick in the 1984 Draft, there were skeptics.

How could a player from a small Catholic college called Gonzaga make it in the NBA? And how could anyone standing 6–1 and weighing less than 180 pounds hope to survive the rough and tumble ways of professional basketball?

"I just always thought I could compete," says Stockton simply. "Not that I thought I was better than Magic Johnson or players like that. But I knew I could compete with them."

And that, Utah Coach Jerry Sloan will tell you, is exactly why Stockton has become one of the greatest point guards in the history of basketball. Before Stockton only two players had handed out more than 1,000 assists in a season. Isiah Thomas and Kevin Porter each did it one time.

**Passing Zone: Stockton has become one of the greatest assist men in NBA history**

## CAREER RECORD

| PERSONAL | | | | | | | | | | | |
|---|---|---|---|---|---|---|---|---|---|---|---|
| **Birthplace/Date** | Spokane, Washington/3.6.62 | | | | | | | | | | |
| **Height /Weight** | 6-1/175 | | | | | | | | | | |
| **AWARDS** | | | | | | | | | | | |
| **MVP** | None | | | | | | | | | | |
| **All- Star Selections** | 1989-94 | | | | | | | | | | |
| **Finals MVP** | None | | | | | | | | | | |
| **CAREER** | | | | | | | | | | | |
| **University** | Gonzaga (1980-84) | | | | | | | | | | |
| **Pro. Career** | 10 seasons, Utah Jazz (1984-94) | | | | | | | | | | |

| PLAYING RECORD | G | FG | Pct | FT | Pct | Reb | Ast | Stl | Bl | Pts | ppg |
|---|---|---|---|---|---|---|---|---|---|---|---|
| **Regular Season** | 816 | 3883 | .517 | 2745 | .822 | 2128 | 9383 | 2031 | 164 | 10,870 | 13.3 |
| **Playoffs** | 84 | 421 | .475 | 322 | .821 | 269 | 929 | 178 | 26 | 1,215 | 14.5 |
| **All-Star** | 5 | 15 | .500 | 4 | .667 | 10 | 45 | 11 | 1 | 38 | 7.6 |

Starting with the 1987–88 season, Stockton dished out more than 1,100 assists for five straight seasons.

Until Stockton only Boston Celtics great Bob Cousy—with eight— had won more than three consecutive assists titles. Stockton had won six in a row entering the 1993–94 season. Magic Johnson had the highest career average for assists per game with 11.35. Stockton's is at 11.38 and climbing.

He has had 28 assists in one game and twice passed out 11 in a single quarter. Perhaps equally amazing, however, is the fact that Stockton missed just four games through his first nine seasons. Indeed, Stockton, hadn't missed a game in four years when the 1993–94 season opened.

"The guy just loves to compete," says Sloan. "John Stockton will fight you every minute he's on the court."

If Stockton were only a remarkable play-maker he would be an All-Star. But Stockton has twice led the NBA in steals, made the NBA All-Defensive Second Team three times, and averaged more than 13 points a game while making 51 percent of his shots, many of those from three-point range.

That's why Stockton became an easy choice for USA Basketball's 1992 "Dream Team" and why he has appeared in every All-Star Game since 1989.

"A lot of people wonder where this team would be without John Stockton," says teammate and fellow All-Star Karl Malone. "Well, I don't want to find out. He's too good. That's all anyone needs to know."

**"HE DOES SO MANY THINGS SO WELL THAT TO TRY TO COMMENT ON EACH OF THEM WOULD BE TOO MUCH WORK. LET'S PUT IT THIS WAY, HE'S PERFECT—AND HE'S IMPROVING."**

Frank Layden, Utah Jazz President.

**Karl Malone scores more, but Stockton remains the Jazz point man**

# ISIAH THOMAS

## The Key To The Motor City

Long before Isiah Thomas established himself as one of the game's most fierce competitors in league history, he had to conquer the mean streets of Chicago's South Side.

He grew up on playgrounds in some of the toughest neighborhoods in the city. It's there Thomas learned a single lesson that would carry him through a brilliant college career at Indiana University and then an equally impressive run in the NBA: Never back down.

Listed at 6–1 and weighing just 182 pounds, Thomas played only two college seasons for Indiana University's legendary Coach Bobby Knight. He led the Hoosiers to the NCAA title in 1981, his wizard-like ballhandling skills and soft shooting touch, advanced well beyond his 20 years.

"Isiah wasn't used to losing at any level, high school or college, by the time he got to Detroit," recalled former teammate Kelly Tripucka. "He, probably more than anyone else with the Pistons, created that winning atmosphere in Detroit."

Though one of the youngest players in the league, Thomas averaged 17.5 points and made the NBA All-Rookie Team. Often matched against players sometimes as much as six inches taller, Thomas fought with a will of iron. His quickness, partic-

**To The Rescue: Thomas presided over the Pistons offense for 13 years**

## CAREER RECORD

**PERSONAL**

| | |
|---|---|
| **Birthplace/Date** | Chicago, Illinois/4.30.61 |
| **Height /Weight** | 6-1/182 |

**AWARDS**

| | |
|---|---|
| **MVP** | None |
| **All-Star Selections** | 1982-1993 (did not play 1991, injured) |
| **Finals MVP** | 1990 |

**CAREER**

| | |
|---|---|
| **University** | Indiana (1979-81) |
| **Pro. Career** | 13 seasons, Detroit Pistons (1981-94) |

| PLAYING RECORD | G | FG | Pct | FT | Pct | Reb | Ast | Stl | Bl | Pts | ppg |
|---|---|---|---|---|---|---|---|---|---|---|---|
| Regular Season | 979 | 7194 | .452 | 4036 | .759 | 3478 | 2858 | 1861 | 249 | 18,822 | 19.2 |
| Playoffs | 111 | 825 | .441 | 530 | .769 | 765 | 524 | 234 | 38 | 2261 | 20.4 |
| All-Star | 12 | 76 | .571 | 27 | .771 | 10 | 27 | 31 | 0 | 185 | 15.4 |

"I BELIEVE GOD MADE PEOPLE TO PERFORM CERTAIN ACTS. FRANK SINATRA WAS MADE TO SING. JESSE OWENS WAS MADE TO RUN. AND ISIAH THOMAS WAS MADE TO PLAY BASKETBALL."

Will Robinson, former Coach.

ularly while dribbling the ball, made him one of the most dangerous players in the league. He could break full-court presses by himself, moving the ball from hand to hand while charging full speed up the court.

But that was only part of the Thomas attack. He could improvise and flip shots around 7-foot centers close to the basket. Outside, Thomas could move full speed in one direction, stop and jump straight into the air for a jump shot. One-on-one, not a single player in the league could regularly stop Thomas by himself.

Most important to the Pistons, Thomas directed the team like he was a coach on the floor. Thomas studied films of opposing players trying to find their weaknesses. Chuck Daly, who coached Thomas during the Pistons title years, remembers watching Thomas break down an opposing team.

"He has a superior intellect," says Daly. "At every step of his career, he has shown that he knows how to win and has done just that."

With Thomas running the show, the Pistons became one of the dominant teams of the late 1980s and early 1990s. Detroit won NBA titles in 1989 and 1990 with a punishing defense and a perfectly executed offense. When it mattered most, particularly in the playoffs, Thomas always pushed his game to another level.

He set an NBA record by scoring 25 points in a single quarter against Magic Johnson's Los Angeles Lakers in the 1988 Finals. In 1990, Thomas was named Most Valuable Player of the championship series against Portland.

**No.1 With A Bullet:** Thomas could stop and shoot, or blow by defenders for easy layups

# DOMINIQUE WILKINS

## The Human Highlight Film

**The nickname followed Dominique Wilkins from the University of Georgia to the Atlanta Hawks. Less than a month into his first NBA season everyone knew why.**

At 6–8 and gifted with one of the most explosive vertical leaps ever seen, Wilkins arrived with a dazzling display of offensive weapons. Able to jump straight up and over most defenders, Wilkins could knock down jump shots from virtually anywhere on the court.

He could dunk flying in from the right side, left side or down the middle. He could grab a rebound, plant his feet and then elevate up and over 7-foot centers. Wilkins got up and down so quickly that defenders sometimes simply moved out of his way.

They call him the "Human Highlight Film," and the nickname fits.

"During the past decade the two most vicious offensive players in the NBA have been Dominique and Michael Jordan," says Johnny Kerr.

"Neither one just drives to the basket; they explode to the basket. Even Dominique's double-pump move when he drives to the basket is a power move because he does it with such authority."

**Wilkins likes the look of another slam dunk**

## CAREER RECORD

| PERSONAL | | | | | | | | | | | |
|---|---|---|---|---|---|---|---|---|---|---|---|
| **Birthplace/Date** | Paris, France/1.12.60 | | | | | | | | | | |
| **Height /Weight** | 6-8/215 | | | | | | | | | | |
| **AWARDS** | | | | | | | | | | | |
| **MVP** | None | | | | | | | | | | |
| **All-Star Selections** | 1986-91, 1992 (didn't play due to injury), 1993-94 | | | | | | | | | | |
| **Finals MVP** | None | | | | | | | | | | |
| **CAREER** | | | | | | | | | | | |
| **University** | Georgia (1979-82) | | | | | | | | | | |
| **Pro. Career** | 12 seasons, Atlanta Hawks (1982-94), Los Angeles Clippers (1994) | | | | | | | | | | |
| **PLAYING RECORD** | G | FG | Pct | FT | Pct | Reb | Ast | Stl | Bl | Pts | ppg |
| **Regular Season** | 907 | 9020 | .467 | 5455 | .814 | 6295 | 2376 | 1274 | 596 | 24,019 | 26.5 |
| **Playoffs** | 51 | 488 | .429 | 350 | .822 | 332 | 135 | 71 | 32 | 1345 | 26.4 |
| **All-Star** | 7 | 34 | .395 | 25 | .781 | 25 | 11 | 246 | 4 | 95 | 13.6 |

One of the quickest players ever at his size and as fast as anyone in the league, Wilkins has used all his raw talents to become a scoring machine. Just three years into the league Wilkins averaged 27.4 points. A year later, Wilkins improved to 30.3 points a game and won his first NBA scoring title.

Born in Paris, France as Jacques Dominique Wilkins, he also won two Gatorade Slam-Dunk Championships, including the 1985 contest where he defeated Michael Jordan. But Wilkins is more than a sideshow. As his career progressed, so too did his all-around abilities. Wilkins averaged a career best 9.0 rebounds a game during the 1990–91 season to go with a 25.9 points per game scoring average.

A year later Wilkins set the single-game record for consecutive free throws made by hitting 23 in a row against the Bulls.

After rupturing an Achilles tendon 42 games into the 1991–92 season, many thought Wilkins' high-wire act would come to an end. But Wilkins spent more than six months strengthening his legs and, at the age of 32, came back with one of the most impressive single-season performances of his career.

Wilkins averaged 29.9 points a game, the third best of his career. He also developed into a consistent threat from beyond the three-point line by hitting a career-high 38 percent of his long-range attempts.

"When he gets the ball on a fast break his natural instincts and talent take over along with his flair for showmanship," says former teammate Glen "Doc" Rivers. "He is just a tremendous professional basketball player."

In February, after almost 12 seasons in Atlanta, Wilkins was traded to the Los Angeles Clippers in a deal that sent Danny Manning to the Hawks.

**The Human Highlight Film: Wilkins rises up and over three Houston Rockets**

"IN HIS PRIME, DOMINIQUE WAS UNSTOPPABLE. ALL YOU COULD HOPE FOR WAS TO SLOW HIM DOWN A BIT, TO DENY HIM OPEN-COURT OPPORTUNITIES."

Pat Riley

Stretch Run: Wilkins can score from virtually anywhere on the court in just about any fashion including the finger roll

# THE ALL-STAR GAME

It started as an idea. With the NBA trying hard to find its way into the hearts and minds of sports fans, why not gather the league's best players every year for an All-Star Game? In the 33 years between 1951 and 1983, the idea turned into an event as big as any in professional sports. Games were sold out quickly, fans gathered around televisions to watch the proceedings live and players worked to become among the few chosen to participate. Since 1984, the game has been included as part of a gala All-Star Weekend devoted to basketball, complete with additional skill competitions and entertainment for fans of every age.

Nothing mirrors the NBA's dramatic rise more closely than the entertainment spectacle that has become All-Star Weekend.

Once considered an idea that had little chance of working, the NBA All-Star Game has turned into a world-wide event and one of the most successful exhibitions in all of professional sports.

"It's more than a game now," says Detroit Pistons personnel director Billy McKinney. "It's a happening. I remember back in the 1970s when it was a big deal. But even then, the game was nothing like it is now. And it's not just the game. Everything surrounding the game is impressive."

Indeed, the game has merely become the cornerstone of an entertainment-filled weekend.

But it certainly didn't start out that way. Back in 1951, NBA publicist Haskell Cohen had an idea. Why not hold a mid-season classic honoring the league's best players? After all, the NBA was trying to find its place in the sporting landscape. During the 1950–51 season, there were only 11 teams, one of which, Washington, disbanded midway through the season. But there were also some great players,

one of whom was George Mikan, the league's first dominant center and the key to the Minneapolis Lakers. Though the game was growing in popularity, very few people thought that an All-Star Game would prove profitable.

**Founding Father:** Boston Celtics owner Walter Brown's vision and determination led to the first NBA All-Star Game in 1951. A crowd of 10,094 flocked to Boston Garden to see the East complete an easy 111–94 victory and Ed Macauley win the MVP trophy

One of those who did, however, was the late Boston Celtics owner Walter Brown. He had not only started to build one of the greatest franchises in league history, but Brown believed in the NBA's future. He also thought an All-Star Game would be a good idea, not only for the league's image but financially as well.

At a time when Brown's own wife was telling him to get out of the basketball business, Brown charged ahead.

"Things were going so badly that even my wife wanted me to get out of the business," said Brown, some years later. "But I thought the All-Star Game would be a good thing. I told the league I would take care of all the expenses and all the losses if there were any.

"Even up until the last week, the game was in doubt. A few days before the game, Maurice Podoloff, the commissioner, called me on the phone and asked me to call it off. He said that everyone he had talked to said it would be a flop, and that the league would look bad."

Thanks in part to Brown's perseverance and bravery, the league has never looked better.

The first All-Star Game took place March 2, 1951 in Boston Garden, where 10,094 gathered to see the 20 best basketball players in the league. The Eastern Division romped to an easy 111–94 victory.

# THE FIRST ALL-STARS

The 1951 All-Star Game was not only a success, but it proved size isn't everything. Though Minneapolis Lakers center George Mikan headed the Western Division squad, he wasn't enough to offset the deep and talented Eastern Division roster.

The East was led by legendary coach Joe Lapchick, who had the head job with the New York Knicks. But Lapchick didn't have to worry about any fancy plays or creative defenses.

The East roster included Philadelphia's Joe Fulks and Paul Arizin, Syracuse sensation Dolph Schayes and Boston pair Ed Macauley and Bob Cousy. Indeed, the East had five of the league's top nine scorers and it showed.

The East All-Stars broke to a 31–22 lead and led by 19 points after three quarters. Though neither team shot particularly well, fans got what they expected: plenty of highlights.

Over the years, the All-Star Game would become a showcase for the wondrous scoring talents of the participants.

# THE SELECTION PROCESS

In the years since, the game has become a glowing example of the NBA's influence and popularity. As creative as the players themselves, league executives have turned a simple game into a weekend that starts gathering momentum just weeks into the regular season.

The process itself has become part of the show. Ballots are made available to fans attending games around the league. Fans are asked to vote for five players—two guards, two forwards and a center—they want to see starting for the Eastern Conference and Western Conference squads. Players receiving the most votes then occupy the five starting positions on each team for the All-Star Game.

Reserves are chosen by the respective head coaches. The coaches are determined by regular season records. The coach of the team with the best record in each conference through the first three months of the current season earns the right to coach that confer-

## AT&T Long Distance Shootout Champions

1986 — Larry Bird, Boston

1987 — Larry Bird, Boston

1988 — Larry Bird, Boston

1989 — Dale Ellis, Seattle

1990 — Craig Hodges, Chicago

1991 — Craig Hodges, Chicago

1992 — Craig Hodges, Chicago

1993 — Mark Price, Cleveland

1994 — Mark Price, Cleveland

ence's All-Star team.

But that's only part of the All-Star Weekend fun. In 1984, as the league exploded in world-wide popularity, events surrounding the game were added to satisfy demand. Not only were All-Star Games now played before sellout crowds in huge arenas, but media coverage turned the game into one of the country's most anticipated sporting events.

Indeed, reporters from around the world cover the event with the game televised around the globe. And no one, it seems, ever goes away disappointed. Thanks in large part to the players and coaches, the floor often seems more like a stage. Not only are the game's best players more rested, but they are surrounded

## Gatorade Slam-Dunk Champions

1984 — Larry Nance, Phoenix

1985 — Dominique Wilkins, Atlanta

1986 — Spud Webb, Atlanta

1987 — Michael Jordan, Chicago

1988 — Michael Jordan, Chicago

1989 — Kenny Walker, New York

1990 — Dominique Wilkins, Atlanta

1991 — Dee Brown, Boston

1992 — Cedric Ceballos, Phoenix

1993 — Harold Miner, Miami

1994 — Isaiah Rider, Minnesota

by stars at every position. The result is usually a high-scoring game revolving around an array of slick passes, slam dunks and long-range jumpers.

The league, responding to the overwhelming popularity of the game, created All-Star Weekend. The first Gatorade Slam-Dunk Championship was held in 1984 at Indiana along with the first Schick Legends Classic (replaced in 1994 by the Schick Rookie Classic). Two years later, in 1986, the AT&T Long Distance Shootout was instituted.

All-Star Saturday immediately became as popular as the All-Star Game itself as some of the league's biggest stars competed head-to-head. Boston's Larry Bird won the first three AT&T Long Distance Shootouts, a shooting contest that takes place from three-point range.

Players shoot from five positions on the court in a set time period. The player who makes the most shots advances until two are left in the finals.

Chicago's Michael Jordan and Atlanta's Dominique

## A WEEKEND AT MICHAEL'S HOUSE

The scene had been set for Michael Jordan. Leading the league in scoring and fast becoming one of the league's best defensive players, Jordan and the Chicago Bulls played host to the 1988 All-Star Game.

Though only half over, the season was becoming Jordan's greatest. So when Jordan decided to compete in the Gatorade Slam-Dunk Championship on All-Star Saturday he became the immediate favorite.

And Jordan didn't disappoint. Matched against Atlanta's Dominique Wilkins in the finals, Jordan prevailed with a variety of thundering dunks. As he had done the previous year, Jordan defended his Slam-Dunk title by taking off from the free-throw line and flying toward the basket, finishing with a one-handed dunk.

But that victory was only the beginning for Jordan. In a brilliant individual performance, he dominated the All-Star Game and carried the East to a 138–133 victory.

Jordan hit 17-of-23 shots and scored 40 points in 29 incredible minutes. He added eight rebounds, four steals and canned all six of his free throw attempts. Ironically, Wilt Chamberlain also hit 17-of-23 shots when he set the All-Star Game scoring record with 42 points 26 years earlier.

But not even Wilt scored with the style and grace that was Jordan's.

Wilkins each won a pair of Slam Dunk titles, with Jordan winning the 1987 event in Seattle by taking off from the free-throw line and sailing toward the basket before dunking. Although the format has changed

Mark Price on the way to victory in the 1993 Three-Point Contest

# THE LAST MAGIC SHOW

The 1991–92 season opened ominously. The great Earvin "Magic" Johnson had become ill during the preseason. For weeks, not even Johnson knew what was wrong.

Then he found out.

Doctors confirmed that Johnson was HIV positive. He had contracted the virus that leads to the deadly disease of AIDS. Strong as ever, Johnson was forced to announce his retirement from the game. Though he would attempt a brief comeback a year later, he had played his last NBA season.

The league had lost one of its greatest showmen, a player whose smile and exuberance were matched only by his ability to play the game.

But fans, many of whom had become interested in the NBA because of Johnson's exploits, couldn't let go. They voted Johnson a starter on the Western Conference All-Star team despite his retirement. And Johnson, never one to back away from a request, decided to make one last appearance.

He also made sure the memory of his greatness wouldn't soon fade. Despite not playing a single regular-season game, Johnson turned the 1992 Orlando All-Star Game into his own show.

He scored 25 points, grabbed five rebounds and passed out nine assists, including several of the patented no-look variety. The East, like everyone else, could only watch in amazement. Johnson led the West to a 153–113 victory, the second most lopsided result in All-Star Game history, and was unanimously named the game's Most Valuable Player.

It was a performance only a magician could appreciate.

A Magic Moment: Johnson came out of retirement to dazzle the world in the 1992 All-Star Game

over the years, dunkers are scored on their dunking ability and creativity.

One of the most stunning Slam-Dunk performances came in 1986 when 5–7 Spud Webb beat all competitors, most of whom were at least a half-foot taller, for the title.

In 1994, the Legends Game was replaced by the first Schick Rookie Game. Two coaches—former NBA stars Doug Collins and K.C. Jones—held a mock draft to determine the competing teams. The coaches alternated picks and chose from the league's 1993–94 rookies, including Golden State's Chris Webber, Chicago's Toni Kukoc, Orlando's Anfernee Hardaway and Dallas' Jamal Mashburn. The versatile Hardaway gained MVP honors in the inaugural Rookie Game.

But the All-Star Game remains the primary attraction.

Given the freedom not usually afforded during regular season games, players are allowed to show all their moves and reach deep into their bags of tricks. There are spectacular dunks, remarkable passes and just enough defense and shotblocking to produce a spectacular show.

Despite never playing together, the game also proves that great players can adjust to virtually any situation. Detroit's Isiah Thomas, one of the game's greatest point guards, was named Most Valuable Player of the 1984 and 1986 All-Star Games.

In 1984, Thomas scored 21 points and passed out 15 assists in one of the highest scoring classics in history. It was Thomas who helped key a 22-point overtime period that carried the East to a 154–145 win over the West. Two years later, Thomas did the scoring. He bombed the West for 30 points and handed 10 assists as the East rallied to a 139–132 victory over Magic Johnson's Western Conference squad.

Another of the more impressive efforts belongs to Tom Chambers, who turned the 1987 game around by himself. Chambers was in his fourth season as a member of the hometown SuperSonics. But this was Chambers' first All-Star Game and it was clear he wanted the locals to go home happy.

With 34,275 fans packed into the Seattle Kingdome, Chambers led a West comeback. He scored four of his game-high 34 points in overtime as the West held on for a 154–149 victory.

One of the more competitive games was played in 1993 at Utah. And it seemed only fitting. The Jazz had long been one of the league's toughest teams thanks to the intense play of superstars Karl Malone and John Stockton.

So as the game headed into overtime, Phoenix's Paul Westphal, who was coaching the West team, turned the game over to Utah's dynamic duo. Malone and Stockton combined to carry the West to a 135–132 victory in only the fifth overtime game in All-Star history.

The two shared the Most Valuable Player award, which was the second for Malone, who won in 1989 as well.

Though All-Star Weekend remains one of the most anticipated events of the season, 1994 marked a departure. Not only was the Rookie Game instituted into All-Star Saturday, but for the first time since 1980 the All-Star Game carried on without Larry Bird, Magic Johnson or Michael Jordan. And for the first time ever, not a single Celtic or Laker competed in the All-Star Game in this season of transition. The torch was officially passed to a long line of future and current stars.

The 1994 MVP was Jordan's former teammate, Scottie Pippen, who had a game-high 29 points, 11 rebounds and four steals as the East won 127–118.

And just as Walter Brown predicted back in 1951, the All-Star Game has become the showcase for the greatest basketball players in the world.

# ALL-STAR GAME RESULTS

| Year | | Score | |
|------|------|---------|----------|
| 1951 | East | 111–94 | West |
| 1952 | East | 108–91 | West |
| 1953 | West | 79–75 | East |
| 1954 | East | 98–93 | West (OT) |
| 1955 | East | 100–91 | West |
| 1956 | West | 108–94 | East |
| 1957 | East | 109–97 | West |
| 1958 | East | 130–118 | West |
| 1959 | West | 124–108 | East |
| 1960 | East | 125–115 | West |
| 1961 | West | 153–131 | East |
| 1962 | West | 150–130 | East |
| 1963 | East | 115–108 | West |
| 1964 | East | 111–107 | West |
| 1965 | East | 124–123 | West |
| 1966 | East | 137–94 | West |
| 1967 | West | 135–120 | East |
| 1968 | East | 114–124 | West |
| 1969 | East | 123–112 | West |
| 1970 | East | 142–135 | West |
| 1971 | West | 108–107 | East |
| 1972 | West | 112–110 | East |
| 1973 | East | 104–84 | West |
| 1974 | West | 134–123 | East |
| 1975 | East | 108–102 | West |
| 1976 | East | 123–109 | West |
| 1977 | West | 125–124 | East |
| 1978 | East | 133–125 | West |
| 1979 | West | 134–129 | East |
| 1980 | East | 144–135 | West (OT) |
| 1981 | East | 123–120 | West |
| 1982 | East | 120–118 | West |
| 1983 | East | 132–123 | West |
| 1984 | East | 154–145 | West (OT) |
| 1985 | West | 140–129 | East |
| 1986 | East | 139–132 | West |
| 1987 | West | 154–149 | East (OT) |
| 1988 | East | 138–133 | West |
| 1989 | West | 143–134 | East |
| 1990 | East | 130–113 | West |
| 1991 | East | 116–114 | West |
| 1992 | West | 153–113 | East |
| 1993 | West | 135–132 | East (OT) |
| 1994 | East | 128–119 | West |

# THE NBA DRAFT

The evolution of the NBA Draft has matched that of the league itself. In the early days, teams gathered around a table in their offices and called off the names of the players selected on a conference call as an official at the league's New York headquarters recorded the information. Few teams did extensive scouting. In the years since, however, the draft has become one of the NBA's biggest shows. Every team studies films, scouting reports and pages of vital information on players from all over the world. The draft itself is now an internationally televised event with 20,000 fans or more packing arenas every year to watch the future unfold.

No one event can change the direction of a franchise like the NBA Draft. In the early years as the league evolved, luck and intuition filled the void for teams that didn't have either the money or personnel to scout college players.

In 1955, Leonard Koppett, a veteran basketball writer, described that year's draft session in a column for the New York Post. According to Koppett, NBA Commissioner Maurice Podoloff sat at the head of a table and called off the names of the league's nine teams.

"Since it is a relatively small family in the NBA, with everyone on quite friendly terms these days, there's a good deal of kidding," wrote Koppett.

"So when Fort Wayne's Charley Eckman chose Dick Howard, Boston's Red Auerbach quipped, 'Is that a relative, Charley?'

"'Wife's cousin,' Eckman shot back."

The atmosphere has changed considerably since. In fact, the entire process has changed dramatically just in the last 10 years.

"Back then teams didn't even have full-time scouts," says Chicago Bulls vice president of operations, Jerry Krause. "You were lucky if you had an assistant coach much less a scout. No one had the things

**Team officials prepare for the 1993 NBA Draft at the Palace of Auburn Hills in Michigan**

**Commissioner David Stern congratulates 1992 No.1 pick Shaquille O'Neal of the Orlando Magic**

# COIN FLIPS AND FLOPS

From 1966, through 1984, there were 19 coin flips to determine which team would get the No. 1 pick in the annual NBA Draft. For the record, the coin came up "heads" just seven times, including the last three.

But not all the coin flip winners turned out to be winners on the court. In 1967, Detroit won the flip and took Jimmy Walker, who went on to a solid nine-year career. Baltimore took Earl Monroe with the second pick. Monroe wound up in the Hall of Fame.

In 1972, the flip went to Portland. The Trail Blazers decided on LaRue Martin, a center from Chicago's Loyola University. He lasted four seasons in the NBA. Buffalo, which lost the flip, took Bob McAdoo, who led the NBA in scoring in each of his first three seasons.

Then again, the simple flip of a coin forever changed the fortunes of at least three teams. In 1969, Milwaukee landed Kareem Abdul-Jabbar, perhaps the greatest all around center in NBA history. The Phoenix Suns ended up with the second pick that season and took Neal Walk, who played eight seasons with three different teams.

The Los Angeles Lakers called heads and took Earvin "Magic" Johnson with the first choice in 1979. Chicago landed David Greenwood with the second pick. The Lakers, with Johnson leading the team, won a championship in Johnson's first season. By the time Chicago won its first title, Greenwood had retired.

In 1974, Portland won the flip and selected center Bill Walton. Philadelphia ended up with Marvin Barnes, who signed instead with St. Louis in the American Basketball Association and played just six professional seasons. Walton led Portland to the 1977 NBA title.

## HISTORY OF COIN FLIPS

| YEAR | WINNER | PLAYER SELECTED | LOSER | PLAYER SELECTED |
|------|--------|-----------------|-------|-----------------|
| 1966 | New York | Cazzie Russell | Detroit | Dave Bing |
| 1967 | Detroit | Jimmy Walker | Baltimore | Earl Monroe |
| 1968 | Sam Diego | Elvin Hayes | Baltimore | Wes Unseld |
| 1969 | Milwaukee | K. Abdul-Jabbar | Phoenix | Neal Walk |
| 1970 | Detroit | Bob Lanier | San Diego | Rudy Tomjanovich |
| 1971 | Cleveland | Austin Carr | Portland | Sidney Wicks |
| 1972 | Portland | LaRue Martin | Buffalo | Bob McAdoo |
| 1973 | Philadelphia | Doug Collins | Cleveland | Jim Brewer |
| 1974 | Portland | Bill Walton | Philadelphia | Marvin Barnes |
| 1975 | Atlanta | David Thompson | Los Angeles | Dave Meyers |
| 1976 | Houston | John Lucas | Chicago | Scott May |
| 1977 | Milwaukee | Kent Benson | Kansas City | Otis Birdsong |
| 1978 | Portland | Mychal Thompson | Kansas City | Phil Ford |
| 1979 | Los Angeles | Magic Johnson | Chicago | David Greenwood |
| 1980 | Golden State | Joe Barry Carroll | Utah | Darrell Griffith |
| 1981 | Dallas | Mark Aguirre | Detroit | Isiah Thomas |
| 1982 | Los Angeles | James Worthy | San Diego | Terry Cummings |
| 1983 | Houston | Ralph Sampson | Indiana | Steve Stipanovich |
| 1984 | Houston | Hakeem Olajuwon | Portland | Sam Bowie |

that are available today. But that didn't mean you couldn't find players. You just had to dig a little more that's all."

Since the beginning, however, the draft has had a very simple mission: to promote competitive balance throughout the league. Teams selected in inverse order of their regular-season records. Thus, the weakest teams were awarded the first shot at available new talent.

In the hope of solidifying franchises, early teams were also allowed a "territorial pick." Each team could select one player from its geographic area to maintain local interest in the professional team.

That's how Oscar Robertson, who attended the University of Cincinnati, ended up playing for the Cincinnati Royals.

Over the years, however, territorial picks were eliminated. In 1966, the coin flip was introduced to determine the No. 1 pick in the draft. The idea was to maintain integrity in the game since the team with the worst record wouldn't be guaranteed of landing the first choice.

In some cases the coin flip changed the fortunes of entire franchises. In 1969, the Milwaukee Bucks won a coin flip with Phoenix and ended up with Kareem Abdul-Jabbar. Two years later, the Bucks

won an NBA championship. Ten years later, the Los Angeles Lakers flipped with Chicago and won the right to choose first. The Lakers selected Earvin "Magic" Johnson and in 1980 won the first of five NBA titles. Phoenix still hasn't won a championship while Chicago didn't win its first until 1991.

# THE LOTTERY

To completely take away any incentive a poor team might have for losing games and thus getting into the coin flip, the league instituted the NBA Draft Lottery in 1985. Initially the lottery was used to determine the order of selection for non-playoff teams or the teams owning those picks through trades. The Lottery determined the order for the first round only, and the order for subsequent rounds went in inverse order of regular season records.

The New York Knicks came away with the first choice in the 1985 NBA Draft and selected Patrick Ewing.

The process was further refined for the 1990 NBA Draft. The Lottery, which included 11 teams due to expansion, was weighted to favor the worst teams. The team with the worst record had 11 chances to land the No. 1 pick. The second worst team had 10 chances and so on.

For the 1994 NBA Draft, the lottery system was modified yet again. Ironically, the incredible luck of the Orlando Magic led to the most recent change. Orlando gained the No. 1 pick in 1992 and selected 7–1 center Shaquille O'Neal. In 1993, the Magic finished just one game out of the playoffs. As a lottery team, Orlando had the lowest odds of gaining the top pick again. But it happened. The Magic, like Houston in 1983 and 1984 when the coin flip still existed, had back-to-back No. 1 picks.

In an attempt to further improve the odds for the league's worst teams, the new lottery system increases the chance of the team with the worst record getting the top pick from 16.7 percent to 25 percent.

Two other key changes over the years involved players and the length of the draft. Prior to 1971, players could not be drafted into the NBA until their college classes had graduated. In other words, a college junior was not eligible to play in the NBA. That changed when Spencer Haywood filed a lawsuit against the league

## HITTING THE LOTTERY JACKPOT

| YEAR | TEAM | FIRST PLAYER CHOSEN |
|------|------|---------------------|
| 1985 | New York | Patrick Ewing |
| 1986 | Cleveland | Brad Daugherty |
| 1987 | San Antonio | David Robinson |
| 1988 | Los Angeles Clippers | Danny Manning |
| 1989 | Sacramento | Pervis Ellison |
| 1990 | New Jersey | Derrick Coleman |
| 1991 | Charlotte | Larry Johnson |
| 1992 | Orlando | Shaquille O'Neal |
| 1993 | Orlando | Chris Webber* |

\* Traded to Golden State for Anferee Hardaway, and three future No. 1 draft picks.

for refusing to allow him to enter the draft before the expiration of his collegiate eligibility. A year later, underclassmen who demonstrated financial hardship were allowed into the draft. In 1976, the draft was opened to all players with or without financial hardship. To become eligible for the draft, underclassmen had to renounce their remaining eligibility in a letter to the commissioner 45 days prior to the draft. That rule remains in place today.

The length of the draft has changed dramatically as well. After years with no limits to the number of rounds, the league instituted a 10-round draft in 1974. In other words, each team had 10 opportunities to select players.

The draft was reduced to seven rounds in 1985, three rounds in 1988 and the present two rounds in 1989. Those changes, along with the booming popularity of college basketball and professional game, have turned the NBA Draft into a major international media event.

# DRAFTED...BUT NOT FOR KEEPS

The 1993 NBA Draft was held at the Palace of Auburn Hills where the Detroit Pistons play their home games. More than 15,000 fans jammed the arena. NBA Commissioner David Stern conducted the draft while representatives from all 27 NBA teams huddled at individual desks to make their selections. Virtually every top pick including Chris Webber, Anfernee Hardaway and Jamal Mashburn was on hand and introduced by the commissioner upon being chosen.

And since draft picks can be traded between teams, the NBA Draft has become one the most important offseason events in the league. Indeed the 1993 NBA Draft included one of the most stunning deals in league history when Orlando used the No. 1 choice to grab Webber and then, less than an hour later, traded Webber to the Golden State Warriors for Hardaway, whom the Warriors had chosen at No. 3, and three future first-round draft choices.

Since teams now have entire departments devoted to scouting players complete with state-of-the-art video equipment and large travel budgets, the NBA Draft is a bigger event than ever.

Anxious fans settle in for the 1992 NBA Draft in Portland

# THE DREAM TEAM

There had been plenty of great teams with two and sometimes three All-Stars occupying starting positions. The Boston Celtics had numerous All-Star players during their championship romp through the 1960s. The Los Angeles Lakers of the late 1960s had future Hall of Famers Wilt Chamberlain, Jerry West and Elgin Baylor on the same team. But no team, neither in the Olympics nor even an NBA All-Star Game, had ever been assembled with the talent and brilliance of USA Basketball's 1992 Dream Team. From top to bottom, position to position, the players represented some of the greatest talent in the history of the game, including three of the most dominant individuals of all time in Michael Jordan, Magic Johnson and Larry Bird. In Barcelona, in front of all the world, the dream became a reality.

By the time the last player was chosen, not even USA Basketball coach Chuck Daly could believe the collection of talent he would take to Barcelona for the 1992 Olympic Games.

Daly had coached the Detroit Pistons to consecutive NBA titles and he had just seen Chicago win back-to-back championships. But never had Daly seen anything like the group that took the floor for the first Dream Team practice in early July, 1992.

There were stars at every position, scoring at every spot on the floor and enough size to beat any team that had ever played. A game plan didn't exist that Daly couldn't use. The players were versatile, quick, strong and driven to succeed. No one had ever seen anything like this.

"You will never see that again," said Daly shaking his head. "I mean, just look at those guys. They are all superstars except for Christian Laettner and he was the best college player in the country that year! You had Michael Jordan, Larry Bird, Magic Johnson and Charles Barkley, and that's just the start."

It proved to be the beginning and the end for the rest of the world. Even before the Games started, opposing teams wondered just how bad the beatings would be. Indeed, even some of the greatest foreign

BELOW Dream Weavers: USA Basketball's 1992 Dream Team included some of the brightest stars ever to play the game; (OPPOSITE) Jordan helped the Dream Team to victory

players, stars like Toni Kukoc and Dino Radja, were resigned to defeat.

"They should just give the United States the gold medal and get it over with," said Radja, then a forward for Croatia and currently a member of the Boston Celtics.

"The United States is going to win every game in the Olympics by 25 or 30 points," predicted Kukoc, Radja's teammate with Croatia and now Scottie Pippen's teammate in Chicago. "If the Americans have a bad day, maybe they'll win by only 15 points."

And that was nearly a month before the Games started.

But Kukoc and Radja had seen enough of the NBA superstars on global television to know what to expect. And Bill Wennington, who played in the NBA as well as in Europe, had an even clearer understanding of what would happen.

Said Wennington, "The world will end before the U.S. is beaten."

Once the Dream Team arrived in Barcelona the worst fears of their victims were realized. The team had size with 7-foot centers David Robinson and Patrick Ewing and the 6–11 Laettner. They had power in Charles Barkley and Karl Malone, speed in John Stockton, versatility in Pippen and Clyde Drexler, extraordinary scoring in Michael Jordan, Larry Bird and Chris Mullin and the ultimate leader in Magic Johnson.

They had no holes, not a single spot for opponents to attack. Try to shut down the

## THE DREAM TEAM

| PLAYER | TEAM | HEIGHT | POSTION |
|---|---|---|---|
| Charles Barkley | Phoenix | 6-6 | Forward |
| Larry Bird | Boston | 6-9 | Forward |
| Clyde Drexler | Portland | 6-7 | Guard |
| Patrick Ewing | New York | 7-0 | Center |
| Magic Johnson | L.A. Lakers | 6-9 | Guard |
| Michael Jordan | Chicago | 6-6 | Guard |
| Christian Laettner | Duke University | 6-11 | Forward |
| Karl Malone | Utah | 6-9 | Forward |
| Chris Mullin | Golden State | 6-6 | Guard/Forward |
| Scottie Pippen | Chicago | 6-7 | Forward |
| David Robinson | San Antonio | 7-1 | Center |
| John Stockton | Utah | 6-1 | Guard |

middle and Bird, Mullin and Jordan would destroy you from the outside. Guard players too closely and Barkley, Pippen and Drexler would blow past for an easy basket. Use a single defender on Ewing or Robinson and either would score at will.

There was no hope—and everyone seemed happily resigned to that.

"No one could beat that team," says Pippen. "There has never been a team that could beat that team and there might never be one."

Few would disagree.

The Dream Team breezed through the Olympic field with the greatest of ease. They won by an average of nearly 44 points a game. Daly's only real problem was trying to find enough playing time for all his players.

Johnson, who ran the team on the floor, had a similar problem. Instead of trying to find a player to pass the ball to, Johnson found it difficult to figure out which one he should give it to.

"You can't even believe how I feel to be part of it," said Johnson during the Games. "There's Michael Jordan on one side, Scottie Pippen on the other, Larry Bird positioning himself for a jumper. You have so many options. On your regular team you pick and choose. But here you don't have

to do that. It's just amazing."

In the gold-medal game against future Bulls teammate Kukoc, Pippen played just 23 minutes, and Malone and Stockton, Utah's dynamic duo during the regular season, played only 11 and 8 minutes, respectively.

Indeed, neither injury, illness nor even retirement affected the Dream Team. Bird, who missed 37 games during the 1991–92 season with a bad back, had trouble moving without pain. Johnson, who retired prior to the 1991–92 season after testing positive for the HIV, had played only one NBA game, the 1992 All-Star Game, in the previous 13 months.

Stockton had broken a bone in his leg during practices for the Olympics while Jordan and Pippen, whose seasons had barely ended when Dream Team practices started, were virtually exhausted.

No one noticed. The collection of talent was so overwhelming that even the competition could be found looking on in amazement.

"It was an honor to play against them," said Kukoc.

And it was an honor to be one of them.

"That basketball team," says Barkley. "Words cannot express how good it was."

A dream come true.

# DREAMS AND NIGHTMARES

## USA Basketball's road to the 1992 Olympic Gold

| USA | 116-48 | Angola |
|-----|--------|--------|
| USA | 103-70 | Croatia |
| USA | 111-68 | Germany |
| USA | 127-83 | Brazil |
| USA | 122-81 | Spain |
| USA | 115-77 | Puerto Rico |
| USA | 127-76 | Lithuania |
| USA | 117-85 | Croatia |

**The Lull Before The Storm: Scottie Pippen (8), Michael Jordan, Magic Johnson (15) and Patrick Ewing (6) prepare to battle for Olympic gold in Barcelona**

# THE NBA GOES GLOBAL

For much of its existence, the NBA remained an American enterprise. But now, with television contracts in more than 140 countries and offices around the world, the league is beginning to make the NBA experience an international one. It started with the McDonald's Open, an annual tournament that featured one NBA team. Now there are 3-on-3 World Tours sponsored in part by Converse, NBA players competing in the World Championship of Basketball, expansion to Canada, regular season games played in Japan and a biennial World Club Championship featuring the NBA Champion. Suddenly the game belongs to everyone.

NBA Commissioner David Stern remembers the request. He was talking to members of the Chinese government during a trip to China. One of them turned to Stern and asked if he would bring the Red Oxen to China.

Stern understood.

"They wanted to see the Chicago Bulls," recalls Stern. "They wanted to know if we could put together a game in China that would include the Bulls."

There had been other requests from inside the Soviet Union, Japan, South America and virtually every European country. Thanks to Stern's marketing genius and the basketball genius of the NBA players, interest in the NBA game extended around the globe.

"Sports really is the international language," says Stern. "And we think basketball is up there on top of the list in terms of dialect."

In 1993 alone, NBA All-Star center Hakeem Olajuwon along with Stacey King of the champion Bulls joined three other professionals for a full week of NBA related activities in Sydney and Melbourne, Australia.

During the preseason, Phoenix played in Munich, Germany, in the McDonald's Open against championship clubs from five countries; New York and Houston played in Mexico City; Portland and Cleveland squared off in Toronto, Canada; Atlanta and Orlando met in London's Wembley Arena; Denver and Miami in San Juan, Puerto Rico.

And that's just the beginning. More than 50 countries carried the 1993 NBA Finals between Chicago and Phoenix live. Meanwhile, the global distribution of NBA games for the 1993–94 season included 141 countries and access to 400 million households worldwide.

Though the momentum had been building for years, it got a big boost during the 1992 Barcelona Olympics when USA Basketball's Dream Team stole the international show.

"Since the impressive performance of the Dream Team at the Olympics, basketball has gained unprecedented worldwide attention, especially among young people," says Stern.

One grassroots example of the international lure of basketball was the overwhelming response to the 1993 Converse/NBA 3-on-3 World Tour. The event matches teams of three players each

**The 1993 Converse/NBA 3-on-3 World Tour stops in Paris, France**

in a variety of age, size and skill levels. The games are usually played outdoors, which make it one of the largest spectator events in Europe.

**A Helping Hand: Denver Nuggets star center Dikembe Mutombo (right) helps youngsters during a 1993 NBA tour through Africa**

The 1993 Tour stopped in 13 cities, attracting more than 27,000 players and more than 527,000 spectators. A two-day tournament in Paris drew more than 180,000 fans. And it will only get bigger. In 1994 the event expanded to 25 cities in 11 countries with expectations of more than a million spectators.

Stern has also made a commitment to the continent of Africa. During the summer of 1993, NBA players and coaches combined on clinics in Kenya and Zambia with additional stops in Johannesburg, Soweto and Durban. When the NBA contingent arrived in Soweto, they found exactly eight basketballs and little knowledge of the game. But by the time that Denver Nuggets star Dikembe Mutombo, then Washington Bullets Coach Wes Unseld and former NBA stars Alex English and Bob McAdoo had departed, there were 200 basketballs, 20 baskets and a pledge from Stern to return.

By late 1993 the first names of the next Dream Team, or Dream Team II as it has been called, were in place for the United States' entry in the 16-team World Championship of Basketball, which was played in Toronto and Hamilton, Ontario, Canada in August 1994.

The location turned out to be a fitting one. In 1994, Toronto became the league's 28th franchise and will begin play with the 1995–96 season. Why Toronto? That's easy, according to Stern.

He described Toronto as the largest unserved market in North America and added that it had already demonstrated spectacular support for sports franchise after sports franchise.

Stern pointed out that a country of 28 million potential sports fans presented a spectacular opportunity for the NBA, and Toronto might only be the beginning. The league is considering adding at least one more Canadian franchise due to the overwhelming interest beyond the NBA's traditional geographic boundaries.

"No question," says former Los Angeles Lakers star Magic Johnson. "People love the NBA game."

## DREAM TEAM II? STAY TUNED!

If the United States entry in the 1994 World Championship of Basketball looked impressive, it should. With the 1996 Atlanta Olympics just two years off, USA Basketball was getting its act together for another gold-medal run.

The players selected for the World Championship competition in Toronto and Hamilton, Ontario, Canada, August 4–14, included some of the league's up and coming superstars. Players such as Miami guard Steve Smith, New Jersey forward Derrick Coleman, Orlando center Shaquille O'Neal, Charlotte center Alonzo Mourning and forward Larry Johnson and Seattle's Shawn Kemp are some of the most talented young players in the league.

Add veteran stars such as L.A. Clippers forward Dominique Wilkins, Indiana's Reggie Miller, Cleveland's Mark Price, Phoenix' guard Dan Majerle, Golden State's Tim Hardaway and Detroit's Isiah Thomas and Joe Dumars, and Dream Team II only looks stronger.

# GLOSSARY OF TERMS

**Air Ball:** When a player shoots a shot that doesn't touch the rim it is sarcastically referred to as an "air ball."

**Alley-oop pass:** The pass is usually thrown as a player runs toward the basket. The receiving player catches the ball in the air and either dunks or lays it in the hoop without touching the ground.

**Assist:** A player earns an assist when his pass to another player leads directly to a basket.

**Backcourt:** As it refers to players, backcourt generally means guards. A team with a great backcourt would have two very talented guards.

**Bench:** Where substitutes and coaches reside during games. A "bench" player is another term for a reserve.

**Bounce pass:** Passing the ball from one player to another by bouncing it on the floor.

**Center:** Usually the tallest player on a team's starting unit with a variety of skills that sometimes include shotblocking, rebounding and scoring. New York's Patrick Ewing, San Antonio's David Robinson, Orlando's Shaquille O'Neal and Charlotte's Alonzo Mourning are examples of top-flight centers.

**Draft:** A selection process to determine on which NBA teams the top newcomers will play.

**Dunk:** The act of slamming the ball through the basket with one or two hands.

**Fast break:** A play that occurs when the offensive team quickly gets the ball out ahead of the defensive team. The offensive team usually has a one or two-man advantage as it goes in for a score.

**Field goal:** Either a two-point or three-point basket can also be referred to as a field goal.

**Foul:** A violation commited by one player against another player. After accumulating six personal fouls in a game, a player is disqualified for the rest of the game.

**Free throw:** When a foul is commited, the player fouled usually gets to take two shots from the free-throw line which is 15 feet from the basket. The free throws are worth one point each.

**Frontcourt:** As it refers to players, frontcourt usually means forwards and centers.

**Halftime:** The time in between the first half and the second half. Each half consists of two 12-minute quarters. Teams break between the second and third quarters and change the baskets at which they shoot.

**Jump shot:** A shot taken away from the basket. Players usually jump into the air, set themselves and take the shot. Sometimes referred to as a "jumper."

**Lane:** The painted area running from the end line under the basket out to the free-throw line. Offensive players can not be in the lane more than three seconds.

**Lottery:** The process that determines the first 11 picks in the NBA Draft.

**Overtime:** When a game is tied at the end of regulation play the two teams play a five-minute overtime period. A game can include as many overtime periods as are necessary to determine a winner.

**Paint:** The area under the basket, and extending to the foul line. Also called the "lane," it is always painted a different color from the rest of the floor.

**Pivot:** This takes place when a player who is holding the ball steps and turns once or more than once in any direction with the same foot, while the other foot — called the pivot foot — is being kept at its point of contact on the floor.

**Point guard:** Usually a team's primary ballhander. He leads the offense and distributes the ball to the team's best scorers. Utah's John Stockton, New Jersey's Kenny Anderson, Seattle's Gary Payton and Phoenix's Kevin Johnson are some of the league's best point guards.

**Power forward:** Usually occupies one of two forward spots on a five-man unit. Known primarily for their rebounding and defensive skills. Utah's Karl Malone, Chicago's Horace Grant and Portland's Buck Williams are examples of power forwards.

**Quadruple-double:** Refers to a player who accumulates ten or more in at last four of five statistical categories—points, rebounds, steals, blocked shots, assists—in a single game. Through the 1993–94 season, there have been only four quadruple-doubles in NBA history.

**Rebound:** The gathering or controlling of a missed shot.

**Screen:** This is a legal action of a player who, without causing undue contact, delays or prevents an opponent from reaching a desired position.

**Shot clock:** The 24-second clock used to time possessions. The offensive team has 24 seconds in which to get off a shot.

**Shooting guard:** Occupies one of two guard positions and usually is one of the team's primary offensive weapons. Former Chicago Bulls star Michael Jordan was a shooting guard. Others include Indiana's Reggie Miller, Phoenix's Dan Majerle, Golden State's Latrell Sprewell and New York's John Starks.

**Sixth man:** Usually refers to a team's top reserve.

**Small forward:** Occupies one of two forward spots, the small forward is most often known for his scoring. Though not necessarily smaller in size, these players are better known for shooting and scoring skills than rebounding or defensive skills. The Los Angeles Clippers' Dominique Wilkins and Chicago's Scottie Pippen are considered small forwards.

**Steal:** The action of a defensive player in either taking the ball away from an offensive player or intercepting a pass is known as a steal.

**Technical foul:** Assessed for a number of violations including fighting, verbal abuse of a referee, a second illegal defense call and flagrant foul.

**Triple-double:** Refers to a player who accumulates double figures, 10 or more, in at least three of five statistical categories—points, rebounds, steals, blocked shots, assists—in a single game.

**Turnover:** A play that results in a change of possession with the control of the ball going from one team to the other.

# BaSKETBaLL HALL OF FAME

B y 1968, the basketball Hall of Fame was an idea whose time was long overdue. Though a memorial had been agreed upon following the 1939 death of Dr. James Naismith, the game's creator, it took nearly 30 years to make the dream a reality.

The Naismith Memorial Basketball Hall of Fame came alive on February 18, 1968, on the Springfield College campus in Springfield, Mass. In 1985 a modern, three-level structure was built on the banks of the Connecticut River in downtown Springfield, the town where Dr. Naismith first tossed a round ball through a peach basket in 1891.

The Hall of Fame recognizes basketball at every level from high school to the Olympics, amateur and professional. An Honors Committee, composed of 24 members representing various levels of basketball, votes each year on nominees, who need 18 votes to be elected to the Hall of Fame. The first Hall of Fame elections were held in 1959, nine years before a building even existed. Since then there have been coaches, players and individual contributors enshrined as well as four teams.

Two of the most unique individuals are John Wooden and Bill Bradley. Wooden was named as a player in 1960 and as a coach in 1972. Bradley, who played for the New York Knicks, is a United States Senator and was inducted in 1982.

The following are brief biographies of NBA-related players in the Hall of Fame:

**Nate (Tiny) Archibald:** 6–1, 160-pound guard; born April 18, 1948. Attended Arizona Western and Texas-El Paso; played 13 seasons with four teams. Became first player to lead NBA in scoring (34.0) and assists (11.4) in the same season (1973–74). A six-time All-Star.

**Paul Arizin:** 6–4, 200-pound forward; born April 9, 1928. Attended Villanova; played 10 seasons with Philadelphia. One of the highest scoring players of his era from 1950 through the 1961–62 season. Nine times an All-Star.

**Rick Barry:** 6–7, 205-pound forward; born March 28, 1944. Attended Miami. Played 14 professional seasons, 10 of those in the NBA. One of basketball's greatest scorers and shooters. A

career 90 percent free-throw shooter, utilizing a distinctive underhanded shooting style. Seven-time All-Star.

**Elgin Baylor:** 6–5, 225-pound forward; born September 16, 1934. Attended College of Idaho and University of Seattle. Played 14 seasons with the Minneapolis and Los Angeles Lakers. Averaged more than 34 points a game for three consecutive years in the early 1960s. 11-time All-Star.

**Walt Bellamy:** 6–10½, 245-pound center; born July 24, 1939. Attended Indiana; played 14 seasons with six teams. Nicknamed "Bells," Bellamy averaged career highs of 31.6 points and 19.0 in his rookie season. Four-time All-Star.

**Dave Bing:** 6–3, 180-pound guard; born November 24, 1943. Attended Syracuse.

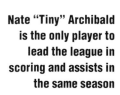

Nate "Tiny" Archibald is the only player to lead the league in scoring and assists in the same season

**Rochester's Bob Davies was one of the first great shooting guards**

One of the NBA's greatest shooting guards, Bing played 12 seasons for three teams; led the league in scoring (27.1) in 1967–68. Seven-time All-Star.

**Bill Bradley:** 6–5, 205-pound forward; born July 28, 1943. Attended Princeton. A Rhodes Scholar, Bradley keyed the Knicks' glory days in the 1960s and early 1970s. Became a U.S. Senator from New Jersey. Appeared in one All-Star Game.

**Al Cervi:** 5–11½, 155-pound guard; born February 12, 1917. Did not attend college. Nicknamed "Digger," Cervi started professional career in 1937. Due to military service he didn't return to professional basketball until 1945. Cervi finished his NBA career with Syracuse at age of 36. One of the great early guards, he retired before the All-Star Game was instituted.

**Wilt Chamberlain:** 7–1, 275-pound center; born August 21, 1936. Attended Kansas. A.k.a. "Wilt the Stilt" and "the Big Dipper," Chamberlain is one of the greatest scorers in NBA history. Averaged 50.4 points one season and had 30.1 career average. Played 14 years with three teams. 13-time All-Star.

**Bob Cousy:** 6–1½, 175-pound point guard; born August 9, 1928. Attended Holy Cross. One of the more dazzling ballhandlers in NBA history, Cousy played 13 seasons for the Boston Celtics. Finished with Cincinnati. Set NBA record leading league in assists eight straight seasons. An All-Star 13 times.

**Billy Cunningham:** 6–6, 220-pound forward; born June 3, 1943. Attended North Carolina. Played nine NBA seasons with Philadelphia and two in the ABA. Four-time NBA All-Star and legendary leaper. Cunningham could do everything from rebounding to scoring.

**Bob Davies:** 6–1, 175-pound guard; born January 15, 1920. Attended Franklin & Marshall and Seton Hall. Davies' professional career started in 1946. Played 10 years with Rochester as a scoring guard. An All-Star four times.

**Julius (Dr. J) Erving:** 6–6½, 200-pound forward; born February 22, 1950. Attended Massachusetts. One of the most acrobatic and creative players in NBA history, Erving became known as "Dr. J." Started in the ABA before finishing career with Philadelphia. An All-Star every one of his 16 professional seasons.

**Walt (Clyde) Frazier:** 6–4, 200-pound guard; born March 29, 1945. Attended Southern Illinois. Cool and calm on the floor, Frazier was one of the most versatile guards of his era. Played 13 NBA seasons, the first 10 with New York where he led the Knicks to two championships. A seven-time All-Star.

**Joe Fulks:** 6–5, 190-pound forward; born October 26, 1921. Attended Millsaps and Murray State. Known as "Jumpin' Joe," Fulks played eight seasons with Philadelphia. One of professional basketball's greatest scorers in the late 1940s. A two-time All-Star.

**Harry Gallatin:** 6–6, 215-pound forward/center; born April 26, 1927. Attended Northeast Missouri. Played 10 years, nine with New York. A brilliant rebounder, Gallatin was nicknamed "the Horse." A seven-time All-Star.

**Tom Gola:** 6–6, 205-pound forward; born January 13, 1933. Attended LaSalle. Played 10 seasons with three teams. A versatile player with size, Gola helped make Philadelphia a consistent playoff team from the mid-1950s to the early 1960s. A four-time All-Star.

**Hal Greer:** 6–2, 175-pound guard; born June 26, 1936. Attended Marshall. A brilliant scoring guard, Greer played 15 NBA seasons, the last 10 with Philadelphia. Averaged more than 20 points a game first seven seasons in Philadephia. A 10-time All-Star.

**Cliff Hagan:** 6–4, 215-pound forward; born December 9, 1931. Attended Kentucky. A great scorer, Hagan led St. Louis to the 1958 championship. Finished his professional career in the ABA. A four-time All-Star.

**John Havlicek:** 6–5, 205-pound forward/guard; born April 8, 1940. Attended Ohio State. Brilliant in every phase of the game, Havlicek played on Boston teams that won eight championships. Nicknamed "Hondo," he was drafted by professional football's Cleveland Browns. A 13-time All-Star.

**Connie Hawkins:** 6–8, 215-pound forward; born July 17, 1942. Attended Iowa. After a period out of professional basketball and two ABA seasons, Hawkins joined Phoenix in 1969. Considered one of the greatest pure talents in history. An All-Star four times.

**Elvin Hayes:** 6–9, 235-pound forward/center; born November 17, 1945. Attended Houston. Missed just nine games in 16-year career. As great a scorer as he was a rebounder, Hayes helped Washington to the 1978 title. A 12-time All-Star.

**Tommy Heinsohn:** 6–7, 218-pound forward; born August 26, 1934. Attended Holy Cross. A rugged scorer and rebounder, Heinsohn helped Boston to eight titles in nine-year career. Later coached the Celtics to two championships. Five-time All-Star.

**Dan Issel:** 6–9, 240-pound forward; born October 25, 1948. Attended Kentucky. Played first six professional seasons in ABA, the last nine with Denver Nuggets. A great shooter and rebounder, Issel averaged more than 21 points a game 11 times. Seven-time All-Star.

**Harry (Buddy) Jeannette:** 5–11, 175-pound guard; born September 15, 1929. Attended Washington & Jefferson. One of the game's top guards in the late 1930s and 1940s. Won four MVP awards and four championships in two leagues.

**Neil Johnston:** 6–8, 215-pound forward/center; born February 4, 1929. Attended Ohio State. One of his era's greatest scorers, Johnston averaged more than 22 points a game five straight seasons for Philadelphia in the 1950s. Played minor league baseball. Six-time All-Star.

**K.C. Jones:** 6–1, 200-pound guard; born May 25, 1932. Attended San Francisco. A defensive specialist, Jones played with Bill Russell in college and then at Boston. Helped lead the Celtics to eight championships in his nine NBA seasons. Later became a highly successful NBA coach. .

**Sam Jones:** 6–4, 205-pound guard, born June 24, 1933. Attended North Carolina College. A key to the Boston dynasty, Jones averaged 17.5 points during 12-year career. Member of 10 championship teams in Boston. Five-time All-Star.

**Bob Lanier:** 6–11, 260-pound center; born September 10, 1948. Attended St. Bonaventure. One of the greatest centers in NBA history, Lanier played 14 seasons with Detroit and Milwaukee. Averaged more than 20 points a game eight straight seasons. Eight-time All-Star.

**Clyde Lovellette:** 6–9. 235-pound foward; born September 7, 1929. Attended Kansas. Helped Minneapolis to 1954 title as rookie. Solid scorer and rebounder. Played 11 seasons winning two more championships with Boston. Three-time All-Star.

**Pete Maravich:** 6–5, 200-pound guard; born June 22, 1947. Attended Lousiana State.

Nicknamed "Pistol Pete" for his extraordinary shooting and scoring skills, he was a ball-handling marvel. Averaged 24.2 points during 10-year career. Four-time All-Star.

**Slater Martin:** 5–10, 170-pound guard; born October 22, 1925. Attended Texas. Member of Minneapolis teams that won four championships. Later helped lead St. Louis to 1958 title. A seven-time All-Star.

**Dick McGuire:** 6–0, 180-pound guard; born January 25, 1926. Attended St. John's and Dartmouth. One of the great early point guards. Nicknamed "Tricky Dick" for ball-handling and passing skills. Seven-time All-Star.

**George Mikan:** 6–10 1/2, 245-pound center; born June 18, 1924. Attended DePaul. The first dominant center in

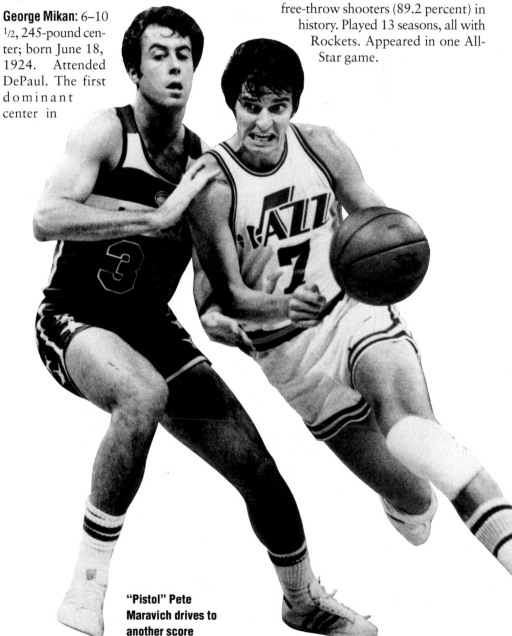

professional basketball history, Mikan led the Minneapolis Lakers to five championships. The greatest scorer of his era, Mikan averaged 23.1 points over his seven-year NBA career. Four-time All-Star.

**Earl Monroe:** 6–3 1/2, 185-pound guard; born November 21, 1944. Attended Winston-Salem State. One of the flashiest guards ever, Monroe was known as Earl "the Pearl" for his smooth moves. Played on New York title team in 1973. Four-time All-Star.

**Calvin Murphy:** 5–9, 165-pound guard; born May 9, 1948. Attended Niagara. One of the greatest small players ever to play the game, Murphy could score, pass and shoot as well as anyone in his era. One of the best free-throw shooters (89.2 percent) in history. Played 13 seasons, all with Rockets. Appeared in one All-Star game.

"Pistol" Pete
Maravich drives to
another score

**Bob Pettit:** 6–9, 215-pound forward; born December 12, 1932. Attended Louisiana State. A brilliant scorer, Pettit never averaged less than 20.4 points during 11-year career. Sixth highest career scoring average (26.4) in history. An 11-time All-Star.

**Andy Phillip:** 6–2½, 195-pound guard/forward; born March 7, 1922. Attended Illinois. Professional career started in 1947. Played on 1957 Boston Celtics championship team. Five-time All-Star.

**Jim Pollard:** 6–3½, 190-pound forward; born July 9, 1922. Attended Stanford. Known as for his jumping ability, Pollard helped lead Minneapolis to five championships. Four-time All-Star.

**Frank Ramsey:** 6–3, 190-pound guard/ forward; born July 13, 1931. Attended Kentucky. A key contributor to seven Boston championships, Ramsey shot better than 80 percent from the foul line. One of basketball's best "sixth men" ever.

**Willis Reed:** 6–9½, 235-pound center; born June 25, 1942. Attended Grambling. A gifted shooter and defender despite his size, Reed led the New York Knicks to two championships. Spent 10-year career with Knicks. A seven-time All-Star.

**Oscar Robertson:** 6–5, 210-pound guard; born November 24, 1938. Attended Cincinnati. Until Michael Jordan, Robertson was considered the greatest all- around guard. Averaged a stunning 30.8 points, 11.4 assists and 12.5 rebounds during 1961-62 season. A 12-time All-Star.

**Bill Russell:** 6–9½, 220-pound center; born February 12, 1934. Attended San Francisco. Led the Boston Celtics to 11 championships during 13 year career. Averaged incredible 22.6 rebounds a game during his career. A 12-time All-Star.

**Dolph Schayes:** 6–8, 220-pound forward; born May 19, 1928. Attended New York University. Great at virtually every aspect of the game, Schayes could rebound, score and shoot as well as any player in his era. Played 16 seasons, 15 with Syracuse. An 11-time All-Star.

**Bill Sharman:** 6–1, 190-pound guard; born May 25, 1926. Attended University of Southern California. One of Boston's key offensive threats during the 1950s and early 1960s. Played on four championship teams. A career 88.3 percent free-throw shooter. Played minor league baseball. Eight-time All-Star.

**Nate Thurmond:** 6–11, 230-pound center; born July 25, 1941. Attended Bowling Green. A solid, if not dominant big man during the 1960s and early 1970s, Thurmond could score, rebound and block shots. Five-time All-Star.

**Jack Twyman:** 6–6, 210-pound forward; born May 11, 1934. Attended Cincinnati. Played nine of 11 seasons in Cincinnati. One of the era's top scoring forwards, averaged 31.2 points during 1959–60 season. Six-time All-Star.

**Wes Unseld:** 6–7 1/2, 245-pound center; born March 14, 1946. Attended Louisville. named Rookie of the Year and Most Valuable Player during 1968–69 season. Spent entire 13-year career with Bullets franchise. A five-time All-Star.

**Bill Walton:** 6–11, 235-pound center; born November 5, 1952. Attended UCLA. One of the greatest college players ever. Walton led Portland to the 1977 title and helped Boston to 1986 championship. Career cut short by chronic foot injuries. Played in one All-Star Game.

**Bobby Wanzer:** 6–0, 172-pound guard; born June 4, 1921. Attended Colgate and Seton Hall. Played 10 years with Rochester. A great free-throw shooter, Wanzer developed into a reliable scorer while leading the Rochester offense. Five-time All-Star.

**Jerry West:** 6–2½, 180-pound guard; born May 28, 1938. Attended West Virginia. One of the greatest shooting guards in history, West averaged 27.0 points during his 14-year career. Teamed with Wilt Chamberlain to lead Los Angeles to 1972 championship. A 12-time All-Star;

**Lenny Wilkens:** 6–1, 185-pound guard; born October 28, 1937. Attended Providence. One of the game's smartest point guards, Wilkens started his coaching career while still a full-time player. Won 900th game in January 1994. An All-Star nine times during his 15-year career.

**Lenny Wilkens was an All-Star point guard before he retired and developed into one of the game's greatest coaches**

# INDEX

**159** ●